# 3ds max 4

## From Objects to Animation

Boris Kulagin

A-List, LLC
c/o CHARLES RIVER MEDIA, INC.
20 Downer Avenue, Unit 3
Hingham, MA 02043
781-740-0400
781-740-8816 (FAX)
chrivmedia@aol.com
http://www.charlesriver.com

This book is printed on acid-free paper.

All brand names and product names mentioned in this book are trademarks or service marks of their respective companies. Any omission or misuse (of any kind) of service marks or trademarks should not be regarded as intent to infringe on the property of others. The publisher recognizes and respects all marks used by companies, manufacturers, and developers as a means to distinguish their products.

3ds max 4: From Objects to Animation
By B. Kulagin
  ISBN: 1-58450-082-4
  Printed in the United States of America

  01 01 7 6 5 4 3 2 1

A-List, LLC titles are distributed by Charles River Media and are available for site license or bulk purchase by institutions, user groups, corporations, etc. For additional information, please contact the Special Sales Department at
781-740-0400.

Book Editors: John Paul Mueller, Rebecca Mueller, Olga Kokoreva, Jessica Mroz

# CONTENTS

# Introduction

## What's in this Book

A s its name implies, this book describes how to work with Discreet's 3D-graphics application 3ds max 4. (Discreet is the new name for Kinetix.) Many books on this application have been published, among which are good and poor, large and small, and original and translated versions. But how does this book differ from them? With certain reservations, all books on 3ds max 4 fall into two categories: "A Guide to 3ds max 4" and "3ds max 4 through Examples". Books from the first group present a scrupulous description of all — or almost all — commands and features of the application. The second group provides solutions to some specific problems that might arise while working with 3ds max 4.

Pros and cons of either category are evident.

The books that fall into the "Guide ..." category present comprehensive information on the commands and features of the application. However, to use this information, you need to have a certain working experience with 3ds max 4. The size of these books often repels novices. Such books abound with examples which, as a rule, are restricted to instructions like "create a sphere" or "apply such-and-such a method by clicking such-and-such a button". Sometimes books of this sort are so terse that a novice can't even understand what the author means.

Conversely, books from the "... through Examples" category fix a reader's attention on particular features of the application. Almost every example there begins with "load such-and-such a project from the CD" and ends with "look at the result, which is on the CD in ...".

I've worked with people who tried to learn from these books. Their unanimous opinion was that it was impossible to use such a scattered knowledge in actual practice.

Neither of the categories is able to help a novice create a project that would encourage him or her. Yet, it's obvions that a successfully finished job gives a person the feeling that "I can do it just as smart as those guys making TV clips!"

It was then that an idea emerged to write a book that would describe in detail the whole path of creating a picture or a clip. This path would run from initial modeling to animation and rendering. And the readers wouldn't be ashamed to show their creation both to 3ds max 4 experts and to ordinary people such as their friends and family.

# Who Should Read This Book

From the very beginning, we thought that this book should be designed primarily for those who already made their first (second, third...) step in creating 3D graphics. That is, those who know how to create cubes, balls, and more complicated shapes and how to animate them, using the keyframe animation method. However, we then concluded that it would be unfair to "cut off" those making their very first steps. Thus, the decision was made to write a book for both advanced and beginner users.

It's for this reason that the book has several levels of presenting material.

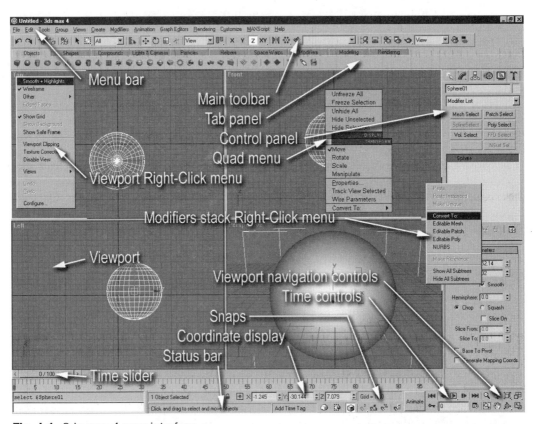

**Fig. I.1.** 3ds max 4 user interface

First, instructions are given to perform some actions. These are presented as a list. For example:

❑ Open the file *scene*.max.

For those readers who don't know how to do this, another level is provided. It has a special style. For example:

Menu Bar → File → Open

Finally, there are many notes, tips, and digressions highlighted as follows:

**NOTE** This text can be skipped depending on your choice. Generally, it has no effect on fulfilling the current task. However, I advise novices to pay attention to the information shown in these paragraphs.

One more word about keyboard shortcuts. In this book, they're represented by: <Ctrl>+<A>. The names of keys are enclosed in angle brackets "<>" while the "+" character means that the keys must be pressed simultaneously.

Information on 3ds max 4 terms can be found in Appendix 1 at the end of this book.

User interface deserves special mention. The 3ds max 4 main window is shown in fig. I.1, along with user interface elements.

## How to Fulfil the Tasks

The lessons in this book *do not* follow the "from easy to difficult" principle. They are *equivalent* and rather difficult, so they can be fulfilled in an arbitrary order. However, I advise novices to do them sequentially. The reason is that the first lessons cover some details crucial to understanding the subsequent material. As you advance through this book, your attention is progressively less drawn to *how* to perform an action while the emphasis is done on *what* you should do.

Notice the comments at the end of each lesson. There you can find suggestions on how to improve the result obtained.

The last and important point. I fulfilled all the lessons by myself while I was writing this book. This is why the ways of solving some problems might be far from optimum. Moreover, flaws are not unlikely. So, if you believe you can do better, go ahead! Don't be afraid of experiments. No book can teach you unless you persistently look into 3ds max 4 features.

## Hardware Requirements

Unlike other high-class 3D-graphics applications, 3ds max 4 is able to run on computers which can't be considered as powerful from the up-to-date standpoint. The minimal hardware configuration is as follows: an Intel Pentium III processor with clock rate no less than 500 MHz, 128 MB of RAM, video adapter with hardware support of Direct3D or OpenGL, with no less than 32 MB video RAM. Microsoft Windows 2000 operating system is highly recommended, though, 3ds max 4 can work under Windows 98 SE or Windows NT 4.0 with Service Pack 6. A 17-inch monitor (or larger) is highly recommended.

I strongly recommend that you purchase a three-button mouse if you don't have one already. In 3ds max 4 the central mouse button is used intensely for navigation in the viewport. In this book I head for using a three-button mouse.

# Initial Settings

You're free to set up 3ds max 4 according to your preferences. However, if you want the pictures on your screen to correspond to the illustrations in this book, you need to do the following. First, set the monitor resolution to 1152×864 pixels or more (if possible). Second, in 3ds max 4, open the setups:

> Menu Bar → Customize → Preferences → **General** tab

and clear the **Use Large Toolbar Buttons** checkbox. Then, exit 3ds max 4 pressing <Alt>+<F4>, and run the application again.

Besides, enable the display of the Tab Panel:

> Main menu → Customize → Show UI → Tab Panel

# What Was Not Included in this Book

The MAX Script language — a wonderful tool for enhancing 3ds max 4 capabilities — is completely left out. I didn't touch on this topic for two reasons. First, I'm not good at programming. Second, programming in MAX Script could easily be the subject of a whole book.

Whenever possible, I tried to use only the standard features of 3ds max 4. That's why you won't see descriptions of plug-ins in this book.

Moreover, only the new features of 3ds max 4 were used in the lessons. Although I tried to use as many of them as possible, some of the features were left out.

# What Else Can Be Used

First of all, your 3ds max 4 *User Manual* must become your handbook.

Online help and the online tutorial shipped with the application also have much to offer you. It might be that 3ds max 4 is the only 3D-graphics application to provide its users with such splendid online help and such truly useful online tutorial.

Finally, a brief reference book on 3ds max 4 features will do no harm.

# What's on the CD

The CD-ROM accompanying this book comprises everything you need to fulfil the lessons. You can also find both the intermediate and final stages of projects, rendered images, and clips in AVI format.

# To the Readers

At the beginning of any project, virtually every 3D novice feels fear (yes, fear indeed) that he or she will never be able to do the job. It's this feeling that keeps many beginners from going on. Believe me, there's nothing to be afraid of! Remember, "Perseverance wins" and "Fear hath a hundred eyes". Everything is possible when you work hard and apply your abilities. I was a layman, once, myself.

Someone might say, "I'm not talented". Another might say, "My computer isn't powerful enough". These are lame excuses for idleness. Only hard work, persistence, and patience make a person an artist. Any real artist will support this.

Now I'm going to give you a bit of bad news. Even after finishing all the lessons, you won't master 3D-graphics. You have to reconcile yourself to the fact. This book is merely a way to overcome your fear of the abyss of 3D-graphics. Who knows, maybe this abyss will turn into your stairway to the summit of mastery some day.

One more bit of advice. Often 3D novices, inspired with some experience and knowledge, try to make the images look like "real life". They get much disappointed when they fail. Don't be upset! There's one slogan I really like (maybe I invented it myself): "If you can't copy the reality, make your work look better than reality." I don't suggest that you create cubes and balls and tell others they can't make heads or tails of art. Try to make people *believe* your images are real, even though you've overdone them with effects or emphasized minor details. Keep in mind that you model a person's perception rather than real life. Moreover, you model perception through a camera, albeit a virtual one.

The last point: don't stick to 3ds max 4 only. Study other applications, 2D ones to begin with. They'll help you to impart a "marketable state" to your creations. You should also study applications enabling video production and special effects. It will allow you to assemble images and add sound and effects to them. It's important to read books on fine arts, photography, and cinematography. Believe me, it won't be out of place.

All materials presented in this book are based on my own experience, and, thus, represent my own point of view. 3D artists are creative individuals who constantly improve their skills. If I were writing this book now, some things would be done using different techniques. Still, I hope that you like the wonderful 3D-art world in general and this book in particular.

# Lesson 1

# Still Life

I n this lesson, we'll create a still life − a bouquet of dahlias in a crystal vase in front of a mirror. The result can be found in Lesson01.tif file, which is located on the companion CD in the Lessons\Lesson01\Images directory. You can open the file without exiting 3ds max 4.

Menu Bar → File → View File...

## Aims of this Lesson

After studying this lesson, you'll know how to:

❑ Use 3ds max 4 to model relatively simple objects using various methods.

❑ Create and properly use complex materials.

❑ Set up scene lighting and simulate some visual effects.

❑ Use new features and functionalities introduced with 3ds max 4. Specifically, you will learn various methods, such as linking objects and working with the Light Lister.

## Preliminary Notes

This lesson is the only one in the book that covers, in detail, all the manipulations needed to perform each of the operations. Generally, 3ds max 4 provides several methods of performing each specific operation. These operations will be described as follows:

Method1 *or* Method2

In the following lessons, I won't describe alternative methods of performing the same action. Rather, I'll concentrate on the methods which I personally consider to be the most efficient and convenient. Also, I strongly recommend that you pay special attention to the techniques of using the Right-click menu and keyboard shortcuts. This is a good working style that you should adopt, especially in regards to the latest trends in 3ds max 4 practice.

## Modeling the Crystal Vase

Let's start with the vase. Why? Because it's a simple object. This simple object is also very instructive because of the large variety of methods that can be used to create it. For example,

I've counted eight various ways to create this vase, to say nothing of the exotic methods, such as extruding with the use of Displace.

**NOTE** 3ds max 4 gurus will notice that I've omitted a description of Loft, which is one of the most popular methods. This is deliberate, since I'm convinced that it's high time to get out of the habit of using Loft for just any occasion. Sure, this is a very powerful instrument; but nowadays, using other methods is easier and quicker just because of Loft's power and versatility.

While creating the model of the vase (in fact, several models), we'll use various modeling methods. This example will demonstrate the expediency of a particular method for a specific case, rather than their strong and weak points.

## Using Curves

The simplest and, at the same time, the most familiar method that comes to mind is modeling with curves (the Shapes method) and subsequently creating a surface of revolution (the Lathe method).

❑ Go to the **Left** viewport.

❑ Maximize the window:

Viewport Navigation Controls → Min/Max Toggle *or* <W>

**TIP** You should fall into a habit of working in a maximized window. First, it will help you control the parameters more precisely. The second advantage is that you won't harm your eyes, especially if you have a small display.

3ds max 4 introduced a new capability of sizing the viewport. To accomplish this, place the mouse pointer over the intersection point of the viewport splitter bars. The cursor will change to cross-hairs with bi-directional arrows. Click the left mouse button and drag the center to change the viewport proportions.

❑ Create a curve similar to the one shown in fig. 1.1:

Tab panel → Shapes → Line *or* Control panel → Create → Shapes → Line *or* <Ctrl>+Right-click menu/TOOLS → Line

While creating the curve (strictly speaking, a broken line or open polygon), click (press and release) the left mouse button rather than drag the mouse with the button pressed. If you make a mistake, don't worry. You'll be able to correct the spline parameters later.

**TIP** While creating a curve, you can enable snap to grid. This will help you create the curve. Furthermore, it will simplify any future positioning of the rotation axis during the process of creating the lathe surface.

Snaps → 3D Snap Toggle *or* <S>

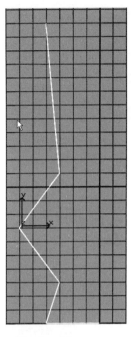

◀ **Fig. 1.1.** The initial curve for modeling the vase

*NOTE* No one is safeguarded against errors. Because of this, every application, including 3ds max 4, provides the Undo functionality. If you aren't satisfied with the result, do the following: **Menu Bar → Edit → Undo...** or press <Ctrl>+<Z>. If you don't like the changes in the viewport, press <Shift>+<Z> or select **View** in the menu bar and then select **Undo...**

❏ Convert the resulting line to Editable Shape

Right-click menu/TRANSFORM → Convert to... → Convert to Editable Shape

Now it is time to correct the vertices.

❏ Switch to the Vertex mode

Right-click menu/TOOLS 1 → Sub-objects → Vertex *or* Control Panel → ... → **Selection** rollout → **Vertex** button

❏ Select the vertex (fig. 1.2) and change its type to Bezier:

Right-click menu → Bezier

Two small green squares will appear. These are handles.

❏ Switch to the Move mode:

Right-click menu/TRANSFORM → Move *or* Main toolbar → Select and Move

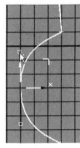

**Fig. 1.2.** The result of changing the vertex type to Bezier

*TIP* Default settings of 3ds max 4 don't provide a keyboard shortcut for switching to the Move mode. However, you can assign it anytime:

Menu Bar → Customize → Customize User Interface → **Keyboard** tab

Select **Move Mode** in the **Action** list. Place the cursor to the **Hotkey** area, then press <Alt> and <M> keys simultaneously.

Make sure that this combination hasn't been assigned yet. If it has, the **Assigned to:** field will display the command to which this shortcut has been currently assigned. In this case, try another combination. Click **Assign**, then **Save**.

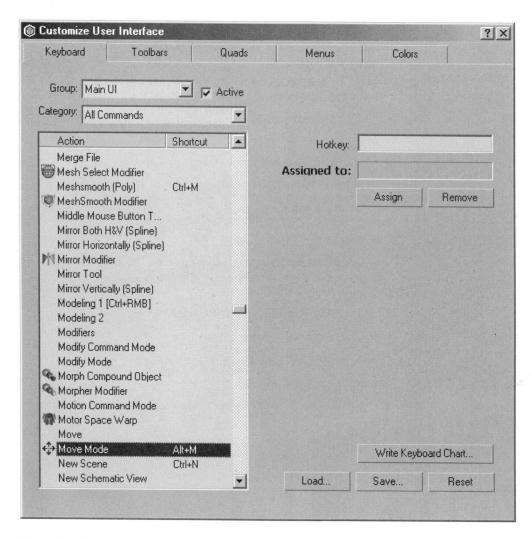

- In the Move mode, move the handles as shown in fig. 1.2.
- Select another vertex (fig. 1.3) and change its type to Bezier Corner:

    Right-click menu/TOOLS 1 → Bezier Corner

- By moving the handles, make your curve look like the one shown in fig. 1.3. Try to experiment with the vertices to achieve a better result.
- Create a surface of rotation (lathe surface):

    Tab panel → Modeling → Lathe *or* Control panel → Modifier List → Lathe

**NOTE**  The modifier stack in 3ds max 4 has been changed significantly as compared to the earlier releases. This was done mainly for the sake of convenience and ease of use. The developers have provided quite a large number of modifier types, which you can view and select by clicking the **Configure Modifiers Set** button. Furthermore, you can make the modifiers set available from Control Panel by enabling the **Show Buttons** option.

The result of this operation isn't the one we expected (fig. 1.4), so let's continue editing.

❏ Switch to the Axis mode to edit the axes:

Control panel/TOOLS 1 → Sub-objects → Axis

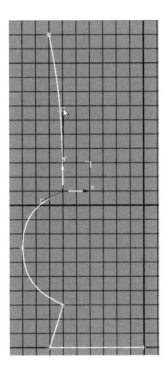

**Fig. 1.3.** The result of changing vertex type to Bezier Corner and subsequent editing of its handles

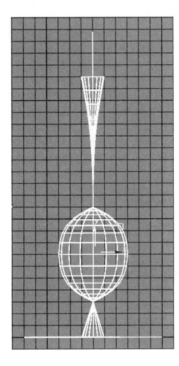

**Fig. 1.4.** The result of applying the Lathe modifier

**Fig. 1.5.** The parameters of the Lathe modifier

Now you can move the axis, thus changing the vase proportions.

❏ Drag the X-axis to the right up to the thick black grid line. As you can see, everything's now in the appropriate place. For the moment, don't worry that the vase is far from perfect. You'll correct this flaw later.

❏ Set up the parameters of the Lathe modifier as shown in fig. 1.5.

❏ Switch to the orthographic view and enjoy your creation:

<Alt>+ drag with the middle mouse button

Viewport Navigation Controls → Arc Rotate *or* <V>. Press and hold on the left mouse button, then drag the cursor within the green circle. Choose the appropriate projection.

**NOTE** Should the vase get outside the viewport during rotation, click the **Zoom Extents** button [icon] in the **Viewport Navigation Controls** panel or press <Ctrl>+<Alt>+<Z>. To exit this mode – and most other navigation modes – you just need to click the right mouse button or press the <Esc> key.

❏ Set the Smooth+Highlights rendering mode for the viewport:

Viewport Right-click menu → Smooth + Highlights *or* <F3>

Don't be surprised or upset by the fact that you can't see the inner surface of the vase. The point is that in 3ds max 4 — as in many other 3D-graphics applications — surfaces are one-sided. To get a double-sided image in the viewport, set the **Force 2-Sided** checkbox in the viewport parameters. For the time being, though, don't do this!

Well, there's little to enjoy right now. However, let's go on.

❏ Press the <L> key to enter the **Left** viewport.

❏ Jump to the bottom of the modifier stack:

Control Panel → Modifier Stack → Line

**NOTE** At any time, you can check the editing result by clicking the **Show end result on/off toggle** button [icon] in the Control Panel.

❏ Select all vertices, except for the lowest right one, and move them closer to the central line (fig. 1.6) by dragging the X arrows.

Now create the outline of the inner surface of the vase. Use the Outline operation for this purpose.

❏ Switch to the Spline mode to start selecting splines:

Right-click menu/TOOLS 1 → Sub-objects → Spline *or* Control Panel → ... → **Selection** rollout → **Spline** button

❏ Select your spline.

❏ Switch to the Outline mode:

Control panel → ... → **Geometry** rollout → **Outline** button

❏ Drag the selected spline and watch the result (fig. 1.7).

**TIP** 3ds max 4 introduces new capability of expanding Control Panel. To do so, simply drag the inside edge of Control Panel to the viewports. Besides, you can also rearrange the rollouts in Control Panel by clicking the rollout title bar and dragging it to the selected location.

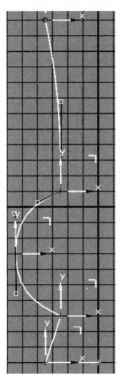

**Fig. 1.6.** The result of moving the vertices

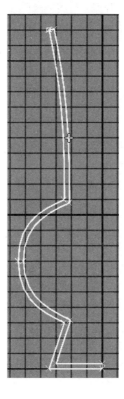

**Fig. 1.7.** The result of outlining

❑ Make the top rim of the vase into a rounded shape.

**TIP** It's easy to enlarge the part being edited up to the viewport size. To do so, use the Region Zoom mode (by clicking the **Region Zoom** button in the Viewport Navigation Controls panel or by pressing the combination <Ctrl>+<W>), then select the part of the model that you want to enlarge. Also, it is very convenient to use the <[> and <]> keys for zooming in the viewports. If you have IntelliMouse, you can do the same thing by rolling the mouse wheel.

❑ Select the vertices as shown in fig. 1.8, and change their type to Bezier Corner.

**NOTE** You can select multiple vertices (or other elements of an object) in two different ways: by pressing <Ctrl> (a "+" character appears next to the mouse pointer) or by drawing a rectangle enclosing all necessary elements.

What a nuisance! The handles responsible for the curvature of the upper segment can't be reached... However, there's a solution to this problem.

❑ Insert one more vertex:

Right-click menu/TOOLS 2 → Refine

❑ Select the newly inserted vertex and change its type to Bezier.

❑ Change the positions and orientation of the focuses of the ellipse (fig. 1.9).

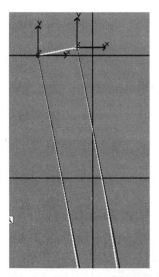

**Fig. 1.8.** The result of setting the Bezier Corner type for the vertices

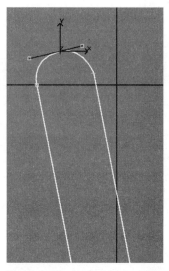

**Fig. 1.9.** The result of inserting the vertex

There's also another method. Although it incurs additional overhead, it enables you to do this without inserting an additional vertex:

❑ Select the vertices that you need.

❑ Convert them to the Smooth type, and the result will be awful.

❑ Reconvert the vertices to Bezier Corner.

❑ Adjust the handles.

Now it's necessary to reshape the inner surface of the bottom.

❑ Switch the viewport to the Pan mode:

Middle mouse button *or* Viewport navigation controls → **Pan** button *or* <Ctrl>+<P> keyboard shortcut

❑ Go down to the generating line of the vase bottom.

**NOTE** Of course, there's another way to accomplish this task. Click the **Zoom Extents** button, or press <Ctrl>+<Alt>+<Z>, then click **Region Zoom** button and press <Ctrl>+<W>.

Make the contour of the vase bottom look more realistic. Select and delete the segment connecting the outer and inner outlines since you don't need it.

❑ To select the segment, click it with the mouse:

Right-click menu/TOOLS 1 → Sub-Objects → Segment *or* Control panel → ...
→ **Selection** rollout → **Segment** icon

❑ Delete the selected segment by pressing <Del>.

❑ Select the vertex belonging to the inner contour, which is nearest to the center of rotation.

❑ Move this vertex upwards. Use the handles to make the segments containing this vertex into a curved shape.

❑ Select and delete the vertex located *to the left* of the inner one.

❑ Move the handles of respective vertices to compensate this loss (fig. 1.10).

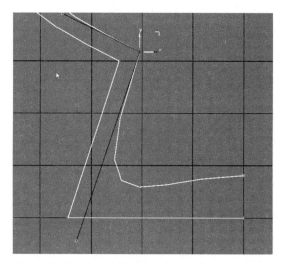

**Fig. 1.10.** The result of editing the vertices

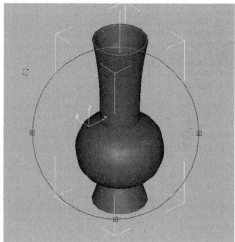

**Fig. 1.11.** The final appearance of the vase

**NOTE** You may need to change the types of the vertices. You already know how to accomplish this.

Now you can admire the result of your labor (fig. 1.11).

❑ Return to the top of the modifier stack (back to the Lathe modifier):

Control panel →... → Modifier Stack → Lathe

❑ Magnify the view in the active viewport to display all visible elements:

Viewport Navigation Controls → Zoom Extents *or* <Ctrl>+<Alt>+<Z>

❑ Rotate the viewport to choose the best projection.

❑ Switch to the Shaded+Highlight mode:

User Viewport Right-click menu → check the **Shaded+Highlight** checkbox or press <F3>

❑ Name the vase CrystalVase_spline.

❑ Enter the name into the appropriate text box in the Control Panel and press <Enter>.

| Name and Color |
| --- |
| CrystalVase_spline |

***TIP*** Assigning unique and meaningful names to all your objects is a good practice. Don't rely on your memory in this matter. Believe me, recalling all the names can be very difficult, especially if you need to return to an old project after several days or even years. If you're working in a group, you'll certainly need to transfer your projects to your colleagues. In this case, easy usage of your projects isn't something to be neglected

***Self-study*** Try to edit the initial curve of the vase by moving and adding vertices or changing parameters of the curve elements. However, don't allow yourself to be carried away by adding too many new elements, especially vertices. If you do, this will complicate your model and eventually slow down your computer. Remember that this is only the initial stage of your project, and you still have a lot of things to do!

Save your project in the file Lesson01-vase1.max:

Menu Bar → Save (*or* Save As) *or* <Ctrl>+<S>

The modeling method we've just looked at is well suited for tasks like this. Its big advantage is that it allows you to control *all* the parameters of a surface. On the other hand, controlling and adjusting surface parameters at the vertex level is a very tedious and time-consuming job.

# Using the Surface Modifier

Modeling using Surface Tools plug-in was one of the most interesting and efficient modeling methods in earlier versions of 3ds max. 3ds max 2.5 finally implemented full-featured NURBS objects, which will be discussed in detail later in this book. This plug-in, created by Digimation and Peter Watje, is now an integral part of 3ds max 4. Peter Watje, by the way, is now working at Discreet.

The essence of this method is very simple. You create a frame of curves making up three- or four-sided polygons. Subsequently, this frame is automatically "skinned over" with a surface.

❑ Reset 3ds max 4:

Main menu → File → Reset

❑ Go to the **Top** viewport (the <T> key).

❑ Maximize it (the <W> key).

❑ Turn on the Snap to grid option:

Snaps → 3D Snap Toggle *or* <S>

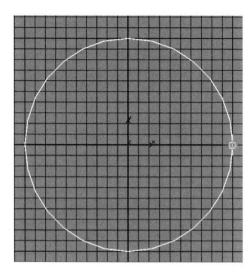

❑ Create a circle with the radius approximately equal to 100 current length units and center it at the origin of the coordinates (fig. 1.12):

<Ctrl>+Right-click menu/TOOLS → Circle *or* Main toolbar → Shapes → Circle *or* Main menu → Create → Shapes → Circle

Move the mouse pointer to the crossing point of the two thick gray lines and click the left mouse button. Create the circle by dragging the mouse in the viewport.

**Fig. 1.12.** Initial circle created for subsequent modeling with the use of the Surface modifier

*TIP* You can create circles and any other primitives (primitive objects) by entering their parameters from the keyboard:

Control panel → Create → Shapes → Circle → **Keyboard Entry** rollout

If the **Keyboard Entry** rollout is minimized, maximize it by pressing the <+> icon.

Leave the **X**, **Y**, and **Z** parameters equal to zero and enter 100 into the **Radius** field. Click **Create**.

❑ Press the <L> key to enter the **Left** viewport.

❏ Adjust the zoom and pan as shown in fig. 1.13, using the middle mouse button combined with the <Alt>, <Ctrl> and <Shift> keys or appropriate button in the Viewport Navigation Controls.

❑ Switch to the Move mode:

Right-click menu/TRANSFORM → Move

❑ Drag the circle along the Y-axis for a distance of 100 units (10 squares). To do so, click the **Y** arrow and drag while pressing the <Shift> key.

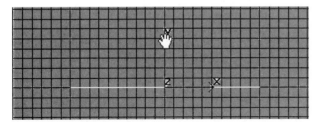

**Fig. 1.13.** The viewport

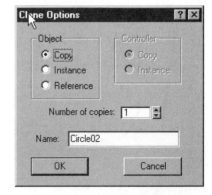

A dialog similar to that shown in fig. 1.14 will appear.

**Fig. 1.14.** The **Clone Options** dialog

---

*TIP* The arrows (called **TRANSFORM Gizmo**) may seem too big or too small for you. If this is the case, you can change their size by pressing <+> or <-> keys on the main keyboard.

Set the **Number of copies** parameter equal to 4 and click **OK**.

Now you have five identical circles.

*TIP* Sometimes it's useful to turn off the grid. To do this, press <G>.

Now it's necessary to arrange the circles so that they resemble a vase.

❑ Select the circle named Circle02.

*NOTE* When you move the mouse pointer over an object, it turns into a cross. If the pointer isn't moved for a while, the name of the object appears on the screen.

❑ Halve the radius of this circle:

Right-click menu/ TRANSFORM → Manipulate

Click the green circle and resize it, at the same time checking the value.

❑ Proceeding the same way, re-scale Circle04 and all the other circles.

❑ Move the circles along the Y-axis and position them as shown in fig. 1.15.

Now you're ready to create a vase using these circles.

❑ Select Circle01.

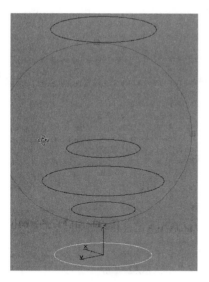

*TIP* Now you can set the viewport to the orthographic view, using the <Alt>+middle mouse button combination or by pressing the <V> key and rotating the viewport as shown in fig 1.15

❑ Apply the Edit Spline modifier to the circle:

Main menu → Modifiers → Patch/Spline Editing → Edit Spline *or* Control Panel → Modify → Modifier List → Edit Spline *or* Main toolbar → Modeling → Edit Spline

**Fig. 1.15.** The result of re-scaling and positioning the circles

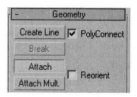

❑ Now, one by one, attach all the other circles to Circle01 in *bottom-up* order. The order for this is essential!

Right-click menu/TOOLS 2 → Attach *or* Control Panel →... → Geometry → Attach

Attach the circles one by one.

❑ Apply the CrossSection modifier to the resulting set of splines:

Tab panel → Modeling → CrossSection *or* Control panel → Modify → Modifier List→ CrossSection

❑ Set up the modifier parameters as shown in fig. 1.16.
❑ The resulting image is shown in fig. 1.17.
❑ Now apply the Surface modifier to the result you've just obtained:

Tab panel → Modeling → Patch Surface *or* Control panel → Modify → Modifier List → Surface

❑ Enable the Smooth+Highlight rendering mode for the viewport.
❑ Set up the modifier parameters as shown in fig. 1.18.
❑ The resulting vase displayed in the viewport will look like the one shown in fig. 1.19.

*Self-study* Try to tweak the parameters of the Surface modifier. To get a better understanding of the effect produced by each setting, switch the viewport to the Wireframe mode.

Now delete everything you've just created!

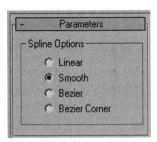

**Fig. 1.16.** The parameters
of the CrossSection modifier

**Fig. 1.17.** The result of applying
the CrossSection modifier

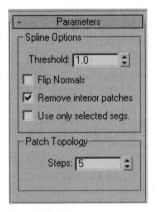

**Fig. 1.18.** The parameters
of the Surface modifier

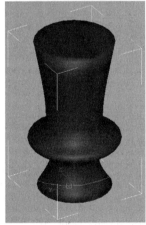

**Fig. 1.19.** The result of applying
the Surface modifier

This isn't a joke. Believe me, it's nearly impossible to create anything worthwhile based on the result of our labor. And starting everything from the scratch will require less effort than further editing the results we've have just produced.

Fortunately, 3ds max 4 provides a large number of methods enabling you to return the project to its initial state as well as to any of the intermediate ones.

*The first method* (first by its position in the list, but not by its importance) is generally used as a last resort. Among other preferences, 3ds max 4 provides the **Auto Backup** option:

Menu Bar → Customize → Preferences → the **Files** tab → → Auto Backup

If this option is set as shown in this figure, 3ds max 4 will automatically save a backup copy of your current file every five minutes. Backup copies will be saved in the AutoBack directory under the names Autoback#.mx. An example illustrating the procedure of loading such a file is shown in fig. 1.20. Notice that this method is intended for emergency situations such as power failures or operating system errors. (In

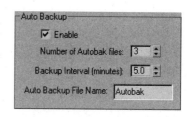

fact, Windows 95/98 operating system hangs quite often.) I recall many cases when the **Auto Backup** feature saved hours of my working time!

**Fig. 1.20.** Opening Auto Backup files

*The second method* enables you to return to the previous state by using the **Undo** command. 3ds max 4 supports multiple levels of undoing. The default number of **Undo Levels** is 20, but you can adjust it as necessary:

> Menu Bar → Customize → Preferences → the **General** tab

The **General** tab of the **Preference Settings** dialog allows you to set any reasonable value of **Undo Level**. Remember, however, that the higher the value, the more system resources get consumed by 3ds max 4; and, consequently, your work is less efficient.

Multilevel Undo can be accomplished either by pressing <Ctrl>+<Z> repeatedly or by opening the **Undo** list:

> Main Toolbar → Undo

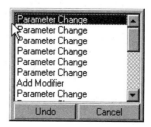

Open the **Undo** list by clicking the counterclockwise arrow button ![icon]. A dialog containing the list of all you previous actions will appear. Select the one you want to return to, and click the **Undo** button. If you undo too far, don't worry. The button with the clockwise arrow undoes your undo actions. You can amuse yourself by watching your work done in reverse or forward order by using these 3ds max 4 features.

*The third method* involves deletion of the assigned modifier from the modifier stack. To delete a modifier, just click the button with a paper bin icon on it. Besides, you can use the modifier stack right-click menu (fig. 1.21). To do so, click the modifier and then select the **Delete** command. If you carefully look at the capabilities provided by this menu, you'll certainly notice that they are not limited to deletion of unnecessary modifiers. You'll learn more about this later in this lesson.

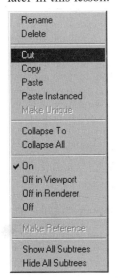

*The fourth method* is to save the current 3ds max 4 status in order to restore it at a later time (**Hold/Fetch**). Most users, including myself, ignore this method; but this is a mistake. I recommend that you use it prior to any action that may cause irreversible changes in your scene:

Main menu → Edit → Hold *or* <Ctrl>+<Alt>+<H>

To fetch the held status:

Main menu → Edit → Fetch *or* <Ctrl>+<Alt>+<F>

**Fig. 1.21.** Right-click menu of the modifier stack

A message will appear. Click **Yes** only after careful consideration. This operation can't be undone! In fact, 3ds max 4 just saves the current state in the file Autoback\Maxhold. By the way, this is a good alternative to the Auto Backup feature described earlier. The only difference is that now you start the process by yourself.

Saving your project periodically is, perhaps, the easiest method.

Now let's go back to our project and delete the modifiers.

❑ Select the object, if you haven't already done so.

❑ Select the Surface and CrossSection modifiers from the modifier stack:

Click the Surface modifier, press and hold the <Ctrl> key, then click CrossSection.

❑ Open the right-click menu of the modifier stack.

❑ Select the **Delete** command.

Now you have to detach all the circles.

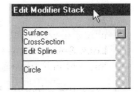

❑ Switch to the Spline mode:

Right-click menu/TOOLS 1 → Sub-object → Spline

❑ Select the uppermost circle and detach it:

Control panel → ... → **Geometry** panel → Detach

❑ Repeat the same procedure with all the other circles.

❑ Leave the Spline mode:

Right-click menu → Sub-objects → Base Object

Now you've returned to the initial state. The only difference is that the names of the circles aren't the same. Also, their types aren't Circle now, but Editable Shape. It doesn't matter, in this case. However, sometimes it does; so I strongly recommend that you save your project prior to any important changes in your scene.

❑ Select all the circles, which are separate objects now.

*TIP* In 3ds max 4, there's no default keyboard shortcut for selecting all objects; however, you can assign it yourself as necessary. For example, you can choose <Grey *> (an asterisk on the gray keypad) for the **Select All** command and <Ctrl>+<Grey *> for **Select None**.

❑ Switch to the **Select and Non Uniform Scale** mode:

Main Toolbar → **Select and Scale** flyout → click and hold the left mouse button, then select the **Select and Non Uniform Scale** button from the drop-down list

*NOTE* A warning may appear. For the moment, ignore it and click **Yes**.

*NOTE* If the object that you're re-scaling behaves somewhat strangely, this means that its pivot point isn't in the center of the object. To put it into the right place, click the **Use Center** flyout available in the Menu Bar → Main Toolbar. Click this toolbar button, and drag the mouse to the **Use Pivot Point Center**. By default, this command has no assigned hotkey, but you can always assign it a keyboard shortcut such as <Ctrl>+<Alt>+<X>. The procedure for assigning hotkeys was described earlier in this lesson.

Moreover, if the **Snap to grid** option is on, the transformation is done with the reference to the point specified by the mouse pointer. If this bothers you, disable the **Snap to grid** option by pressing the <S> key.

A final note. 3ds max 4 has a very useful option; namely, **Lock Selection**. To lock the selection, press the <Space> key. You can judge whether or not this option is on by the color of the **Lock Selection Set** button 🔒, located in the **Status Controls** bar. Notice that you can use this button if 3ds max 4 doesn't react to your pressing the spacebar.

❑ Lock the selection by pressing the spacebar, just to be on the safe side.

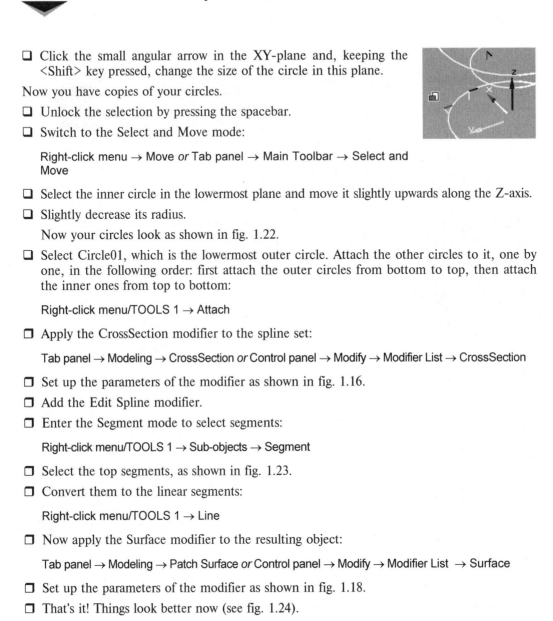

❑ Click the small angular arrow in the XY-plane and, keeping the <Shift> key pressed, change the size of the circle in this plane.

Now you have copies of your circles.

❑ Unlock the selection by pressing the spacebar.

❑ Switch to the Select and Move mode:

Right-click menu → Move *or* Tab panel → Main Toolbar → Select and Move

❑ Select the inner circle in the lowermost plane and move it slightly upwards along the Z-axis.

❑ Slightly decrease its radius.

Now your circles look as shown in fig. 1.22.

❑ Select Circle01, which is the lowermost outer circle. Attach the other circles to it, one by one, in the following order: first attach the outer circles from bottom to top, then attach the inner ones from top to bottom:

Right-click menu/TOOLS 1 → Attach

❑ Apply the CrossSection modifier to the spline set:

Tab panel → Modeling → CrossSection *or* Control panel → Modify → Modifier List → CrossSection

❑ Set up the parameters of the modifier as shown in fig. 1.16.

❑ Add the Edit Spline modifier.

❑ Enter the Segment mode to select segments:

Right-click menu/TOOLS 1 → Sub-objects → Segment

❑ Select the top segments, as shown in fig. 1.23.

❑ Convert them to the linear segments:

Right-click menu/TOOLS 1 → Line

❑ Now apply the Surface modifier to the resulting object:

Tab panel → Modeling → Patch Surface *or* Control panel → Modify → Modifier List → Surface

❑ Set up the parameters of the modifier as shown in fig. 1.18.

❑ That's it! Things look better now (see fig. 1.24).

❑ Rename the vase to CrystalVase_STools and save the project in the file lesson01-vase2.max.

Well, what's your opinion? If you said that this job was tedious, you're right. This method is very tedious for the case we've just looked at. Of course, it isn't fit for modeling lathe surfaces. However, when you need to create a polygonal object, this method will work just fine. Moreover, by adding new curves to your object you'll be able to achieve impressive results.

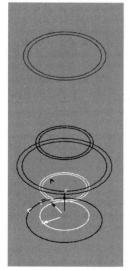

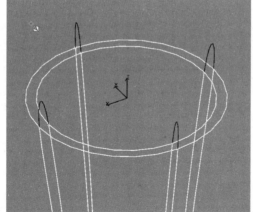

**Fig. 1.23.** Selecting the segments

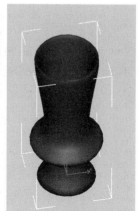

**Fig. 1.24.** The final view of the vase dummy created using the Surface modifier

**Fig. 1.22.** The result of changing and copying the circles

# Using NURBS

Modeling with NURBS (Non-Uniform Rational B-Splines) is now one of the most popular methods for modeling objects of any type. The idea of this method is that you have no way to directly edit faces or polygons. Instead, you deal with control vertices (CVs), which define the control curves. You can use this as a basis to create surfaces. The distinguishing feature of these surfaces is their smoothness. NURBS curves, and therefore NURBS surfaces, can't have any sharp angles or edges.

Now, let's start modeling.

❑ Reset 3ds max 4:

Main menu → File → Reset

❑ Go to the Left viewport.

❑ Maximize the window:

Viewport Navigation Controls → Min/Max Toggle *or* <W>

❑ Create a NURBS curve, as shown in fig. 1.25:

Tab panel → Shapes → NURBS CV Curve *or* Control panel → Create → Shapes → NURBS Splines → CV Curve

❑ Switch to the NURBS modify mode:

Control panel → Modify

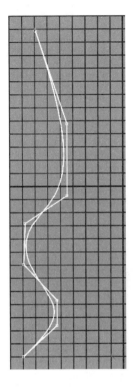

◄ **Fig. 1.25.** The initial NURBS curve

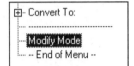

*NOTE* By some unknown reasons, the developers of 3ds max 4 did not include the transition to the Modify mode to the right-click menu. Let us do it ourselves.

Open the **Customize User Interface** window:

Main menu → Customize → Customize User Interface → **Quads** tab

Select the **Default Viewport Quad** option from the drop-down list and TRANSFORM option in the **Label** field. From the list of available commands select the **Modify Mode** command, drag it with the mouse and drop at the right-click menu commands list. Add the separator as necessary. Save the settings by overwriting the DefaultUI.mnu file. Now you can select this command from the right-click menu.

Furthermore, you can also modify the Main menu. As you have already noticed, nearly all objects can be created using the **Create** command from the Main menu. However, NURBS curves were forgotten for some unknown reason. Let us correct this drawback.

In the **Customize User Interface** window, go to the **Menus** tab. Expand the **Create** branch. Create the NURBS menu by clicking **New**... and entering the NURBS name. Find the NURBS option in the **Menus** list and drag it to the menu tree. Add the separator if necessary. Expand the newly created menu branch and add commands for creating NURBS curves and surfaces. To do so, select these commands from the list of available actions (the **Action** list) and drag them to the menu tree (fig.1.26). Save your settings in the DefaultUI.mnu file.

❑ Switch to the CV editing mode (CV stands for Control Vertex):

Right-click menu/TOOLS 1 → Sub-objects → Curve CV Level *or* Control panel →...→ Modifier stack... → expand the subobjects tree by clicking "+" → Curve CV

Now, let's proceed with a detailed discussion of NURBS modeling.

As was mentioned earlier, NURBS curves can't have sharp angles. In other words, a NURBS curve is always smooth, and any point of the curve has a curvature radius, no matter how small it may be. You can change this curvature radius by changing the weight of respective control vertex. This is true for NURBS implementation in 3ds max 4 only. In other 3D graphics software products (Softimage, for instance), NURBS curves may have breakpoints.

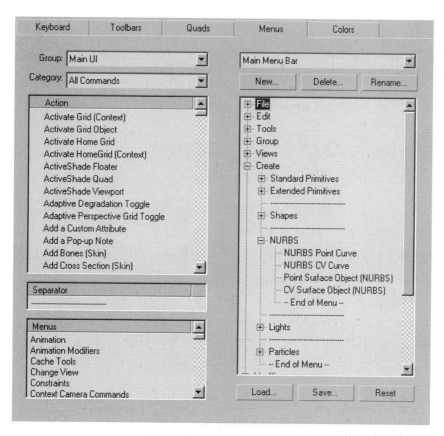

**Fig. 1.26.** Customizing menus

From the point of view generally accepted in such 3D editors, standard 3ds max 4 splines can also be considered as NURBS curves.

❑ Select any vertex and experiment with changing its weight. Notice how the curve will change its shape. Then move the control
vertices and change their weights to produce a curve similar to
the one shown in fig. 1.27.

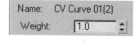

❑ Switch to the curve editing mode:

Right-click menu/TOOLS 1 → Sub-objects → Curve CV

❑ Select your curve.

❑ Switch to the Move mode:

Right-click menu → Move

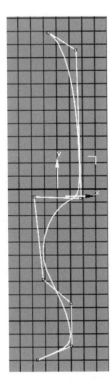

◀ **Fig. 1.27.** The result of changing weights and moving control vertices

❏ Press and hold the <Shift> key while dragging your curve to the right towards the thick gray line.

❏ The **Sub-Object Clone Options** dialog will appear (fig. 1.28). Set the **Independent Copy** radio button and click **OK**.

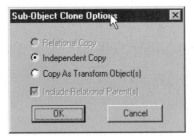

**Fig. 1.28.** The **Sub-object Clone Options** dialog

Now you have two independent curves.

❏ Edit the resulting curve as shown in fig. 1.29:

Right-click menu/TOOLS 1 → Curve CV Level

***TIP*** If the original curve vertices distract you, you can select and hide them all. To do this, click the **All CVs** button, select any vertex of the curve, and click the **Hide** button.

Now we're ready to create a vase.

❏ In the **NURBS** menu (fig. 1.30), click the **Create Lathe Surface** button.

❏ Move the mouse pointer to the outer (leftmost) curve (it will turn blue) and click the left mouse button. You'll get a green surface.

❏ Switch to the surface-editing mode and select the resulting surface. It will turn red:

Right-click menu/TOOLS 1 → Sub-objects → Surface

***TIP*** By default, the **TRANSFORM Degrade** option, which hides objects during transformation, is enabled. This is done in order to speed up the editing process. However, if you wish to view all changes that take place during transformation, you can disable this option:

Right-click menu/TOOLS 1 → TRANSFORM Degrade

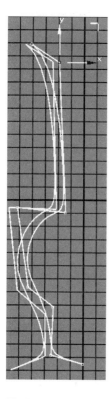

◀ **Fig. 1.29.** The result of editing the second curve

❑ Select the object axis and move it to the right towards the thick gray line. The axis will turn yellow while you move it. You'll get a picture similar to the one shown in fig. 1.31.

❑ Repeat the procedure described above for the other curve.

**Fig. 1.30.** The **NURBS** menu

❑ Delete the curves, since you don't need them any more:

Right-click menu/ TOOLS 1 → Sub-objects → Curve

Select the curves and press <Del>.

**NOTE** The sequence of actions described above isn't quite correct. Don't rush to delete any of the initial curves while editing NURBS surfaces. After the curve has been deleted, the surface becomes independent. The procedures for editing a surface like this will certainly prove to be difficult. On the other hand, independent surfaces present much more editing possibilities.

The final result of your efforts will look similar to what's shown in fig. 1.32.

Now let's examine the normals.

❑ Select the inner surface:

Right-click menu/TOOLS 1 → Sub-objects → Surface

❑ Set the **Flip Normals** checkbox:

Control panel → ... → **Surface Common** rollout → **Flip Normals**

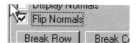

At this point, we need to "join" the two surfaces and create the bottom of the vase.

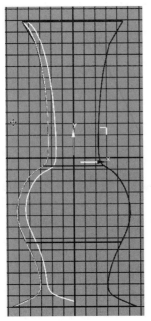

**Fig. 1.31.** The surface of rotation obtained from the first curve

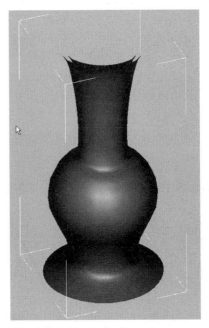

**Fig. 1.32.** The result of creating lathe surfaces

***NOTE*** You won't actually "join" the surfaces. Instead, you're going to create a new surface.

❑ In the **NURBS** menu (fig. 1.30), click the **Create Blend Surface** button 🖾.

❑ Move the mouse pointer to make the outer surface turn yellow and the circle defining the vase neck turn blue.

❑ Drag the mouse pointer to the inner surface until it turns yellow while the inner circle defining the vase neck turns blue.

You probably won't get the desired result from the first attempt. To produce the expected result, you have to set up the corresponding parameters of the surface (fig. 1.33).

***Self-study*** Try to experiment with these parameters and notice their effect on the resulting surface.

Finally, let's make the bottom.

❑ Rotate the vase for better accessibility.

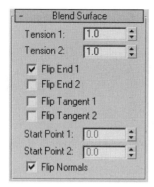

**Fig. 1.33.** The **Blend Surface** parameters

❑ In the **NURBS** menu (fig. 1.30), click the **Create Cap Surface** button 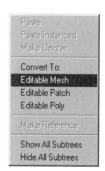.

❑ Move the mouse pointer so that the outer surface turns yellow while the circle defining the bottom turns blue.

❑ Click the left mouse button.

❑ Rename your object to "CrystalVase_Nurbs" and save the project under the name lesson01-vase3.max.

Over the years, I've come to like this method more and more. The most obvious advantage of this method is the capability of controlling object properties through parameters. Using this capability, you can produce the desired result in a reasonable amount of time; provided, of course, that you have sufficient experience and knowledge.

## Correcting the Vase Geometry

Now we have three models. Which one should we choose? To be honest, this choice is of little or no importance. We'll convert our model into a basic 3ds max 4 object; namely, Editable Mesh. Actually, this conversion isn't necessary. You can use any of the modifiers without explicit conversion, because 3ds max 4 will perform this conversion automatically. However, this procedure is worth doing, since each item in the modifier stack requires additional resources.

Personally, I prefer the last version, CrystalVase_Nurbs.

❑ Open lesson01-vase3.max:

Menu Bar → File → Open *or* <Ctrl>+<O>

❑ Select the vase.

❑ Convert it to the Editable Mesh type:

Right-click menu/TRANSFORM → Convert To: → Convert to Editable Mesh *or* Right-click menu of the Modifier Stack → Convert To: Editable Mesh

Now you've deleted all information on how the vase had been created.

*Warning*    This is a very important step. You should take it only when you're absolutely sure that you won't drastically edit the object during intermediate stages.

Now we have to perform some preliminary operations that will be helpful in the future.

❑ Reset all transformations:

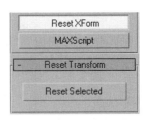

Control panel → Utilities → Reset XForm, Reset Selected

The point of this is that all changes in the position and size of an object are logged in a *transformation matrix*. The viewport that the object was created in is also important. Moreover, orientation of your object doesn't necessarily correspond to the world coordinates. In other words, the "vertical" and "horizontal" axes of your object don't necessarily coincide with those of the world coordinates. The consequences might be unpredictable. The Reset XForm operation rotates your object so that its current orientation in space corresponds to the world coordinates.

Notice the XForm modifier appearing in the modifier list.

❑ Convert the vase to Editable Mesh once again.

**NOTE**    By doing this through the right-click menu of the modifier stack, you'll open the stack. Click the **Collapse All** button and confirm the operation by clicking **OK**.

❑ Apply mapping coordinates:

Tab panel → Modifiers → UWV Map *or* Control panel → ... → UWV Map *or* Main menu → Modifiers → UV Coordinates → UVW Map

❑ Choose the cylindrical mapping. Set the **Cylindrical** radio button in the **Mapping** group in the **Parameters** rollout.

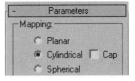

By applying the coordinates, you instruct 3ds max 4 how to apply a map on your object. It must be done now, since subsequent actions will change the geometry of the object and, consequently, the mapping coordinates.

Now let's finish the vase geometry with the free deformation (cylindrical) modifier; namely, FFD (cyl).

❑ Apply the FFD (cyl) modifier:

Tab panel → Modifiers → FFDCyl *or* Control panel → Modifier List → FFD (cyl)

A mesh will appear. This is just the editable mesh of your object.

❑ Set the number of points to 12×2×10 by clicking the **Set Number of Points** button.

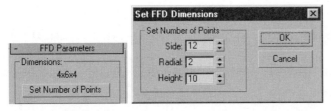

❏ Switch to the Control Points mode:

Right-click menu/ TOOLS 1 → Sub-objects → Control Points *or* Control panel → Modifier stack → expand the FFD (cyl) tree and select the **Control Points** item

❏ Edit the lower part of the vase. To accomplish this, maximize the viewport with the <W> key and then go to the **Left** viewport with the <L> key.

❏ Select lower control points by enclosing them into a rectangle.

❏ Lock selection:

Status Controls → Lock Selection Set *or* <Space>

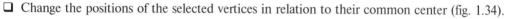

❏ Switch to the Uniform Scale mode to change the size:

Right-click menu/TRANSFORM → Scale *or* Main Toolbar → Uniform Scale

❏ Change the positions of the selected vertices in relation to their common center (fig. 1.34).

❏ Select a group of control points in the lower part of your object.

❏ Move them alternately upwards and downwards along the Y-axis, thus adjusting the shape of the vase:

Right-click menu/TRANSFORM → Move
*or* Main Toolbar → Select and Move

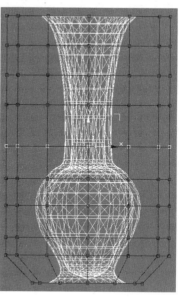

❏ By selecting and moving the control points, try to attain a shape like the one shown in fig. 1.34.

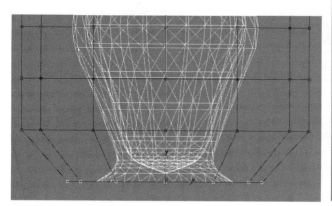

**Fig. 1.34.** The result of scaling the control points

**Fig. 1.35.** The result of moving the control points of the FFD (cyl) modifier

Now let's carry out more sophisticated procedures on the upper control points.

❑ Switch the viewport to the orthographic view. To do so, rotate the viewport by dragging with the middle mouse button while pressing and holding down the <Alt> key:

Viewport Navigation Controls → Arc Rotate

❑ Zoom the region to include the uppermost control points (fig. 1.36):

Viewport Navigation Controls → Region Zoom or <Ctrl>+<W>

❑ Pan through the viewport as necessary:

Viewport Navigation Controls → Pan or <Ctrl>+<P>

Now be very careful!

❑ Press and hold the <Ctrl> key, and select *every other point* of those making up the upper control mesh.

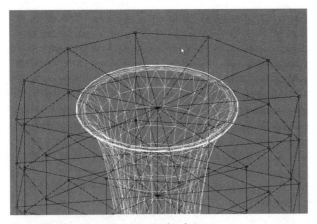

Fig. 1.36. The uppermost control points

Fig. 1.37. The final view of the vase

❑ Lock selection:

Status Controls → Lock Selection Set or <Space>

❑ Switch to the Uniform Scale mode to change the size:

Right-click menu/TRANSFORM → Scale or Main Toolbar → Uniform Scale

❑ Change the positions of the selected vertices in relation to their common center.

❑ Without unlocking the selection, move the selected points slightly upwards along the Z-axis:

Right-click menu /TRANSFORM → Move

***Self-study*** Try to perform similar procedures with other horizontally positioned groups of control points.

❑ Convert the vase to Editable Mesh.

You'll get a picture similar to the one shown in fig. 1.37.

# Creating Material for the Vase

You may have a similar crystal vase at home. If you examine it, you'll notice that there are notches on its outer surface, which make up a simple pattern. Generally, the inner surface has no notches. Now try to model this material.

First of all, you'll need to "separate" the outer surface from the other ones. I've used the word *separate* since the surfaces will actually be separated only from the Material Editor point of view. No modifications will be introduced from the geometrical point of view.

**NOTE** Notice that the method used here for assigning materials to subobjects is now obsolete. 3ds max 4 provides better technique, which is more elegant. On the other hand, however, the method we use is the best to illustrate the principle of dividing an object to subobjects as relates to the materials used.

❑ Select the vase.

❑ Switch to the Modify mode.

❑ Switch to the selection mode:

Right-click menu → Sub-objects → Element *or* Control panel → ... → **Selection** rollout → **Element** button

❑ Select the outer surface (fig. 1.38).

❑ Assign it material ID value equal to 2:

Control panel → ... → Surface Properties → Material ID

Enter "2" and press <Enter>

**NOTE** The NURBS model was intentionally chosen for editing. As a matter of fact, when converting a NURBS object, 3ds max 4 turns every NURBS surface into a distinct element (a group of faces). To verify this, try to move the selected element. You'll notice that the outer surface moves independently from the other surfaces.

**Fig. 1.38.** The selected outer surface of the vase (colored gray)

❏ Select all the remaining surfaces in turn and make sure that material ID value assigned to them is equal to 1.

❏ If this isn't so, change the values to 1.

❏ Switch to the object editing mode:

Right-click menu/TOOLS 1  → Sub-objects → Top-level

❏ Open the Material Editor:

Main Toolbar → Material Editor *or* <M>

❏ Select any unused sample slot.

❏ Change the material type to Raytrace:

Material Editor → **Standard** button

Material/Map Browser → Browse From: New

Material/Map Browser → Raytrace Raytrace

❏ Rename the material to Crystal_main Crystal_main . Enter the name and press <Enter>.

❏ Set the **2-Sided** checkbox ☑ 2-Sided ☐ Wire :

Material Editor → Raytrace Basic Parameters → 2-Sided

❏ Set the **Index of Refraction** value to 2:

Material Editor → Raytrace Basic Parameters → → Index of Refr: 2

Index of Refr: 2.0

❏ Change the transparency color to light blue:

Material Editor → Raytrace Basic Parameters → double-click **Diffuse**

Color Selector → set **Hue** to 133, **Sat** to 23, and **Value** to 228

Hue: 133
Sat: 23
Value: 228

**NOTE** 3ds max 4 supports two color formats: RGB (Red, Green, Blue) and HSV (Hue, Saturation, Value). I recommend you to use the second format. Recall, that in your everyday life, when describing a color, you don't say that it has  "thirty points of red, thirty points of blue and 120 points of green". Rather, we describe the color as "light-green" or "pale yellow"".

❏ Increase the brightness of the material by editing parameters in the **Specular Highlight** group:

Material editor → **Raytrace Basic Parameters** rollout → **Specular Highlight** group → **Specular Level**:100, **Glossiness**:70

Specular Highlight
Specular Color:
Specular Level: 100
Glossiness: 70
Soften: 0.1

Before you start editing transparency and reflection, it is necessary to say some words about these parameters. If you look carefully at a glassware, you'll notice that transparency decreases when nearing the edges of an object (a glass, for example). Reflection, on the other hand, increases. Let us imitate these properties of the materials for our vase.

As the first step, adjust transparency.

> **TIP** To view the changes in the sample slot of material editor, enable the background by clicking appropriate button in Material Editor.

❑ Clear the color checkbox next to the **Transparency** field:

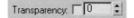

Material Editor → Raytrace Basic Parameters → Transparency

❑ Click the button next to the value and select the Falloff map:

Material/Map Browser → Falloff

❑ Edit the Falloff parameters as shown in fig. 1.39.

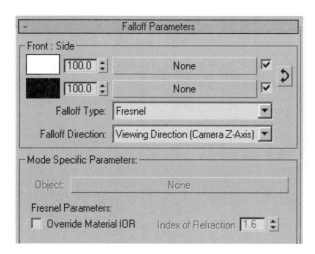

**Fig. 1.39.** Parameters of the Falloff map for transparency

> **TIP** Exchange the places of colors in the **Front: Side** group.
>
> Set the falloff type to Fresnel. As for falloff direction, set it along the Camera Z-Axis.
>
> Disable the **Override Material IOR** parameter (which sets the index of refraction different from the value specified in material parameters).

❑ Resume editing of the material parameters by clicking the **Go to Parent** button.

❑ Copy the map from transparency to reflection using the copy method.

❑ Clear the color checkbox next to the **Reflect** field.

❑ Switch to editing the map applied to the reflection channel, and exchange the order of colors in the **Front: Side** group.

I hope that you have understood how the Falloff map works. White corresponds to the maximum value of the parameter, while black corresponds to zero. Thus, the transparency is at maximum in the center and gradually decreases when approaching edges. Reflection, in contrast to transparency, is at its minimum value in the center and increases when approaching the edges.

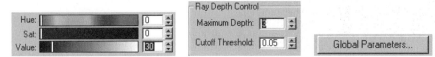

❑ Assign this material to the vase:

Material Editor → **Assign Material to Selection** button

**NOTE** If the button is inaccessible, select the vase without leaving the Material Editor.

You can also apply material to an object by dragging it from the sample slot and dropping it when the mouse pointer is over the object (that is, with the drag-and-drop method).

Now material is applied to your object.

**NOTE** You can judge whether or not the material is assigned to an object by the border of the sample slot. In fig. 1.40, the leftmost slot contains the material applied to an object (inherent white corners of the border can be seen). The material in the middle is being edited, but not applied to an object, and the rightmost slot contains material that isn't applied to any object of the scene.

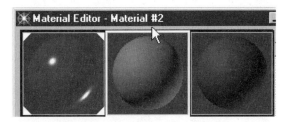

**Fig. 1.40.** Different states of material as related to objects

❑ Perform the test rendering:

Menu Bar → Rendering → Render... *or* <Shift>+<R> → **Render** button

***TIP*** Since you'll perform test rendering often, I recommend that you set the picture size to 320×240 pixels maximum (the **Output Size** group). This will speed up the process.

The result of the test rendering of our vase is shown in fig. 1.41.

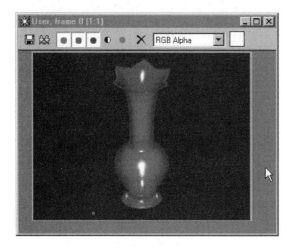

**Fig. 1.41.** The result of rendering the vase

Now you need to notch the outer surface of your vase. 3ds max 4 presents two methods of creating a relief on a surface: Bump and Displacement. Since we're going to view our picture on the computer screen (with resolution no better than 640×480) and the notches aren't very deep, we'll use the Bump map. If you're planning to print the picture (with a resolution of 1500×1500 or better), you'll have to use the Displacement map.

As a relief map, we'll use a simple one that can be found on the companion CD in the \Lessons\Lesson01\Maps\vase_bump.tif file.

Notice that this image has a Grayscale 256 format. However, this isn't a mandatory requirement. 3ds max 4 can use any picture — from black-and-white to fully colored — for a Bump map. However, since we'll only use the brightness parameter (that's *value* in terms of 3ds max 4) and editing a "gray" picture is easier, we'll use the Grayscale format.

❑ Copy the Crystal_main material to another sample slot.

❑ Rename the material to Crystal_Bump. To do so, enter the new name and press <Enter>.

❑ Assign the file vase_bump.tif as a Bump map:

Material Editor → Raytrace Basic Parameters → the **None** button next to the **Bump** field

Material/Map Browser → Browse From: New

Material/Map Browser → select and double-click bitmap, then select the vase_bump.tif file

❑ Rename the relief map to Crystal_Bump_map.

❑ Return to the parameter-editing level:

Material Editor → **Go to Parent** button 

❑ Set the map value to 150 and set the **Bump** checkbox.

Now you need to create a Multi material, which will be the final one for our vase.

❑ Choose an unused sample slot.

❑ Change the material type to Multi/Sub-Object:

Material Editor → the **Type: Standard** button

Material/Map Browser → Browse From: New

Material/Map Browser → select **Multi/Sub-Object** and double-click it with the left mouse button

In the **Replace Material** dialog box, set the **Discard old material** radio button and click **OK**

❑ Set the number of materials to 2:

Material Editor → **Multi/Sub-object Basic Parameters** → the **Set Number** button

Enter "2" and press <Enter>

❑ Set Crystal_main as the first material and Crystal_Bump as the second one with the **Instance** parameter. To do this:

- In Material Editor, drag Crystal_main to the upper button of the sub_material slot.

- Select **Instance** in the **Instance (Copy) Material** dialog box and click **OK**.

- In Material Editor, drag Crystal_Bump to the lower button of the sub_material slot.

- Select **Instance** in the **Instance (Copy) Material** dialog box and click **OK**.

❑ Rename the material to Crystal.

❑ Assign the new material to our vase:

Select the vase

Material Editor → **Assign Material to Selection** button *or* Drag the Crystal material to the vase

❑ Perform test rendering (fig. 1.42).

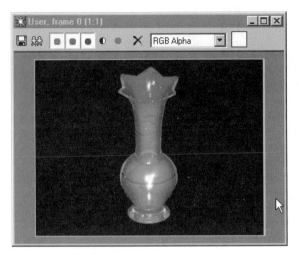

**Fig. 1.42.** Test rendering. The map is visible

The map is now visible, but its position still needs to be corrected.

Let's continue editing. You need to set up mapping parameters. 3ds max 4 allows you to set up mapping coordinates in the viewport without having to perform test rendering.

❑ Switch to the Smooth+Highlight mode for rendering the viewport.

❑ Return to the Material Editor.

❑ Switch to editing of the Crystal_Bump material.

> **NOTE** Since Crystal is a Multi/Sub-object material created with the Instance Method, all subsequent changes in Crystal_main and Crystal_Bump will automatically appear in Crystal.

❑ Switch to editing of the Bump map of the Crystal_Bump material.

❑ Click the **Show Map in Viewport** button ⬡ :

Material Editor → Show Map in Viewport

A picture will appear like that shown in fig. 1.43. As you can see, it has low contrast. This is because our object is transparent. The map can be viewed, however.

❑ Change the tiling along the U-coordinate to 12:

Material Editor → **Coordinates** panel → **U:Tiling** field → → enter "12"

❑ Disable the tiling along the V-coordinate:

Material Editor → Coordinates → clear the **V:Tile** checkbox

You'll see the map tiled around the vase (fig. 1.44).

◄ **Fig. 1.43.** Mapping in the viewport before coordinate correction

*TIP*   3ds max 4 can use two map filtering algorithms. A **Pyramidal** one is rough, but it's less time-consuming, whereas a **Summed Area** algorithm provides better quality. You should use the latter algorithm for mapping:

Material Editor → **Bitmap Parameters** rollout → Filtering → Summed Area

Now you need to correct the vertical mapping. To do this, use the Unwrap UVW modifier.

❑  Close the Material Editor.

❑  Go to the **Left** viewport by pressing <L>.

❑  Switch to the Smooth+Highlight mode if necessary.

❑  Switch to the Polygon mode:

Right-click menu/ TOOLS 1  → Sub-objects → Polygon

❑  Select the polygons as shown in fig. 1.45.

**Fig. 1.44.** Mapping in the viewport after coordinate correction

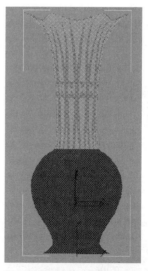

**Fig. 1.45.** The polygons selected for editing the mapping coordinates

*TIP* 3ds max 4 provides very convenient capabilities of displaying faceted surfaces in Smooth+Highlight mode (Viewport right-click menu → **Edged Faces** checkbox or <F4> button) and filling selected faces (the <F2> button).

❑ Use the Unwrap UVW modifier:

Tab panel → Modifiers → Unwrap_UVW *or* Control panel → Modifier List → Unwrap UVW

❑ Switch to the coordinate editing mode (fig. 1.46):

Control panel → ... → Parameters → the **Edit** button

❑ Select all the vertices and lock the selection:

Edit UVWs → the **Lock Selection** button

❑ Perform vertical scaling of the selected vertices up to the size approximately equal to that of the lower part of the map:

Edit UVWs → left-click the **Scale** button and, keeping the left mouse button pressed, select **Scale Vertical**

Notice how your map changes in the viewport.

❑ Move the vertices along the vertical axis so that they're near the center of the lower part of the map:

Edit UVWs → left-click the **Move** button and, keeping the left mouse button pressed, select **Move Vertical**

❑ Edit the size and the position of the selected group of vertices as necessary.
❑ Close the window to exit the editing mode.
❑ Use the Mesh Select modifier:

Control panel → Modifier List → Mesh Select

❑ Switch to the mode for polygon selecting:

Control panel → ... → the **Polygon** button

❑ Invert selection to select the other polygons:

Menu Bar → Edit → Select Invert

*TIP* There's no default keyboard shortcut for inverting selection in 3ds max 4. However, you already know how to assign hotkeys. Assign the combination <Alt>+<Grey *> to the **Select Invert** command.

❑ Use the Unwrap UVW modifier and repeat the procedures described above for the remaining polygons.

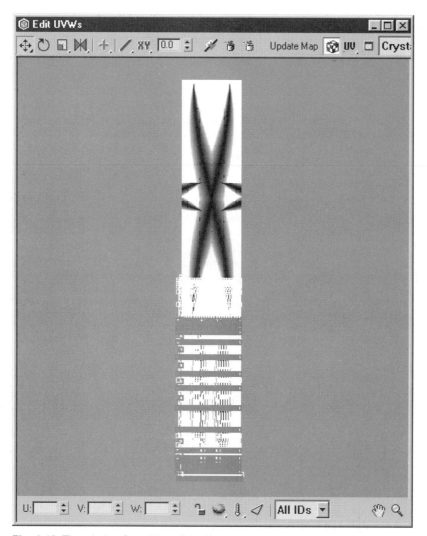

**Fig. 1.46.** The window for editing of the Unwrap UVW modifier

Now everything's correct.

❑ Save the scene under the name of lesson01-vase_ready.max.

After you've performed the test rendering, you'll see a picture similar to the one shown in fig. 1.47.

At the moment, the vase doesn't look quite right. As a matter of fact, the Raytrace material attempts to reflect and refract the environment; however, it has nothing to reflect or refract but itself.

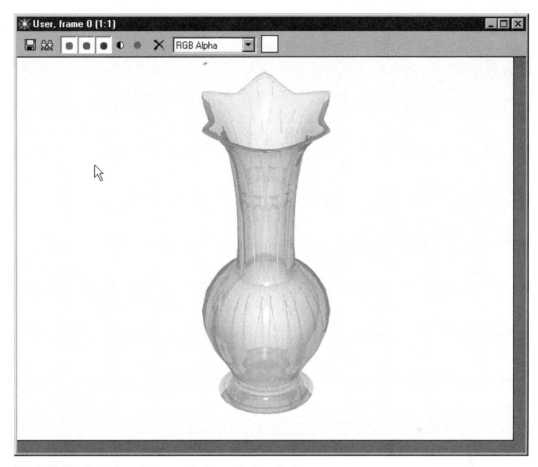

**Fig. 1.47.** The final view of the vase in the rendering window

# Modeling the Dahlia Flower

## Modeling Petals

To model the petals, we'll apply the patch method with the use of the Surface modifier and subsequent editing.

❑ Reset 3ds max 4:

  Main menu → File → Reset

❑ Go to the **Top** viewport.

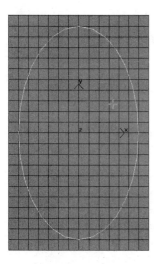

❑ Maximize the window:

Viewport Navigation Controls → Min/Max Toggle or <W>

❑ Turn on Snap to grid:

Status Controls → the **3D Snap Toggle** button or <S>

❑ Create an ellipse 100×200 with its center in the origin of co-ordinates (fig. 1.48):

Tab panel → Shapes → Ellipse or Main Menu → Create → Shapes → Splines → Ellipse

**Fig. 1.48.** An ellipse as a dummy for a petal

*TIP*  By default, ellipses and some other shapes are created using two angle points. Sometimes – for example, in this case – it's useful to switch to creating from the center:

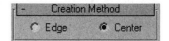

Creation Method → Center

❑ Convert the resulting curve to editable shape:

Right-click menu/TRANSFORM → Convert To: → Convert to Editable Spline

❑ Switch to the modify mode:

Right-click menu/ TOOLS 1 → Sub-objects → Vertex or Control panel → ... → **Selection** rollout → **Vertex** button

❑ Change the shape of the petal according to its image on the CD-ROM in the \Lessons\Lesson01\Maps\ptl.tif file. Select the lateral vertices and move them upward along the Y-axis.

❑ Having selected the two corresponding vertices, give a pointed form to the uppermost and lowermost points of the petal. Select upper and lover vertices and convert them to Bezier Corner.

Right-click menu/TOOLS 1 → Bezier Corner

❑ Switch to the Move mode:

Right-click menu/TRANSFORM → Move

❑ Drag one of the handles closer to the center, up along the Y-axis. If you wish, you can disable the Transform Gizmo, by pressing the <X> key.

You can also change the direction of movement by pressing the <F5>—<F9> keys or clicking appropriate buttons on the Main toolbar.

❑ Perform the procedure mentioned above with the upper vertex. Move the vertices down along the Y-axis.

You'll see a picture similar to the one shown in fig. 1.49.

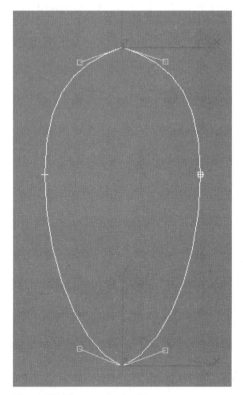

Of course, the model is quite primitive, but this won't stand out when there are more petals.

❑ Use the Surface modifier:

Tab panel → Modeling → Patch Surface *or* Control panel → Modifier List → Surface

❑ Set up the parameters of the Surface modifier as shown in fig. 1.50:

Control panel → ... → **Parameters** rollout

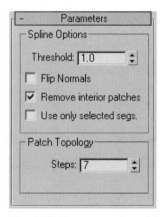

**Fig. 1.49.** The result of editing the vertices of the petal

**Fig. 1.50.** The parameters of the Surface modifier

You'll see a picture like the one shown in fig. 1.51.

❏ Switch the viewport to the orthographic view, using the petal as the center of rotation of the viewport:

Viewport Navigation Controls → **Arc Rotate** button

Left-click the **Arc Rotate** button, then drag the mouse pointer to the **Arc Rotate Selected** button

❏ Dragging the mouse pointer through the viewport, choose the best projection.

Now you need to make the petal look more realistic. For this purpose, change its shape slightly so that it becomes convex.

❏ Use the Edit Patch modifier:

Tab panel → Modeling → Edit Patch *or* Control panel → Modifier List → Edit Patch

***NOTE*** Patch editing is similar to the spline editing process. The only difference is that each vertex has four handles rather than two. However, there's also the following analogy: Vertex corresponds to Vertex, Segment corresponds to Edge, and Spline corresponds to Patch.

**Fig. 1.51.** The result of using the Surface modifier

❏ Switch to the Vertex mode to edit vertices:

Right-click menu/TOOLS 1 → Sub-objects → Vertex *or* Control panel → ... → **Selection** rollout → **Vertex** button

Now it's obvious that we're short of vertices.

❏ Switch to the patch editing mode:

Right-click menu/TOOLS 1 → Sub-objects → Patch *or* Control panel → ... → **Selection** rollout → **Patch** button

❏ Select a patch.

❏ Divide it into several smaller ones:

Right-click menu/TOOLS 1 → Subdivide Patch *or* Control panel → ... → **Geometry** rollout → **Subdivide** button

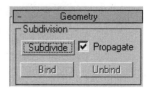

❏ Switch to the vertex editing mode:

Right-click menu → Sub-objects → Vertex

❏ Select the vertices as shown in fig. 1.52.

❏ Move them slightly along the Z-axis:

Right-click menu/TRANSFORM → Move

❏ Rename the object to Ptl01:

Control panel → Modify → enter the name and press <Enter>

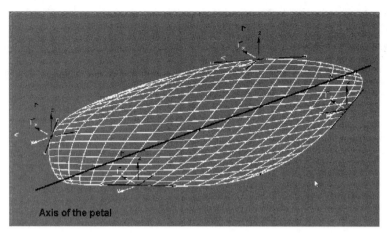

**Fig. 1.52.** The result of selecting and moving the vertices

Let's create a material for the petals.

❐ Open Material Editor:

Main Toolbar → Material Editor *or* <M>

❐ Select the first sample slot and set up the material parameters according to the fig. 1.53:

Material Editor → Shader Basic Parameters → Shader: Blinn:

Material Editor → Shader Basic Parameters → 2-Sided

Material Editor → Blinn Basic Parameters → Diffuse → Hue: 0, Sat: 0, Value: 200

Unlock the diffuse and ambient colors.

Move the diffuse color to ambient, using the Copy method.

Material Editor → Blinn Basic Parameters → Ambient → Hue: 0, Sat: 0, Value: 64

Material Editor → Blinn Basic Parameters → Specular → Hue: 0, Sat: 0, Value: 255

Material Editor → Blinn Basic Parameters → Specular Highlights → Specular Level: 10, Glossiness: 0, Soften: 1.0

❐ Assign a bitmap as a diffuse map:

Material Editor → Maps → the **None** button in the **Diffuse Color** line

Material/Map Browser → Browse From: New

Material/Map Browser → Bitmap

❐ Select the ptl.tif file located on the companion CD in the \Lessons\Lesson01\Maps directory.

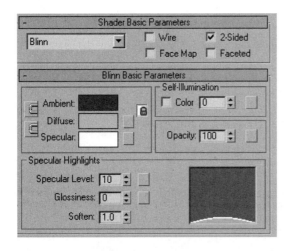

**Fig. 1.53.** The parameters of the Petal material

❏ Click the **Show Map in Viewport** button.

❏ Rename the map to ptl_diffuse.

❏ Return to the basic parameters of material:

Material Editor → **Go To Parent** button

❏ Assign Self_illumination and Bump to the ptl_diffuse map:

Material Editor → Maps → drag the map from the **Diffuse Color** slot to Self_illumination

Select the Instance method and click **OK**

Enter 20 into the **Self illumination** field

Material Editor → Maps → drag the map from the **Diffuse Color** slot to **Bump**

Select the Instance method and click **OK**

Enter 20 into the **Bump** field

❏ Rename the material to Petal.

❏ Assign this material to the object of the same name. To do so, select the object and, in the Material Editor, click the **Assign Material to Selection** button.

❏ Close the Material Editor window.

❏ Switch to the Smooth+Highlight mode.

Although we've instructed 3ds max 4 to show the map in the viewport, we can't see it. Can you guess why? Right. The point is that we haven't assigned UVW Mapping to the object.

❏ Press <T> to switch to the **Top** viewport:

Tab panel → Modifiers → UVW Map Modifier *or* Control panel → Modifier Stack → UVW Map

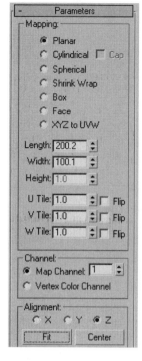

◄ **Fig. 1.54.** Mapping coordinates parameters for the petal

Normally, the correct mapping coordinates are assigned automatically. If the automatic assignment isn't correct, set up the parameters as shown in fig. 1.54. The resulting image must look like the one shown in fig. 1.55.

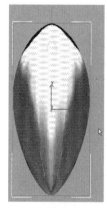

**Fig. 1.55.** A mapped petal

❏ Get rid of the black contour by changing the mapping sizes:

Control panel → ... → **Parameters** rollout → **Length** and **Width** fields

❏ Besides, you can use new 3ds max 4 functionality – manipulator helpers.

Right-click menu/TRANSFORM → Manipulate

Drag the green square in such a way as to stretch the map in order to get rid of the black contour.

I need to mention that we have made a mistake by starting to edit the object before assigning mapping coordinates. Assigning mapping coordinates immediately after applying the Surface modifier would be more appropriate. Unfortunately, simply moving of the UVW Map modifier within the modifier stack can't solve this problem. You can try to move the UVW Map modifier downward within the stack and view the results. In our case this is not highly important because distortions are not very significant. However, keep this in mind and don't reproduce this mistake in your future projects.

However, let us proceed further.

❏ Convert the object to Editable Mesh:

Right-click menu → Convert To: → Convert to Editable Mesh

One petal is ready. Now we'll create a corolla using the Snapshot method. This method is complicated, so be very careful.

❑ Switch to the **Left** viewport by pressing the <L> key.

❑ If required, change the zoom so that the object takes up the entire viewport space:

Viewport Navigation Controls → Zoom Extents or <Ctrl>+<Alt>+<Z>

❑ Use the Bend modifier:

Tab panel → Modifiers → Bend or Control panel → Modifier List → Bend

❑ Set up the parameters, as shown in fig. 1.56 (a).

❑ Press <F> to switch to the **Front** viewport.

❑ Use the Bend modifier once again, by dragging it within the modifier stack while pressing and holding the <Shift> key.

❑ Set up the parameters, as shown in fig. 1.56 (b).

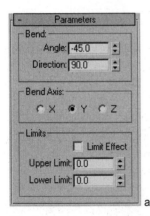 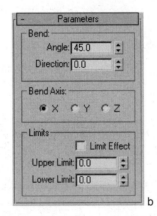

**Fig. 1.56.** The parameters of the first (a) and the second (b) Bend modifiers

❑ "Crumple" the petal a little with the Noise modifier. Set its parameters as shown in fig. 1.57:

Tab panel → Modifiers → Noise or Control panel → Modifier List → Noise

❑ Again, go to the **Left** viewport by pressing the <L> key.

❑ Rotate the petal around the Z-axis as shown in fig. 1.58:

Right-click menu/TRANSFORM → Rotate

❑ Hold the current state:

Menu Bar → Edit → Hold or <Ctrl>+<Alt>+<H>

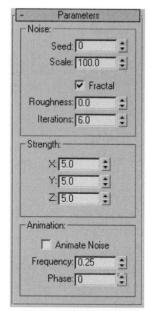

**Parameters**

Noise:

Seed: 0

Scale: 100.0

☑ Fractal

Roughness: 0.0

Iterations: 6.0

Strength:

X: 5.0

Y: 5.0

Z: 5.0

Animation:

☐ Animate Noise

Frequency: 0.25

Phase: 0

◄ **Fig. 1.57.** The parameters of the Noise modifier

Now the most exciting things are about to start!

☐ Click the **Animate** button .

☐ Go to the last frame:

Time controls → **Go To End** button ▶▶| or the <End> key

☐ Jump to the first Bend modifier in the modifier stack.

☐ Change its parameters as shown in fig. 1.59 (a).

☐ Move through the stack up to the second bend modifier.

☐ Change the modifier parameters as shown in fig. 1.59 (b).

Try to playback the resulting animation:

Time Controls → **Play Animation** button

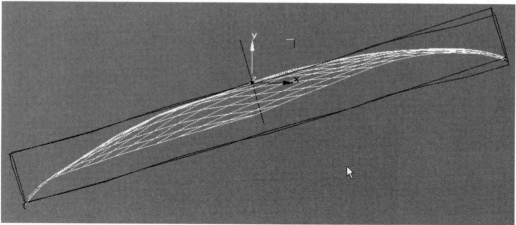

**Fig. 1.58.** The initial position of the petal

☐ Once again, go to the last frame by pressing the <End> key.

☐ Rotate the petal, change its size, and move it as shown in fig. 1.60.

Right-click menu/TRANSFORM → Rotate, Move, Scale

☐ Disable the animation by clicking the **Animate** button .

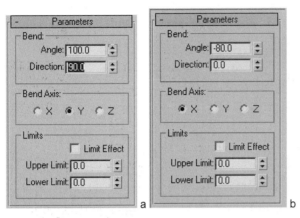
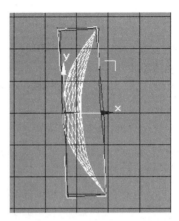

a                                                        b

**Fig. 1.59.** The parameters of the first (a) and the second (b)     **Fig. 1.60.** The final position of the petal
Bend modifiers in the last frame

❑ Copy the intermediate stages. For this purpose, select the **Tools** command in the Menu
Bar and go to the **Snapshot** dialog (fig. 1.61). Set the **Range** radio button, set **Copies** to 6,
and set the **Mesh** radio button in the **Clone Method** group.

❑ Press <Del> to delete the initial object.

❑ Position the resulting petals as shown in fig. 1.62.

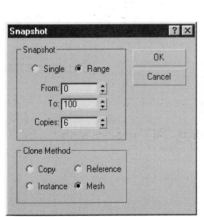
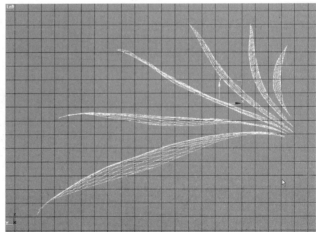

**Fig. 1.61.** The **Snapshot** dialog box     **Fig. 1.62.** Final view of the petals

❑ Select all the petals and group them:

Menu Bar → Edit → Select All *or* <Grey *> if you have assigned this hotkey

Menu Bar → Group → Group

Enter the PETALS00 name and click **OK**

Now you need to change a very important parameter of the object; namely, a *pivot point*. This is the reference point for all transformations.

❐ Press <T> to switch to the **Top** viewport.

❐ Switch to the pivot point editing mode:

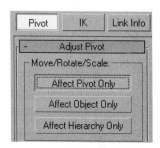

Control panel → Hierarchy → **Pivot** button → **Adjust Pivot** rollout → **Affect Pivot Only** button

❐ Move the pivot point along the Y-axis to the point from where the petals are growing.

❐ Switch to the modify mode:

Control panel → Modify

❐ Change the transformation center to **Use Pivot Point Center**:

Tab panel → Main Toolbar → left-click the **Use... Center** button and, keeping the left mouse button pressed, select **Use Pivot Point Center**

❐ Switch to the object rotation mode:

Right-click menu/TRANSFORM → Rotate

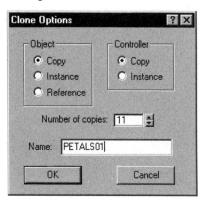

❐ Make sure that the Angle Snap mode is on:

Status controls → **Angle Snap Toggle** button or the <A> key

❐ While keeping the <Shift> key pressed, rotate the PETALS00 object by 30° clockwise.

❐ In the **Clone Options** dialog (fig. 1.63), set the **Number of copies** parameter to 11 and set the **Copy** radio buttons in the **Object** and **Controller** groups.

**Fig. 1.63.** The **Clone Options** dialog box

❐ The result is shown in fig. 1.64.

The corolla is beautiful, but not perfect! Notice that the petals penetrate each other. There's no other way of eliminating this problem but to pull them apart manually.

❐ Press <T> to switch to the **Top** viewport.

❐ Keeping the <Ctrl> key pressed, select every third group of petals.

❐ Lock the selection by pressing the spacebar.

❐ Press <L> to switch to the **Left** viewport.

❐ Move the selected petals slightly downwards along the Y-axis, so that they don't run through the adjoining ones.

    *TIP* If you're editing a large number of objects, it's useful to *freeze* some of them. In this case, you may freeze the objects you've performed actions upon.

❐ Freeze the selected petals:

    Control panel → Display → **Freeze** rollout → **Freeze Selected** button *or* the <6> key

❐ Press <T> to switch to the **Top** viewport.

❐ Select the other four groups of petals.

❐ Lock selection by pressing the spacebar.

❐ Press <L> to switch to the **Left** viewport.

❐ Decrease the sizes of the petals a little:

    Right-click menu/TRANSFORM → Scale

❐ Move the selected petals slightly upwards along the Y-axis:

    Right-click menu/TRANSFORM → Move

❐ Unfreeze all petals:

    Control panel → Display → **Freeze** rollout → **Unfreeze All** button *or* the <7> key

That's all there is to it! The result is shown in fig. 1.65.

**Fig. 1.64.** The corolla

**Fig. 1.65.** The final view of the corolla

Now you need to combine the petals into one group.

❏ Select all the petals, group them and name the final object CROWN:

Menu Bar → Edit → Select All *or* <Grey *>

Menu Bar → Group → Group

Enter the name and click **OK**

❏ Perform the test rendering (fig. 1.66).

**Fig. 1.66.** The result of rendering the corolla

In my opinion, the result is worth the effort.

**Self-study**   To make the flower look more realistic, ungroup all its petals using the **Group**, **Explode** commands in the Menu Bar. Select all the petals on a certain level (for example, all the petals of the lowermost level). Go to the **Top** viewport and rotate them by approximately 30°. Repeat the same procedure for the other petals, changing the rotation angle each time. Then group the petals again.

Now add the final stroke.

❏ Apply the Noise modifier to the entire group.

❏ Change the parameters of the modifier, thus introducing some chaos to the positions of the petals.

❏ Save the image in the lesson01_dahlia_corolla.max file:

Menu Bar → Save As

*Self-study*    The method described above is appropriate for flowers with many petals, such as roses and asters. Try to create them by yourself.

# Modeling Leaves and the Stalk

To model the leaves, we'll use a somewhat different method than the one described in the previous section. However, this method is also based on patch editing. In this case, we'll use the opacity map in the Material Editor rather than draw the leaves.

❏ Reset 3ds max 4:

Main menu → File → Reset

❏ Switch to the **Top** viewport.

❏ Maximize the window:

Viewport Navigation Controls → Min/Max Toggle *or* <W>

To ensure that the size of the leaf corresponds to that of the object, you need to do the following:

❏ Assign background to the viewport:

Menu Bar → Views → Viewport Background

❏ The **Viewport Background** dialog will appear. Set up the parameters as shown in fig. 1.67.

*NOTE*    The **Aspect Ratio** → **Match Bitmap** command maintains the proportions of the initial image. The **Lock Zoom/Pan** command keeps the size and position of background in line with the actions performed on the viewport.

❏ Click **Files** to load the Leaf_f.tif file, which is located at the companion CD in the \Lessons\Lesson01\Maps directory. Click **OK**.

❏ An image of a dahlia leaf will appear. Change the Zoom of the viewport so you can see the entire leaf (fig. 1.68):

<Ctrl>+<Alt>+middle mouse button *or* Viewport Navigation Controls → Zoom *or* <Z>

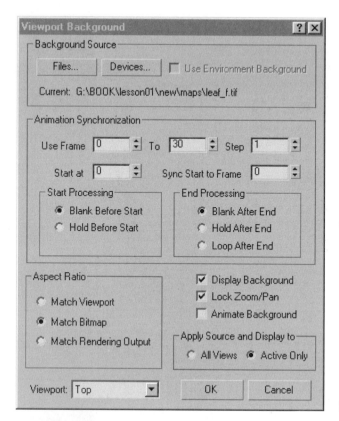

**Fig. 1.67.** The background parameters

**Fig. 1.68.** The viewport
with a dahlia leaf as the background

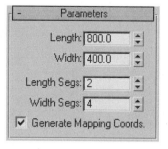

**Fig. 1.69.** The **Parameters** rollout

❏ Create a patch grid in accordance with the background dimensions:

Tab panel → Objects → Quad Patch *or* Control panel → Create → Geometry → Patch Grids → Quad Patch

❏  Switch to the Modify mode:

Right-click menu → Modify Mode *or* Control panel → Modify

❏  In the **Parameters** rollout (fig. 1.69), set up the following parameters: **Length Segs** to 2 and **Width Segs** to 2. Set the **Generate Mapping Coords** checkbox.

The geometry of the leaf is set.

❏  Rename the object to Leaf and convert it to Editable Patch:

Right-click menu/TRANSFORM → Convert To: → Convert to Editable Patch

The correct mapping is a matter of particular importance.

❏  Switch off the background:

Viewport Right-click menu → clear the **Show Background** checkbox

❏  Press <M> to switch to the Material Editor.

❏  Select the first sample slot.

❏  Set up the material parameters as follows:

Material Editor → Shader Basic Parameters → Anisotropic

Material Editor → Anisotropic Basic Parameters → Ambient → → Hue: 88, Sat: 159, Value: 45

Material Editor → Anisotropic Basic Parameters → Diffuse → → Hue: 88, Sat: 159, Value: 141

Material Editor → Anisotropic Basic Parameters → Ambient → → Hue: 88, Sat: 80, Value: 210

Material Editor → Anisotropic Basic Parameters → Specular Highlight → Specular Level: 20, Glossiness: 40, Anisotropy: 50, Orientation: 0

❏  Rename the material to Leaf_top.

❏  Assign the file Leaf_f.tif to Diffuse channel as a diffuse map:

Material Editor → Maps → **None** button in the **Diffuse Color** line

Material/Map Browser → Browse From: New

Material/Map Browser → Bitmap

Select file Leaf_f.tif

❏  Rename the map to Leaf_diffuse.

**TIP**   If you're sure you don't need tiling it along the U- and V-axis, you'll probably want to switch tiling off.

❏ Switch on the display of the map in the viewport:

Material Editor → **Show Map in Viewport** button

❏ Return to the material parameters:

Material Editor → **Go to Parent** button

❏ Assign the material to the object:

Material Editor → **Assign Material to Selection** button

❏ Switch to the Smooth+Highlights mode to render the viewport:

Top Viewport Right-click menu → Smooth+Highlights *or* <F3>

As you can see, the mapping isn't quite right due to the map asymmetry. To be more specific, the center of the leaf doesn't coincide with that of the object. This might present problems while editing the leaf later on. Correct the mapping to gain axial symmetry.

❏ Use the Unwrap UVW modifier:

Tab panel → Modifiers → Unwrap_UVW Modifier or Control panel → Modifier List → Unwrap UVW

❏ Switch to the coordinate editing mode:

Control panel → ... → Parameters → **Edit** button

❏ Select the central vertex in the lower row.

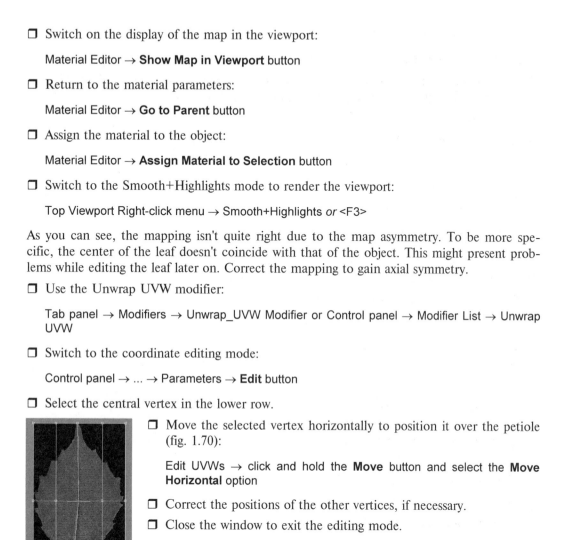

❏ Move the selected vertex horizontally to position it over the petiole (fig. 1.70):

Edit UVWs → click and hold the **Move** button and select the **Move Horizontal** option

❏ Correct the positions of the other vertices, if necessary.

❏ Close the window to exit the editing mode.

**Fig. 1.70.** Correction of applying the leaf map in the **Edit** window of the Unwrap UVW modifier

*NOTE*   Notice that we've corrected the mapping coordinates for all the maps using this mapping channel rather than a specific map. Because of this, we don't need to repeat the correction.

Now apply the remaining maps.

❏ Return to the Material Editor.

❑ Open the **Maps** rollout.

❑ Apply the Leaf_diffuse map to the Bump channel, using the Instance method.

Notice that the relief is somewhat different from the expected result. To be more precise, it has convexities instead of concavities. You can easily solve this problem by entering a negative number into the **Bump** field.

❑ Now apply a map to the opacity.

> Material Editor → Maps → **None** button in the **Opacity Color** line
>
> Material/Map Browser → Browse From: New
>
> Material/Map Browser → Bitmap
>
> Select the Leaf_f_o.tif file

❑ Rename the map to Leaf_opacity.

Now we have to solve another problem. If you perform the test rendering right now, you'll notice that the opacity map we've applied has only solved a part of our problem. Namely, a light green rectangle is visible. As a matter of fact, our material glitters a little. To suppress this glitter, you need to apply the same map to the Specular Level channel and modify it slightly.

❑ Apply the Leaf_opacity map to the Specular Level channel using the Copy method. Notice that it's the Copy method that must be used in the case!

If you perform the test rendering now, you'll see that the leaf is too bright.

❑ Switch to the map editing mode:

> Material Editor → **Maps** rollout → the button with the name of the map in the **Specular Level** line

❑ Go to the **Output** panel to gain access to the output parameters.

❑ Set the **Enable Color Map** checkbox to edit colors.

❑ On the diagram, move the rightmost vertex to the position shown in fig. 1.71. In doing this, you'll reduce the white color.

> ***NOTE*** Despite the fact that you're dealing with colors, only the **Value** channel is really important for the **Specular Level** parameter. This parameter, like most other settings using digital setup, interprets the channel as a number belonging to the range from 0 (black) to 255 (white).

Obviously, the leaf looks much better now!

Create a material for the other side of the leaf.

❑ Drag the Leaf_top material to another sample slot and switch to the editing mode.

❑ Rename the material to Leaf_bottom.

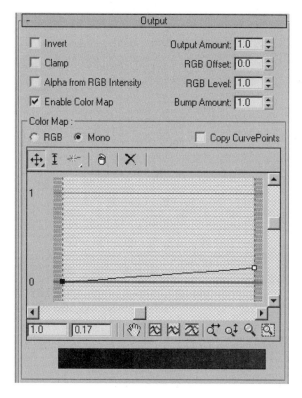

**Fig. 1.71.** Editing the brightness diagram

❏ Go to the diffuse map parameters and replace the Leaf_f.tif file by Leaf_b.tif.

Material Editor → **Maps** rollout → the button in the **Diffuse Color** line

Material Editor → ... → Bitmap Parameters → **Bitmap** button

Select the Leaf_b.tif file

❏ Return to the editing material parameters:

Material Editor → **Go to Parent** button

**NOTE**   Notice that there's no need to change the map in the Bump channel. This has happened, because you used the Instance method for maps in the initial material.

❏ Perform similar changes in the Opacity and Specular Level channels. In other words, replace the Leaf_f.tif file by the Leaf_b.tif file.

❏ Change **Glossiness** to 0:

Anisotropic Basic Parameters → Specular Highlight → Glossiness: 0

Now you have two materials. Let's proceed further to create the double-sided material.

❑ Create a new double-sided material (of the Double Sided type).

❑ Choose any unused sample slot.

❑ Click the **Standard** button and select **Double Sided**:

Material/Map Browser → Browse From: New

Material/Map Browser → Double Sided

❑ Assign the appropriate materials to the Facing Material and Back Material components of the newly created double-sided material. While dragging, use the Instance method in the Material Editor:

- Drag the Leaf_top material to the **Facing Material** button
- Drag the Leaf_bottom material to the **Back Material** button

❑ Rename the material to Leaf.

❑ Apply the Leaf material to the leaf.

Perform the test rendering. Rotate the viewport to view the facing side of the leaf first and then the back side. Notice, that the facing side looks all right, while the back side is far from perfect. To solve the problem, just mirror the maps.

❑ Switch to the editing mode for the Leaf_bottom material.

❑ Start editing the Diffuse Color map.

❑ Change the **U:Tiling** parameter to -1:

Material Editor → ... → Coordinates → U:Tiling

❑ Repeat the same procedure for all the other Leaf_bottom maps.

Since everything's fine now, we can proceed further.

❑ Apply the Edit Patch modifier:

Tab panel → Modeling → Edit Patch Modifier *or* Control panel → Modifier List → Edit Patch

❑ Switch to the vertex editing mode:

Right-click menu/TOOLS 1 → Sub-objects → Vertex *or* Control panel → **Selection** rollout → **Vertex** button

❑ Press <F> to switch to the **Front** viewport.

❑ Select all the vertices located to the left and to the right of the center.

❑ Move them upward along the Y-axis by one unit.

❑ Select all the vertices belonging to the left and right edges.

❑ Move them downward along the Y-axis by one or two units.

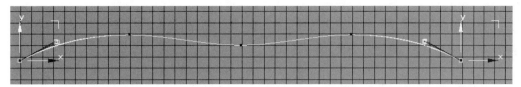

**Fig. 1.72.** The result of editing the vertices

Now you need to change the surface curvature near the edge vertices.

❐ Move the handles with the mouse to change the curvature as shown in fig. 1.72.

Bend the leaf slightly using the Bend modifier.

❐ Go to the **Left** viewport.

❐ Switch to the base object editing mode:

Right-click menu/TOOLS 1 → Sub-objects → Top Level

❐ Use the Bend modifier:

Tab panel → Modifiers → Bend *or* Control panel → Modifier List → Bend

❐ Set up the parameters as shown in fig. 1.73.

**Fig. 1.73.** The parameters of the Bend modifier

❐ Change the position of the modifier center:

Right-click menu/TOOLS 1 → Sub-objects → Center

❐ Move the center along the X-axis to the rightmost position. Create a cane with leaves. The dahlia has five leaves on a stalk.

❐ Press <T> to switch to the **Top** viewport.

❐ Copy the leaf:

Menu Bar → Edit → Clone

Select the **Copy** option and click **OK**

❐ Move and rotate the newly created leaf as if it grew from the same point as the first one.

❐ Mirror the new leaf about the X-axis, using the Copy method:

Menu Bar → TOOLS → Mirror
*or* Tab panel → Main Toolbar → **Mirror** button

Set up the parameters as follows: **Mirror Axis**: X and **Selection**: Copy

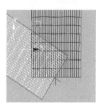

□ Move the new leaf along the X-axis.

□ Select the two new leaves and, while keeping the <Shift> key pressed, move them downward along the Y-axis.

□ Select the Copy method.

□ Slightly increase the size of these two leaves in relation to the common center.

You'll get a picture like the one shown in fig. 1.74.

**Fig. 1.74.** Dahlia leaves

As you may have noticed, the upper leaves are superimposed. To correct the situation, you'll need to do the following: Go to the **Top** viewport, rotate the uppermost leaf a little, and move the leaf into place.

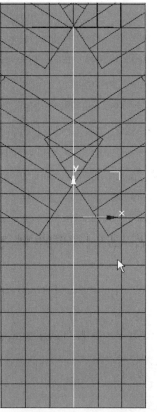

Now we need to create a cane for the leaves. Let's use the Loft method.

**NOTE** As I stated earlier in this lesson, the Loft method isn't always convenient. However, in this case, the power of lofting may be very helpful.

□ Press <T> to switch to the **Top** viewport.

□ Select all leaves.

□ Freeze them, pressing the <6> key.

□ Create a circle with a radius of 15 units:

<Ctrl>+Right-click menu/TOOLS → Circle *or* Tab panel → Shapes → Circle *or* Control panel → Create → Shapes → Circle

□ Create a vertical line that begins at the crossing point of the three upper leaves. Make its length twice as long as the distance between the beginning and the two lower leaves (fig. 1.75).

<Ctrl>+Right-click menu/TOOLS → Line

**NOTE** By "vertical line" I mean the line vertical in the screen coordinates. The line is actually horizontal in the world coordinates.

**Fig. 1.75.** The path for loft

❏ Create a Loft object without removing any selections from this line (which is the path for loft):

Tab panel → Compounds → Loft Compound Object *or* Control panel → Create → Geometry → → Compound Object → Loft

❏ Select the circle as a generating curve to create a shape:

Control panel → ... → **Creation Method** rollout → Instance

Control panel → ... → **Creation Method** rollout → **Get Shape** button → Select the circle

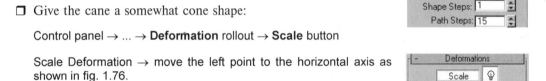

❏ Switch to the Modify mode:

Right-click menu → Modify Mode *or* Control panel → Modify

❏ Set up the Loft parameters:

Control panel → ... → **Surface Parameters** rollout → Mapping → set the **Apply Mapping** checkbox

Control panel → ... → **Skin Parameters** rollout → Options → **Shape Steps**: 1, **Path Steps**: 15

❏ Give the cane a somewhat cone shape:

Control panel → ... → **Deformation** rollout → **Scale** button

Scale Deformation → move the left point to the horizontal axis as shown in fig. 1.76.

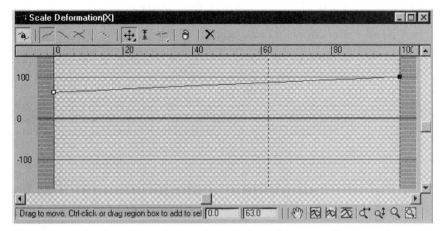

**Fig. 1.76.** The **Scale Deformation** window with the point corrected

Change the outline of the generating circle, thus changing the cross-section of the cane.

❐ Select the circle.

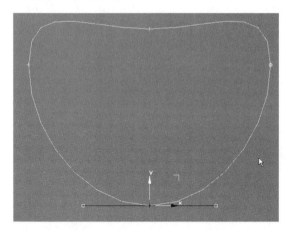

❐ Apply the Edit Spline modifier to it:

Control panel → Modifier List → Edit Spline

❐ Switch to the vertex editing mode:

Right-click menu/TOOLS 1 → Sub-objects → Vertex

❐ Move the vertices to transform the circle, as shown in fig. 1.77.

**Fig. 1.77.** The result of editing the cross-section of the cane

Select the cane and make sure that all your operations within the circle were processed by Loft.

❐ Unfreeze the leaves by pressing the <7> key.

❐ By moving each individual leaf, make them really "grow" out of the cane.

> **TIP**    It would be helpful to turn on the texture display in the Material Editor and to pull the leaves apart in the Smooth+Highlight mode of the viewport.

You probably couldn't achieve the desired result from the first attempt. So, let's try to change the shape of the cane by adding nodes in the places where the leaves grow.

❐ Select the cane.

❐ Switch to the scaling mode of a Loft object:

Control panel → ... → **Deformations** rollout → **Scale** button

❐ Unlock symmetrical editing:

Scale Deformation → **Make Symmetrical** button

❐ Make sure you're actually editing the curve responsible for deformation along the X-axis:

Scale Deformation → **Display X-Axis** button

❐ Add two vertices near the left end of the curve:

Scale Deformation → **Insert Corner Point** button

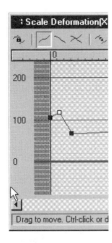

☐ Change their positions by clicking the **Move Control Point** button (fig. 1.78).

*TIP* Monitor the changes in the viewport (fig. 1.79).

**Fig. 1.78.** Changing the positions of the points in the **Scale Deformation** window

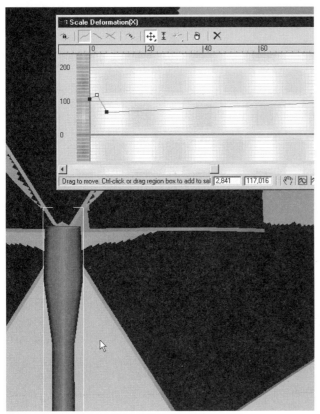

**Fig. 1.79.** The result of changing the positions of the points

❏ In the **Scale Deformation** window, add some more points and create nodes in the places where the leaves join the cane.

Now create a material for the cane.

❏ Press <M> to open the Material Editor.

❏ Use the Leaf_top material as a basis.

❏ Drag it to an unused slot.

❏ Rename the material to Stalk.

❏ Define the Blinn shader for the material:

Material Editor → Shader Basic Parameters → Blinn

❏ Set up the main parameters to obtain a matte material:

Material Editor → Specular Highlight → **Specular Level**: 10, **Glossiness**: 20, **Soften**: 1.0

Now let's settle things concerning the textures.

❏ Switch off the maps applied to the **Specular Level**, **Opacity**, and **Bump** channels, by moving **None** from the button next to the channel or simply clearing appropriate check-boxes.

❏ Apply the map of the Gradient Ramp type to the Diffuse channel:

Material Editor → **Maps** rollout → the button in the **Diffuse Color** line

Change the type by to the **Gradient Ramp** clicking the **Bitmap** button

This new map is ideal for creating regular maps based on color gradient. Using it, we'll create a texture simulating a lengthwise pattern on the branch.

*NOTE*   In-depth description of this map can be found in the 3ds max 4 online Help system.

❏ Build the gradient shown in fig. 1.80.

❏ In order to add a new color to the gradient, left-click the color field.

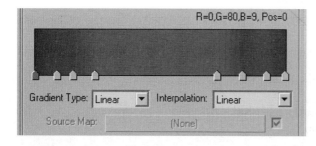

**Fig. 1.80.** Gradient used as a cane map

❏ In order to delete or edit a color, click the right mouse button and select the appropriate menu item.

❏ Set up the following:

- The first and eighth colors (from left to right) — **Hue**: 80, **Sat**: 255, **Value**: 90.
- The fourth and fifth colors — **Hue**: 80, **Sat**: 255, **Value**: 130.
- The second, third, sixth and seventh colors — **Hue**: 45, **Sat**: 255, **Value**: 80.

Use the Copy/Paste operation while doing this.

❏ Right-click the first slider.

❏ Select the **Copy** command in the Right-Click Menu.

❏ Repeatedly right-click the sliders you want to assign the chosen color to, selecting the **Paste** item each time.

❏ Rotate the map about the U-axis so the lighter part of the cane is at the bottom.

❏ Apply the Noise map to the Bump channel:

Material Editor → **Maps** rollout → the button in the **Bump** line

❏ Change the parameters of the Noise map as shown in fig. 1.81.

**NOTE**  Changing the **Noise Threshold High** and **Low** parameters results in two effects. First, the boundaries between colors become more distinct. Second, the color balance changes. As an example, a single noise map is shown in fig. 1.82 with different values of the **Noise Threshold** parameter.

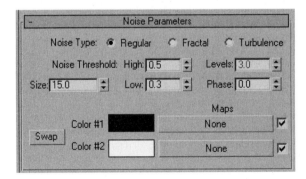

**Fig. 1.81.** The parameters of the Noise map

**NOTE**  3ds max release 4 introduces a new capability of displaying so-called 3-dimensional procedure maps such as Noise in the viewport. The display, however, is quite rough, and now it is not the case when we should use this capability.

❏ Set the **Bump** parameter to 30:

Material Editor → **Maps** rollout → Bump

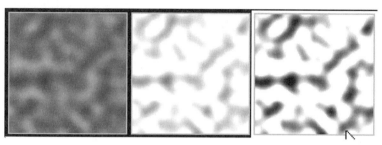

**Fig. 1.82.** A map of the Noise type with different values of the **Noise Threshold** parameter

❏ Exit the Material Editor.

❏ Perform test rendering (fig. 1.83).

**Fig. 1.83.** The cane with the leaves

Now we'll slightly bend the cane and the leaves. However, before bending, we need to convert all the objects to Editable Patch.

❏ Select a leaf and convert it to Editable Patch:

Right-click menu/TRANSFORM → Convert to Editable Patch

❏ Repeat the procedure described above for all the objects in the scene.

Group the branch and the leaves into the **List** group.

❏ Select Leaf## and Stalk objects.

> **NOTE** The **Select by: Name** tool is suitable in this case.

Menu Bar → Edit → Select by: Name *or* <H>

❏ Group the selected objects:

Menu Bar → Group → Group

❏ Go to the **Left** viewport.

❏ Use the Bend modifier:

Control panel → Modify → Bend

❏ By changing the parameters and the position of the center and rotating the object, try to attain a picture like the one shown in fig. 1.84.

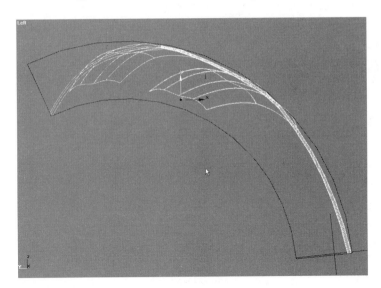

**Fig. 1.84.** The bent cane with the leaves

Now create a stalk. This can be done without using Loft. The idea is to use a truncated cone and then bend it within certain limits.

❏ Press <T> to switch to the **Top** viewport.

❏ Create a cone:

Tab panel → Object → Cone *or* Control panel → Create → Geometry → Standard Primitives → Cone

**NOTE**   You can create primitives with any parameters since they can be modified anytime later on.

❑ Switch to the Modify mode:

Control panel → Modify Mode

❑ Set up the parameters as shown in fig. 1.85.

❑ Rename the cone to Stalk_Main.

❑ Press <L> to switch to the **Left** viewport.

❑ Use the Bend modifier and set up its parameters as shown in fig. 1.86.

❑ Apply one more Bend modifiers.

❑ Set up its parameters as shown in fig. 1.87.

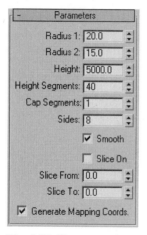

Fig. 1.85. The parameters
of the Modify Mode

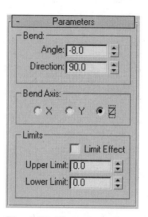

**Fig. 1.86.** The parameters
of the first Bend modifier

**Fig. 1.87.** The parameters
of the second Bend modifier
with limits set up

Notice that the second Bend modifier was applied with limits. Using limits allows you to bend only a specified part of an object; in this case, the upper one.

❑ Move the center of the modifier to the position shown in fig. 1.88:

Right-click menu → Sub-objects → Center

Now we need to create the sepals. It may seem that we've bent the object somewhat prematurely, which we did. However, there's a feature in the latest version of 3ds max that will save you from the tedious procedure of fitting all of the objects together. Be careful, because we're going to use this new feature right now. I hope you'll appreciate it.

❏ Press <V> to switch to the orthographic view.

❏ By changing the position and zoom of the object, try to attain a picture like the one shown in fig. 1.89.

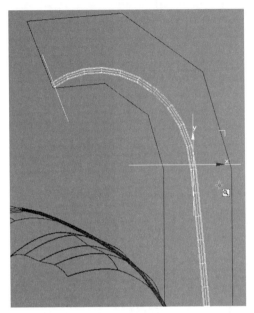

**Fig. 1.88.** The cane bent with the Bend modifiers

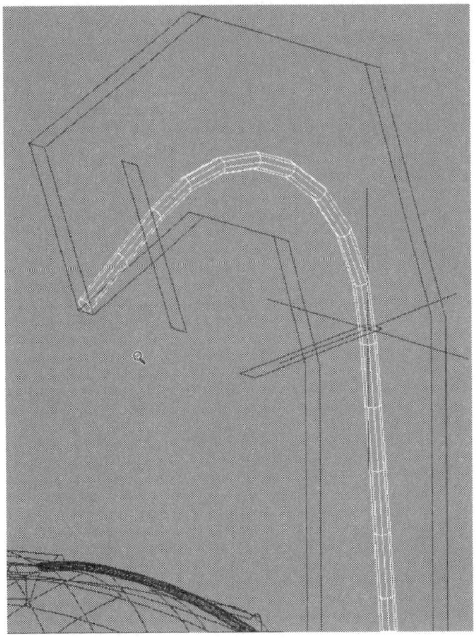

**Fig. 1.89.** The viewport for creating sepals

❏ After setting the **AutoGrid** checkbox, create a six-pointed star:

Tab panel → Shapes → Star *or* Control panel → Create Shapes → Splines Star

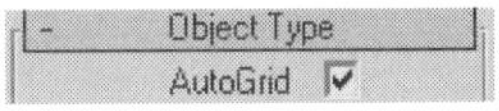

Control panel → set the **AutoGrid** checkbox

Move the mouse pointer to the butt-end of the stalk; notice the coordinate axes changing. Create a star

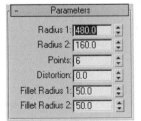

❏ Switch to the Modify mode:

Control panel → Modify Mode

❏ Change the parameters of the star as shown in fig. 1.90.

**Fig. 1.90.** The parameters of the star

You should get an image like the one shown in fig. 1.91.

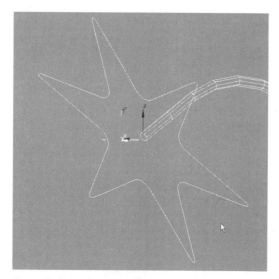

**Fig. 1.91.** The star in the viewport

We'll shape the sepals using my favorite modifier, Bevel.

☐ Use the Bevel modifier:

    Control panel → Modifier List → Bevel

☐ Set up the of the modifier as shown in fig. 1.92.

**Fig. 1.92.** The parameters of the Bevel modifier

**TIP**    You should hide all of the objects except the one you're editing. Hiding objects was possible in the earlier versions of 3ds max 4, but the latest version has an even better feature, Isolate Tool. It hides all of the objects except the one being edited:

<Ctrl>+Right-click menu/DISPLAY → Isolate Tool

You can exit the mode by clicking the **Exit Isolation** button or by repeatedly calling the command from the right-click menu.

☐ Apply the Stalk material to the stalk and sepals.

☐ Enter the Material Editor.

☐ Select the Star01 and Stalk_Main objects.

☐ In the Material Editor, select the Stalk material.

☐ Apply it to the selected objects.

❐ Group the stalk and the sepals, and name the group STALK_MAIN:

Menu Bar → Group → Group

Arrange a number of canes with leaves along the stalk using operations such as copying, moving, rotating, and resizing.

**NOTE** Don't forget that you're not merely modeling a flower, you'll have to put it into a narrow-necked vase as well. Moreover, you'll put in a whole bouquet rather than a single flower.

The result of my own work is illustrated in fig. 1.93.

Now let's join the corolla to the stalk. To do this, we'll use a new feature of 3ds max 4, XRef Objects. Using this feature is advantageous, since XRef objects don't store information about modifiers in memory (this saves computer resources). Besides, if you decide to modify an object in a completed scene, you'll be able to do so at any time. While modifying the object, you can be assured that all the changes within the object will appear in the final version of the scene.

❐ Load the Lesson01_dahlia_corolla.max file as an XRef Object:

Menu Bar → XRef Object

Click the **Add** button

Select the Lesson01_dahlia_corolla.max file

Click the **All** button in the appearing dialog box and then click **OK**

❐ Close the **XRef Object** dialog.

❐ Put the corolla in its place by changing the proportions and rotating it.

Now create a bouquet.

❐ Select all the objects and group them under the DAHLIA name.

❐ By copying, changing the proportions, rotating and moving the flowers, make up a bouquet (fig. 1.94).

**Fig. 1.93.** The stalk with leaves and sepals

**Fig. 1.94.** The bouquet created

❏ Group all the flowers under the name of BOUQUET and save the group in the Lesson01_flower.max file.

If you aren't satisfied with the result, you can always change it.

# Modeling the Environment

Now that we've created the central objects, it's time to proceed with creating an environment.

For modeling a table, we'll use a very simple method; that is, modeling with primitives. 3ds max 4 presents a rather long list of primitives, with a chamfer cylinder among them.

❏ Reset 3ds max 4:

Main menu → File → Reset

❏ Switch to the **Top** viewport.

❏ Maximize the window:

Viewport Navigation Controls → Min/Max Toggle *or* <W>

In the origin of coordinates, create a Chamfer Cylinder object with a radius of about 200 units and a height of 10 units:

Tab panel → Objects → ChamferCyl *or* Control panel → Create → Geometry → Extended Primitives → ChamferCyl

Convert the resulting cylinder to an object resembling a sector (Top view).

❏ Using the cylinder you've just created, create an object, which is a sector of the cylinder. Set up the parameters as shown in fig. 1.95. Be sure to turn on the Smooth mode and to set the **Generate Mapping Coords** checkbox. You'll get an object like the one shown in fig. 1.96.

❏ Rename the object to Table.

Now create the walls.

❏ Press <F> to switch to the **Front** viewport.

❏ Create a 800×400 plane that has one vertical and one horizontal section:

Tab panel → Objects → Plane *or* Control panel → Create → Geometry → Extended Primitives → Plane

❏ Rename the object to Wall.

❏ Press <L> to switch to the **Left** viewport.

❏ Create a similar object and name it Wall2 (fig. 1.97).

Now create the mirrors.

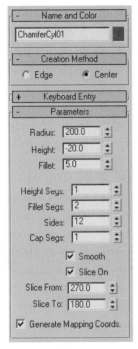

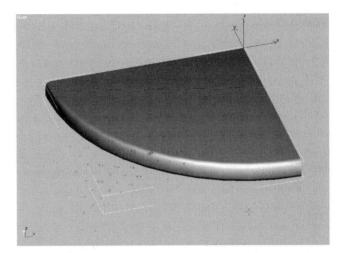

**Fig. 1.95.** The parameters of the table     **Fig. 1.96.** The table

To model the central mirror, you need to create an additional coordinate grid.

❏ Switch to the **Left** or **Front** viewport by pressing the <L> or <F> keys respectively.

❏ Create the grid (fig. 1.98):

Tab panel → Helpers → Grid Object *or* Control panel → Create → Helpers → Standard Grid

Press <T> to switch to the **Top** viewport.

❏ Move the grid by 50 units (five squares) to the left along the X-axis and then rotate it by 45° counter-clockwise so as to place the grid to the position reserved for the mirror to be created.

*TIP* Switch on **Snap to grid** and **Angle snap** by pressing the <S> and <A> keys respectively.

❏ Increase the width of the grid so that it looks like what's shown in fig. 1.99.

❏ Activate the grid:

Right-click menu/TOOLS 1 → Activate Grid *or* Menu Bar → Views → Grids → Activate Grid Object

**Fig. 1.97.** The walls and the table

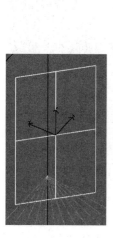

**Fig. 1.99.** The final position of the additional coordinate grid

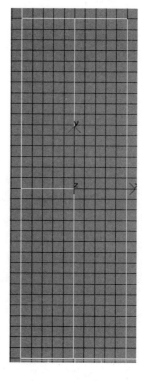

**Fig. 1.98.** The initial position of the additional coordinate grid

Now we can create objects in the plane of the grid.

❑ Switch on **Snap to grid** by pressing <S>.

❑ Create a rectangle with rounded corners that corresponds with the size of the additional grid:

Tab panel → Shapes → Rectangle

Set the **Corner Radius** parameter to 10

❑ Use the Bevel modifier:

Control panel → Modifier List → Bevel

❑ Set up the parameters as shown in fig. 1.100.

**NOTE** Notice that the **Start** checkbox is cleared. This will decrease the size of the model and, at a later time, will enable you to set up lights without any trouble. As stated earlier, surfaces are one-sided in 3ds max 4 by default. This means that they're visible from one side only. Hence, the light easily passes through the surface, provided that its source is at the back side of the surface.

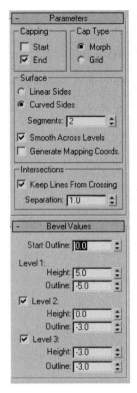

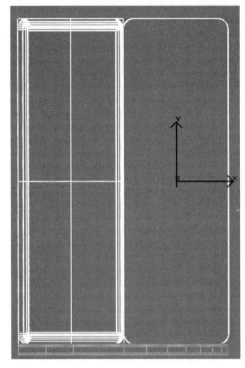

**Fig. 1.100.** The parameters
of the Bevel modifier for
the central mirror

**Fig. 1.101.** The model for a side mirror

Create the side mirrors.

❑ Enter the **Left** or **Front** viewport by pressing the <L> or <F> key respectively.

❑ Activate the home grid:

   Menu Bar → Views → Grids → Activate Home Grid

❑ Create a rectangle similar to the previous one and place it directly against the central mirror (fig. 1.101).

❑ Apply the Edit Spline modifier:

   Control panel → Modifier List → Edit Spline

❑ Select the upper right vertices and delete them:

   Right-click menu/TOOLS 1 → Sub-objects → Vertex

❑ Select the upper vertex and adjust the right handle to get an image like the one shown in fig. 1.102.

Unfortunately, the right segment isn't smooth. Let's try to improve it.

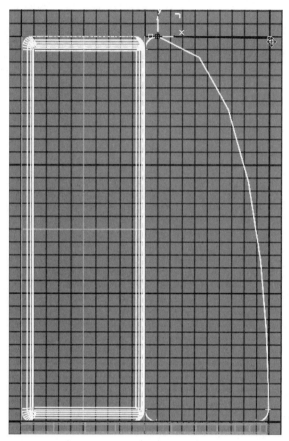

**Fig. 1.102.** The result of editing the vertices of the side mirror

❏ Return to editing the base object.

❏ Click **OK** to ignore the warning.

❏ Open the **Interpolation** rollout and check **Adaptive**.

Notice how the shape of the segment has changed.

❏ Jump to the top of the stack.

❏ Exit the vertex editing mode:

Right-click menu → Sub-objects → Top-level

❏ Select the first mirror and move the Bevel modifier from the modifier stack to the curve corresponding to the second mirror, while pressing and holding the <Ctrl> key. Thus you will create another instance of this modifier.

***NOTE*** You can achieve the same result using the **Copy** and **Paste Instance** commands from the right-click menu of the modifier stack. To make the two instances of the modifier independent, select the **Make Unique** command from the right-click menu of the modifier stack.

❐ Move the side mirror a little so that it doesn't touch the wall or extend beyond the table.

❐ Create a copy of the side mirror and place it on the other wall. Use the Mirror tool to do this:

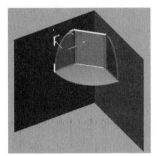

Tab panel → **Mirror** button *or* Menu Bar → TOOLS → Mirror

❐ Copy and mirror the object about the Y-axis. Rotate and move the newly created object, then place it on the opposite wall (fig. 1.103).

❐ Rename the mirrors to Mirror_left, Mirror_center, and Mirror_right.

**Fig. 1.103.** The final view of the environment objects

Now let's create the materials for the environment.

The main material will be plastic, which is very easy to create.

❐ Open the Material Editor.

❐ Select an unused sample slot.

❐ Set a light green diffuse color.

❐ Unlock Diffuse and Ambient colors and decrease the **Value** for Ambient.

❐ Set up the following parameters: **Specular Level** to 5, **Glossiness** to 20, and **Soften** to 1.0.

❐ Rename the material to Green Plastic.

Now create a material for the mirrors.

❐ Select an unused sample slot.

❐ Set a light gray highlight color.

❐ Set a gray diffuse color.

❐ Set a dark gray ambient color.

***NOTE*** The **Saturation** parameter must be zero for the gray color.

Don't change the other parameters.

❐ Assign Raytrace as the reflection map:

Material Editor → Maps → **None** button in the **Reflection** line

Material/Map Browser → Raytrace

For the moment, don't change any settings. You will do it when tuning the final rendering.

❏ Rename it to Mirror.

> **NOTE** Why did we select Raytrace? After all, 3ds max 4 provides two more maps generally used for reflections, namely, Reflect/Refract and Flat Mirror. However, the first one is a good choice only for smoothened surfaces. Therefore, if you use it for a flat surface, you won't see any reflections. Flat mirror uses simple and fast algorithm for creating reflections, and at first may appear to be the best choice for our purposes. However, the Raytrace material is already present in the scene under construction. If we use Flat Mirror, 3ds max 4 will need to compute the scene three times in order to create the reflection map before starting the final rendering. I hope that you have already noticed that rendering of the scene containing the Raytrace material is rather time-consuming. Using Raytrace as reflection map will also increase the rendering time. However, in this case the time required for rendering will not be tripled.

For the moment, you already know how to create Multi/Sub-Object materials and assign them to objects. Now I will discuss newer and more progressive method, based on the drag-and-drop principle.

❏ Select all the mirrors and convert them to Editable Mesh.

Right-click menu/TRANSFORM → Convert To: → Convert to Editable Mesh

❏ Apply the Edit Mesh modifier to them:

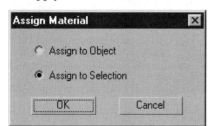

Control panel → Modifier List → Edit Mesh

❏ Drag the Green Plastic material to the selected objects (and set the **Assign to Selection** radio button in the **Assign Material** window), fig. 1.104.

**Fig. 1.104.** The **Assign Material** dialog

❏ Switch to the polygon selection mode:

Right-click menu/TOOLS 1 → Sub-objects → Polygon *or* Control panel → ... → **Polygon** button

❏ Remove the selection from the polygons:

Menu Bar → Edit → Select None *or* the <Ctrl>+<Grey *> combination

❏ Select the polygons that are related to the mirrors (fig. 1.105).

❏ Move the Mirror material to the selected polygons.

❏ Exit the polygon editing mode:

Right-click menu → Sub-objects → Top Level

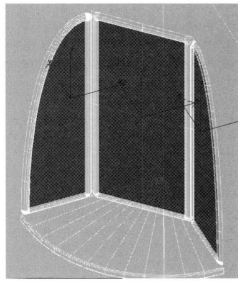

◀ **Fig. 1.105.** The selected polygons related to the mirrors

❑ Go to Material Editor, click the **Pick Material from Object** button and then click the objects.

❑ Rename the composite material to Plastic And Mirror.

Create a material for the walls. It should be similar to the Green Plastic, the difference being that the Ambient and Diffuse colors should be light gray and the **Specular Level** and **Glossiness** parameters should be zero. Rename the created material to Walls. Use a Speckle type procedure map as a map for Bump.

You may want to change the parameters of the map. For example, try to use gray and white colors and decrease the size of the map.

Set Bump to 5.

❑ Save the project in the Lesson01_final.max file.

# Composing the Scene

## Assembling Scene Elements

This is a crucial moment: all the scene elements are now ready and we can assemble them.

> **TIP** I usually freeze all the objects in an initial scene before loading new objects:
>
> Control panel → Display → **Freeze** rollout→ **Freeze Unselected** and **Freere Selected**

❑ Load all the objects like the XRef ones from the files Lesson01-vase_ready.max and Lesson01-bouqt.max:

Menu Bar → File → XRef Objects → Add

Select all the objects

Close the **XRef Objects** dialog

Now all the objects are in the scene and they differ in size and orientation. By moving the objects and changing their sizes, put the vase on the table and the bouquet in the vase.

*TIP* Click the **Degradation Override** button in the Status Controls bar to speed up the process. You'll also need to assign a box output to the bouquet:

Right-click menu/TRANSFORM → Properties → Display as Box

❏ Stir the bouquet when it's in the vase.

❏ Enable access to the elements of the group (in other words, open it):

Menu Bar → Group → Open

❏ Selecting each flower in turn, rotate them so that all the flowers touch the neck of the vase.

❏ Close the group:

Menu Bar → Group → Close

❏ Select the vase and the bouquet and group them together under the name of VASE+BOUQUET.

# Setting Up the Camera

There's always at least one camera in 3ds max 4; namely, **Perspective**. However, it's not easy to operate and its parameters are few in number. Because of this, we'll create a new camera.

❏ Press <T> to enter the **Top** viewport.

❏ Change the zoom so that the window contains all the objects:

Viewport Navigation Controls → Zoom Extents *or* <Ctrl>+<Alt>+<Z>

❏ Create a camera as shown in fig. 1.106:

Tab panel → Lights & Cameras → Targeted camera *or* Control panel → Create → Cameras → Target

❏ Press <C> to enter the mode for the camera view.

❏ Operate the camera using the Viewport Navigation Controls.

One important point: there's little sense in horizontal rendering for such a "vertical" composition. Let's change the size of the image.

❏ Set the image size to 350×500 pixels:

Menu Bar → Rendering → Render

Set **Width** to 350 and **Height** to 500

❏ Close the **Render** window and switch on the Safe Frame mode:

Viewport Right-click menu → check **Show Safe Frame**

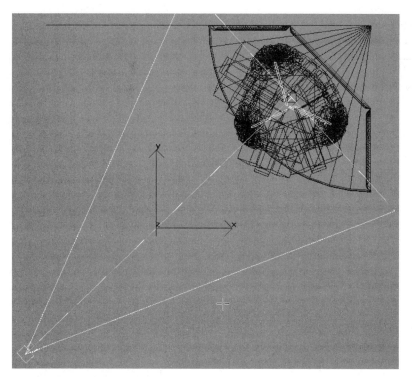

**Fig. 1.106.** The camera

As you can see, the pattern has changed.

❐ Set the camera according to fig. 1.107.

**Fig. 1.107.** The viewport

# Lighting and the Environment

What can bring an ordinary scene (such as ours) to a professional level or, conversely, make all our efforts useless? This would be the lighting, of course. It's lighting that gives volume to objects and makes us believe the scene is almost real.

So, let's analyze our scene. First, a primary light source is necessary to illuminate the scene and create shadows. Second, each mirror is a secondary light source, which will also create shadows. Third, the vase itself is a secondary light source, since it reflects and refracts light. And fourth, the walls create a certain level of diffused light.

Recently there appeared lots of renderers capable of creating interesting lighting effects, such as radiosity — repeated multiple light reflections from objects, reflective and refractive caustic — increase of the luminous intensity due to light diffraction in the course of reflection and refraction (in the lens, for example), soft shadows and shadows from area light. Nearly all these renderers can be used with 3ds max 4. Using these renderers allows to achieve quite a realistic and impressive effects. However, they all have at least two drawbacks — high price and a long time required for the rendering with acceptable quality. Unfortunately, there are also problems of compatibility with 3ds max 4.

We will make an attempt to achieve comparable results and imitate all the effects listed above using native 3ds max 4 tools only.

Let's create the main light source.

❒ Press <T> to enter the **Top** viewport.

❒ Change the zoom so that the window contains all the objects:

   Viewport Navigation Controls → Zoom Extents *or* <Ctrl>+<Alt>+<Z>

❒ Create a directional light source:

   Tab panel → Lights & Cameras → Targeted Directional Light *or* Control panel → Create → → Lights → Target Direct

❒ Create the light source and position it within the scene by changing the source and target position as shown in fig. 1.108.

   ***TIP*** Make sure that the source-target axis intersects the vase center in the Top view. This is very important!

Now let's set the source parameters. Set up the **Hotspot** and **Falloff** values so that the illuminated area doesn't contain anything unnecessary. Enter the light source viewport to do this:

   Viewport Right-click menu → Views → Direct 01 *or* combination <Shift>+<$>

❒ Adjust the falloff (fig. 1.109):

   Viewport Navigation Controls → **Light Falloff** button

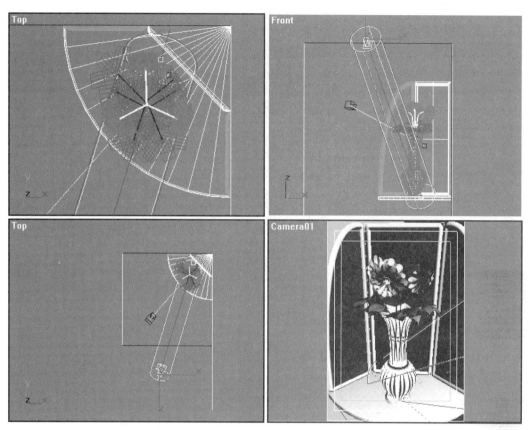

**Fig. 1.108.** Placing the main light source in the scene

❑ Adjust the hotspot by maximizing its value (notice, that this is not required in this particular case):

Viewport Navigation Controls → **Light Hotspot** button [icon]

Now set up the other light source parameters.

❑ Change the light color to light blue.

❑ Set the **Multiplier** parameter to 1.6:

Control panel → ... → **General Parameters** rollout → Multiplier

❑ Switch on the Cast Shadows mode:

Control panel → ... → **General Parameters** rollout → set the **Cast Shadows** checkbox

❐ Set up the shadow parameters:

Control panel → ... → **Shadow Parameters** rollout

**Fig. 1.109.** The result of adjusting light falloff

***NOTE*** Our scene includes objects with the opacity map applied. For their shadows to be cast correctly, we need to use the **Ray Traced Shadows** feature by setting up the corresponding parameters in the **Object Shadows** group (fig. 1.110).

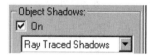

**Fig. 1.110.** The **Object Shadows** group

The latest version of 3ds max 4 allows you to set the shadow density explicitly (the **Dens**. parameter). Since our scene is rather light, it's necessary to decrease the shadow density.

❑ Set the shadow density to 0.8.

❑ Check the **Overshoot** checkbox to ensure that the source illuminates the objects (walls, in particular) that are beyond the Falloff boundaries.

Control panel → ... → **Directional Parameters** rollout → the **Overshoot** checkbox

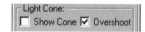

***NOTE*** Pay special attention to the fact that it is impossible to adjust the hotspot. Therefore, in this particular case it is not necessary to adjust the hotspot. Bear in mind that shadows and maps will have effect only within the area limited by the **Falloff** parameter. All objects outside this area will be lighted uniformly and will not cast shadows.

Let us try to render our scene to tune the shadows from the vase. For this purpose, we need to hide unnecessary objects and temporarily disable the raytracing algorithm in materials and maps.

❑ Select the bouquet and hide it.

Right-click menu/DISPLAY → Hide Selection

❑ Start the Material Editor and select any material or map or the Raytrace type. If Material Editor doesn't contain any materials from the scene, load the vase or mirror material using the **Pick Material from Object** button.

❑ In the **Raytrace Controls** rollout (for materials) or **Raytrace Parameters** (for maps), open the **Raytrace Options** dialog and disable raytracing the **Global** column (fig. 1.111).

❑ Perform the test rendering:

Main Toolbar → Quick Render → Production

What a nuisance! And where is the shadow from the vase? I need to admit that I also did not expect such an effect. The reason of this proved to be the following: as a matter of fact, the shadows from the objects that have the falloff map of the Fresnel type assigned to their transparency channel (as in our case) are considered as completely transparent for the light with

the shadows generated using raytracing algorithm. How can we correct the situation? There are two possible methods of solving this problem. The first method is as follows: you simply need to give up using the Fresnel map and use Perpendicular/Parallel type instead. Generally speaking, this solution is acceptable. By tuning the mixing curve settings, you can achieve quite a good results. However, it is highly undesirable to cease using the model that is physically correct.

**Fig. 1.111.** Disabling raytracing

The second method involves using new Studio Max 4 functionality that allows using an object visible for light sources but hidden during the final rendering. Let us use this method.

❏ Create the copy of the vase without changing its position, and save it as Vase_for_Shadows.

    Main menu → Edit → Clone

    Enter the name Vase_for_Shadows

❏ Disable visibility for reflections and refractions when specifying parameters for this object.

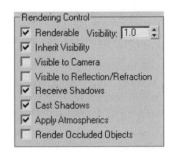

    Right-click menu/TRANSFORM → Properties... → **General** tab → **Rendering Control** group

    Clear the following checkboxes: **Visible to Camera** and **Visible to Reflection/Refraction**

❏ Now create material for this object. Select any unused sample slot and rename the material to Vase_for_Shadows.

❏ Assign the Falloff transparency map with parameters shown in fig. 1.112.

*NOTE*    For standard materials, you need to adjust the opacity value. In contrast, for Raytrace materials you need to edit transparency. By this reason, color selection for the Falloff map in this case is exactly opposite to that for the standard material.

❏ Assign this material to the Vase_for_Shadows object.

❏ To speed up the rendering, it is necessary to exclude the original vase from the process of creating shadows from all light sources. To do so, open the parameters for the CrystalVase_Nurbs and clear the **Cast Shadows** checkbox.

    Right-click menu/TRANSFORM → Properties → ... → **Rendering Control** group

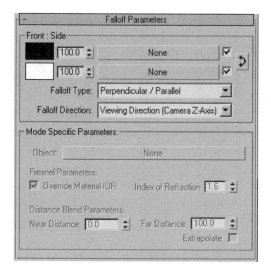

Perform the test rendering. As you can see, now the vase casts shadows.

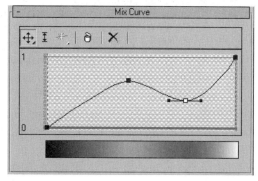

**Fig. 1.112.** Parameters of the Falloff map for the Vase_for_Shadows material

**Fig. 1.113.** Example illustrating adjustment of the Falloff curve

***Self-study*** To make the shadow cast by the vase look more realistic, try to adjust the Falloff map curve as shown in fig. 1.113. You can produce an interesting effect by applying the image used for creating the relief as a map to the Front channel of the Falloff map. Don't forget to adjust the **Tiling** parameter of the map along the U coordinate in accordance to the relief map!

Now let us try to imitate soft shadows. The method that we will use for this purpose is based upon the same principle, as the one used for creating soft shadows by the renderers supporting this option (Mental ray, for example). Smoothing the transitions is the only thing that we won't be able to do.

❐ Select the light source and create its instance:

Main menu → Edit → Clone

❐ Select the Instance method.

❐ Switch to the transform mode in the local coordinate system:

<Alt>+Right-click menu/Scale Keys → Coordinate System → LOCAL *or* Main toolbar → **Reference Coordinate System** list → Local

❐ Move the instance approximately 3 units along Y-axis. Use the coordinate panel for this purpose.

Coordinate panel → **Offset Mode TRANSFORM Type-In** button

Enter 3 into the Y field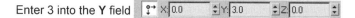

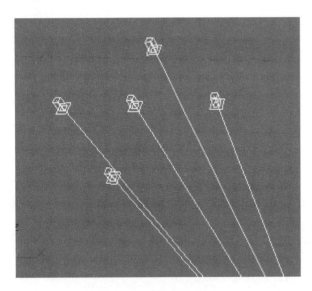

☐ Now create several other instances of the light source and position them as shown in fig. 1.114.

☐ Select these light sources and group them under the MAIN_LIGHT name:

Main menu → Group → Group

**Fig. 1.114.** Group of the light sources for imitation of the soft shadows

Try to perform the test rendering in the camera viewport. Notice that the scene is over-exposed to light. Adjust the multiplier factor by setting it to 0.32.

Control panel → ...→ **Multiplier** parameter.

I would like to draw your attention to the fact that despite you have selected the MAIN_LIGHT group rather than a separate light source, 3ds max 4 allows you to edit common parameters. This is due to the fact that group members are similar objects dependent from one another.

Thus, the shadow becomes blurred. However, this is not sufficient. You can extend the boundary of blurring by simply increasing the distance between the light sources. This can be achieved by increasing the size of the MAIN_LIGHT group.

Main toolbar → Use Pivot Point Center

Main toolbar → Select and Uniform Scale

However, don't overdo! If you make the distance too large, this will lead to the undesirable effect of shadow stratification.

*TIP* To avoid rendering of the whole scene each time, you can use the new 3ds max 4 capability allowing you to render the selected region only. Go to the Main toolbar, open the **Render Type** list, and select the **Region** option. Thus, you'll be able to define the rendering region. To avoid confirming your selection each time you perform the rendering, click the **Render Last** button on the Main toolbar. 🏶 ⬡ [Region ▼] ⬢

❏ Now it is possible to render the whole scene (however, without reflections and refractions).Unhide all the objects in the scene:

Right-click menu/DISPLAY → Unhide All

❏ If you followed my advice and changed rendering type, select rendering of the whole scene:

Main toolbar → Render Type → View

Rendering time has significantly increased. Main part of this time is consumed by rendering the corolla. This is due to the fact that our scene contains a large number of small objects, and the task of creating shadows exceeds the capabilities of Raytrace-based renderer. Therefore, we'll need to find a workaround. It is necessary to create two light sources, one of them will create Raytrace shadows from all objects except for the corolla (this task will be done by the MAIN_LIGHT group), while the other source will create the shadows of the Shadow Map type from corolla only.

❏ Select and ungroup the BOUQUET group:

Main menu → Group → Ungroup

❏ Open access to the elements of the following groups: DAHLIA, DAHLIA01 and DAHLIA02:

Main menu → Group → Open

❏ Select the MAIN_LIGHT group using selection by name::

Main menu → Edit → Select By → Name *or* <H>

❏ When specifying the source parameters, exclude from the process of creating shadows the following groups: CROWN## and STALK_MAIN## (fig. 1.115).

Control panel → ... → **General Parameters** rollout → **Exclude** button        Exclude..

Select the CROWN## and STALK_MAIN## groups, then click the **>>** button.

***NOTE*** The STALK_MAIN## groups contain elements, namely, flower-cups, that may produce undesirable effect of shadow superposition.

❏ Open access to the elements of the MAIN_LIGHT group and select the central light source.

❏ Create a copy of this light source and rename it to the Direct ShadowMapper.

❏ Specify parameters of this light source as follows: change the multiplier value to 1.6 (this value is equal to the sum of the multipliers of all sources).

❏ Change the shadow type to Shadow Map.

☐ In the **Exclude/Include** dialog, set the **Include** radio button and add mirrors and table (fig. 1.116).

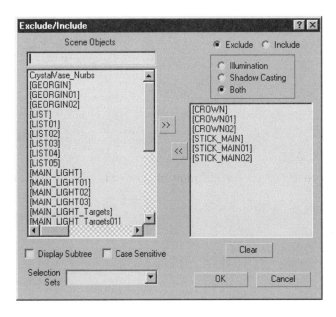

**Fig. 1.115.** Excluding light sources from the MAIN_LIGHT group in the **Exclude/Include** dialog

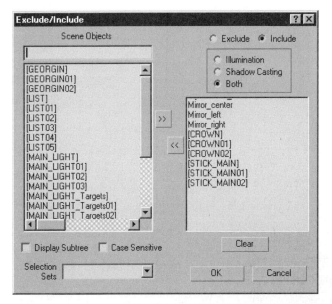

**Fig. 1.116.** Including the light sources from the MAIN_LIGHT group in the **Exclude/Include** dialog

Perform the test rendering. To increase the rendering speed, use the 3ds max 4 capability of separate adjustment parameters of the test and final rendering operations.

❑ Open the rendering settings dialog.

Main menu → Rendering → Render *or* Main toolbar → Render Scene

❑ Switch to the draft rendering mode and copy the settings of the production rendering.

❑ Clear the **Anti-Aliasing** and **Filter Maps** checkboxes.

Render Scene dialog → **MAX Default Scanline A-Buffer** rollout →
**Anti-Aliasing** group

❑ Later on, use the **Quick Render (Draft)** button at the Main toolbar.

The scene is obviously over-exposed to light, but for the moment don't attempt to correct this situation — we will do it later.

Create secondary light sources corresponding to the mirrors. Remember the well-known optical law: "The angle of incidence is equal to the angle of reflection".

❑ Select the targets of the light sources and group them under the MAIN_LIGHT Targets name.

**TIP** To prevent other objects from interfering during selection, it is recommended to set the selection filter for the light sources:

Main toolbar → Selection Filter

❑ Enter the **Top** viewport.

❑ Select previously closed MAIN_LIGHT group and MAIN_LIGHT Targets group. Press and hold the <Shift> button and drag the selection. Create the copy of the light sources using the Copy method as shown in fig. 1.117.

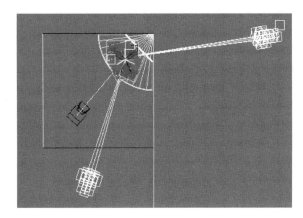

**Fig. 1.117.** The light source simulating reflection from the mirror

❐ Simplify the resulting group by deleting the redundant light sources. Leave only three sources forming the central group and casting the Ray-trace shadows, and edit their position. Close the group.

❐ Notice that now you again can work with the group the same way as with the single light source. Change the shape of the light beam to a rectangular one:

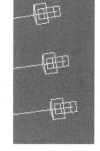

Control panel → ... → **Directional Parameters** rollout

❐ Set the **Rectangle** radio button.

❐ Clear the **Overshoot** checkbox.

❐ Set up **Hotspot** and **Falloff** values so that the illuminated area contains only the main mirror. Thus, we'll simulate reflection from the mirror. Since the walls and mirrors are one-sided, they won't impede the light.

❐ Enter the **Direct08** window:

Viewport Right-click menu → Views → Direct08

❐ Set up **Hotspot** and **Aspect** so that the former is within the plane of the mirror. Move and rotate the light source, if necessary.

❐ Adjust the falloff:

Viewport Navigation Controls → **Light Falloff** button

❐ Adjust the hotspot by maximizing its value.

❐ Make two copies of the light source as shown in fig. 1.118.

❐ Setup the **Falloff**, **Hotspot**, and **Aspect** parameters according to the mirrors.

**NOTE** Don't let the improper shapes of the mirrors to bother you. Creating additional screens may overcome the problem. However, this imperfection doesn't stand out. In order to make the light spot boundaries less noticeable, increase the falloff area relative to the hotspot area.

Starting from release 3, 3ds max 4 presents a tool that enables you to perform this task quickly.

❐ Launch the Light Lister:

Tab panel → Lights & Cameras → Light Lister Tool

A dialog box will appear where you can change the parameters of light sources.

❐ Create a light source that will simulate specks of light on the table that are reflected/refracted by the vase.

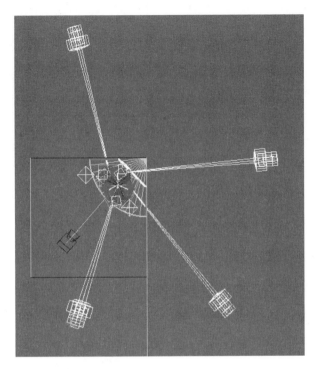

**Fig. 1.118.** The primary and secondary light sources

❑ Create an omnidirectional light source:

Tab panel → Lights & Cameras → Omni Light *or* Control panel → Create → Lights → Omni

❑ Position this source over the table, at the thickening point of the shadow from the vase.

❑ Set the multiplier value to 1.5.

❑ Add attenuation to the scene in such a way as to make the area of limitation cover the table, creating a spot on its surface.

Control panel → Modify → ... → **Attenuation Parameters** rollout

Far Attenuation → check **Use**; set **Start** to 15 and **End** to 30

❑ Include the Table object into the list:

Control panel → Modify → ... → **General Parameters** rollout → **Exclude...** button

❑ Set the **Include** radio button.

❑ Select the Table object, click the ">>" button, and then the **OK** button.

❑ Add some noise to the light to make it more real.

❑ Set a Noise type projector map.

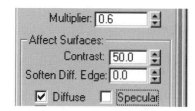

Control panel → Modify → ... → **Projector Parameters** rollout

Click the **None** button

Select Noise

❑ Press <M> to open the Material Editor.

❑ Using the Instance method, move the map to an unused material slot.

❑ Set up the Noise map parameters in the **Noise Parameters** rollout (fig. 1.119).

❑ Copy this light source several times and place the copies at similar positions in the scene.

Create light sources to illuminate the corollas.

❑ Create an omnidirectional light source:

Tab panel → Lights & Cameras → Omni Light *or* Control panel → Create → Lights → Omni

❑ Place it somewhere over the vase, but below the ceiling.

❑ To keep from getting unwanted specks of light, clear the **Specular** checkbox in the **Affect Surfaces** group shown in fig. 1.120.

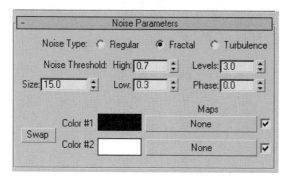

**Fig. 1.119.** The **Noise Parameters** rollout for the light sources imitating the glare from the vase

**Fig. 1.120.** The **Affect Surfaces** group

❑ Set up the **Multiplier** parameter to 0.6 and increase the contrast up to 50.

❑ Include only the corollas into the illumination list.

*Self-study* It's a good idea to set several light sources to illuminate the visible petals of each corolla.

❑ Now you need to add ambient light and change the background color.

❑ Open the **Environment** window (fig. 1.121):

Menu Bar → Rendering → Environment

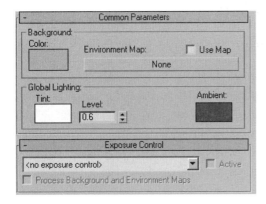

◀ **Fig. 1.121.** Fragment of the **Environment** window

❐ Set the background color to gray and the ambient color to light blue.

❐ Turn down all the light sources by setting the **Level** parameter to 0.6.

***NOTE*** 3ds max 4 introduces new capability of adjusting the level of scene illumination – Exposure Control. This functionality will be discussed in detail in the second lesson.

❐ Perform test rendering to make sure the light sources are set correctly.

The result is satisfactory. However, it is recommended to create a room by copying the walls and positioning them in front of the mirrors. Thus, the central mirror will reflect something besides the vase. Furthermore, it is advisable to illuminate these walls by directional lights.

For the final step, do the following: copy the walls and place the copies in front of the mirrors. Thus the central mirror will reflect something other than the vase.

Now it is time to include Raytrace maps and materials and adjust their parameters.

❐ Open Material Editor and start editing the reflection map of the Mirror material.

❐ Enable raytracing for all maps and materials.

**Raytrace Parameters** rollout → **Options** button → set the **Enable Raytracing** checkboxes.

❐ Enable smoothing for this map by setting the **Antialiasing** checkbox in the **Local** column.

❐ Navigate to the Crystal_main and Crystal_Bump materials and disable anti-aliasing. Besides, to improve the rendering time, disable **Self-Reflections/Refractions** and exclude corolla from raytracing process.

❐ Save your project under the name Lesson01_final.max.

❐ Start the final rendering process. Now you can have a cup of coffee, make a phone call or watch the TV. After some time you'll be able to enjoy the final view of your creation. Save the resulting image in the file by clicking the **Save** button.

# Additional Objects

You may want to add some objects to the composition. In the following sections, I'm only going to show you some outlines and recommendations on how to do this, rather than describe the process of creating new objects in detail.

# A Glass of Water

You won't encounter any problems with this. Just create a curve and make a shape of rotation with it (fig. 1.122). Notice that the walls of the glass are very thin. Because of this, you shouldn't create an inner surface; just turn the upper rim down instead. Use a 2-sided standard glossy material. It must be nontransparent, but with the Thin Walls Refraction map applied to the Refraction channel.

For the water, create the curve shown in fig. 1.123. Its little turn-up simulates surface tension. Use a Raytrace type material, with the refraction coefficient of about 1.33.

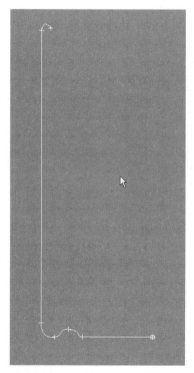

**Fig. 1.122.** The curve for the glass

**Fig. 1.123.** The curve for water

# A Spruce Stick

To create a spruce stick, proceed as follows:

❏ Create the stick however you'd like. For example, it might be a cylinder.

❏ Select only the right and the left side polygons in order to flatten the stick (fig. 1.124):

Control panel → Modifier List → Mesh Select → **Polygon** button

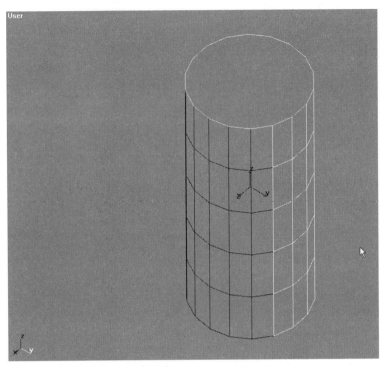

**Fig. 1.124.** The stick

❑ Create a needle; that is, a cone with the minimal values of its parameters.

❑ Check **AutoGrid** and place the needle on the stick.

❑ Select the cylinder, jump down the modifier stack, and set the height of the cylinder to be much greater that its radius.

Now use the compound object named Scatter.

❑ Select the needle.

❑ Create a Scatter object:

Control panel → Create → Geometry → Compound Objects → Scatter

❑ Select the cylinder as an object for scattering.

❑ Set the parameters as shown in fig. 1.125.

You'll get an image like the one shown in fig. 1.126.

Now assemble the main stick with these needles, add some Christmas-tree decorations, and put the stick into the vase.

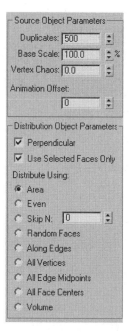

**Fig. 1.125.** The parameters of the Scatter object

**Fig. 1.126.** The final result

# A Carnival Mask

You can put a carnival mask next to the vase.

❐ Draw a contour of a mask (fig. 1.127).

❐ Convert it to the Editable Mesh type:

Right-click menu → Convert To: → Convert to Editable Mesh

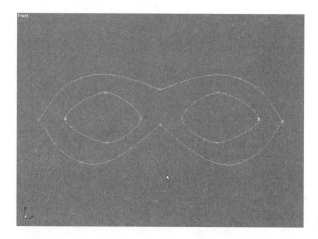

**Fig. 1.127.** A contour of a mask

❏ Bend the mask a little.

❏ For the laces, use curves, with the **Renderable** checkbox checked. The material should be two-sided.

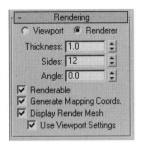

# Summary

The job isn't over yet. Now we're going to discuss its merits and drawbacks.

The main — and most evident — inference is that you always need to outline a plan of action prior to embarking on a new project. Draw what you mean to obtain with a pencil first. This will enable you to better understand which methods to use, what's necessary, and what's optional.

So, what did we do wrong? Or what shouldn't we have done?

We shouldn't have created petals with so many details. The whole scene comprises more than 150,000 faces, 80 percent of which fall on the corolla.

The stalks could have been created using Renderable shapes. There was no need to create nodes. Finally, to choose that complicated material for the stalk was entirely needless.

We were able to make the sepals simpler by decreasing the number of steps for the Bevel modifier.

What else could be done to improve the scene?

Of course, it was worthwhile to make the materials for the table, and to make the mirror frames more complicated (that is, to add wooden texture and metal borders).

The use of the Volume Light effect would have given the impression of a sunny morning to the scene.

Despite all of this, our composition is quite decent. After all, you shouldn't forget that this is a training project.

One more point needs to be made. When creating a scene, whether simple or not, you might perceive your creation in either of the following ways. (Trust my experience and that of my friends.)

First, "This is so good. I have no idea of how to make it better!"

Second, "This won't do at all! I don't know how to do it and I'll never learn!"

Both problems can be easily solved.

In the first place, you should divert your attention from computer graphics and the computer. Go out of town to enjoy nature or meet your friends. Having returned, you'll look at your creation in a new frame of mind.

Secondly, it will be good to show your work to your friends and relatives and to listen to their comments. Don't argue or explain anything. Just take their opinions into consideration and try to understand what people appreciate and what they don't.

# Lesson 2

# A Fantastic Animal

I n this lesson, we'll try to supplement the fauna by fabricating new animals. The result of this lesson is on the CD in \Lessons\Lesson02\Images\Lesson02.tif.

## Aims of this Lesson

After studying this lesson, you'll know how to:

☐ Create complex models of live creatures based on polygons (PolyMesh).

☐ Use MeshSmooth for polygonal objects.

☐ Create skeletons based on bones and deform objects using the bones.

☐ Introduce the models in a real environment.

☐ Set illumination and use visual effects.

## Preliminary Notes

At present, many technologies are used to model organic forms. Among these technologies, the most frequently used ones are NURBS and Metaballs. Despite all their advantages, these methods have a disadvantage, as well. A fully detailed model requires a great number of iterations. This, in turn, results in a heavy consumption of computer resources even while modeling, not to mention rendering and animation.

While modeling, we will use a new type of object — PolyMesh, and combine it with an improved MeshSmooth modifier.

In 3ds max 4, a new type of polygon has appeared. PolyMesh polygons make it much easier to create a polygonal model.

The MeshSmooth feature first appeared as far back as version 1.1 and was then upgraded in version 3. The improvements were so significant that the developers invented a new term — NURMS (Non-Uniform Rational MeshSmooth). The resemblance to NURBS isn't coincidental since NURMS uses similar methods to control surface. However, a dummy is created based on ordinary polygons, which can be easily edited with numerous 3ds max 4 tools. In the latest version of 3ds max 4, the MeshSmooth modifier has become a real editing tool. Besides, a new modifier — HSDS — was added, which provides more flexibility when editing the model. Finally, the interface for mesh objects and polygons was radically renovated, so it's much easier to use now than it was in previous versions.

# Modeling

I'm sure that after having performed the first lesson, you caught on to the main idea. That is, prior to starting a project you should be acquainted with the process of creating models and the final scene. For that reason, you should at least make a sketch of the desired result.

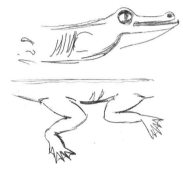

Fig. 2.1 shows the animal that we're going to model. It's "fantastic" since it's somewhat of a collective image of an amphibian which doesn't really exist. From this point on, I'll call it "crocodile", even though it isn't at all.

Study the sketch carefully. As you can see, the crocodile consists of several parts: the head, the body, the tail, and the limbs. We'll model these parts one at a time and finally assemble them.

**Fig. 2.1.** A sketch of a fantastic animal

***NOTE***   You're free to model the animal as a whole, but this requires a certain amount of experience.

## Modeling the Body and the Limbs

Let's begin with the body, which will define the animal's proportions.

❒ Reset 3ds max 4.

    Main menu → File → Reset

❒ Enter the **Top** viewport and maximize it with the <W> key.

❒ Press <S> to switch on snap to grid.

❒ Create a 200×100×90 box (length x width x height) and position it symmetrically in reference to the origin of coordinates:

    <Ctrl> + Right-click menu → Box

❒ Set **Segs** as follows: **Length** to 3, **Width** to 2, and **Height** to 2.

❒ Switch to the orthographic view by rotating the viewport with the <Alt> key and the central mouse button or by pressing the <V> key. Also, switch off the grid (the <G> key), see fig. 2.2.

***TIP***   3ds max 4 features a new method for manipulating the parameters of objects and modifiers. By this I mean manipulators that are enabled with the **Select and Manipulate** button in the Main ToolBar or with the **Manipulate item** command in the Right-click menu (sub-menu **Transform**). By default, 3ds max 4 provides quite a few manipulators. However, you can easily increase the number of manipulated objects and modifiers if you have selected the **Bonus Scripts** option during the installation. Just move the SuperManipulators.mzp file from the folder 3dsmax\scripts\MaxScriptTools to scripts\startup and restart the application.

❏ Convert the box to editable mesh:

Right-click menu → Convert To: → Convert to Editable Poly

Now everything's ready for editing the object on a vertex-and-polygon level.

Since the animal is symmetrical, there's no need to edit the whole body.

❏ Press <T> to enter the **Top** viewport.

❏ Select and delete the right polygons (fig. 2.3):

Right-click menu → Sub-object → Polygon

❏ Switch to the orthographic view.

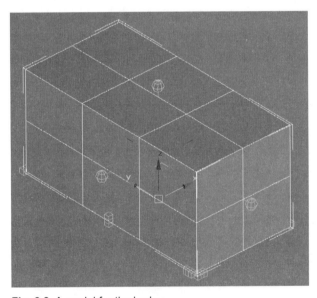

Fig. 2.2. A model for the body

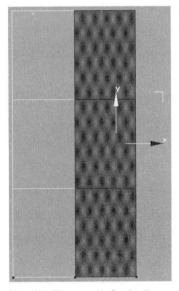

Fig. 2.3. The result of selecting the polygons

**TIP**  Use the **Undo View Change** option; that is, the <Shift>+<Z> combination.

As for me, I prefer to work in a viewport set as follows: rendering type is Smooth+Highlight or Facets+Highlight, faces are shown as **Edged Faces** or as **Shade Selected Faces**. You can easily toggle between these modes using <F2>, <F3>, and <F4>.

Slightly flatten the upper part of the body.

❏ Select the vertices (fig. 2.4, a):

Right-click menu → Sub-objects → Vertex

❏ Move them along the X-axis to the center (fig. 2.4, b).

Right-click menu → Move

Bend the back.

❏ Select the vertices (fig. 2.4, c).

❏ Move them along the Z-axis in an upward direction (fig. 2.4, d).

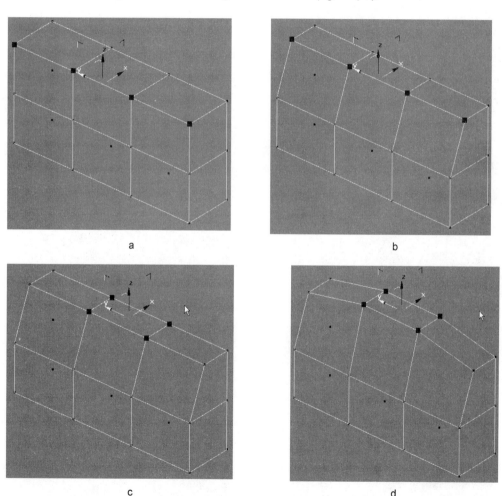

a                                          b

c                                          d

**Fig. 2.4, a, b, c, d.** The sequence of steps while editing the body

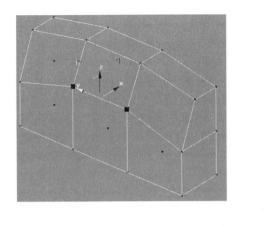

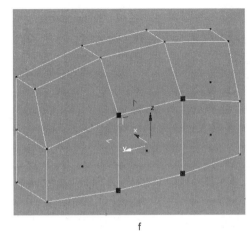

e    f

**Fig. 2.4, e, f.** The sequence of steps while editing the body

Make the belly bulge a little.

☐ Select vertices on the side of the body and move them along the Z-axis in an upward direction (fig. 2.4, e).

☐ Select vertices on the belly and move them along the X-axis from the center (fig. 2.4, f).

Shape the tail.

☐ Change the view to facilitate further editing.

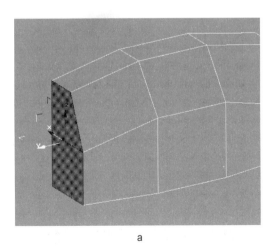

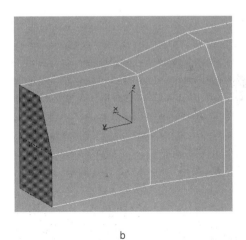

a    b

**Fig. 2.5, a, b.** The sequence of steps while editing the tail

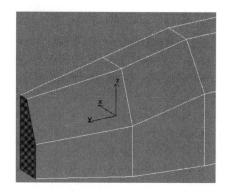

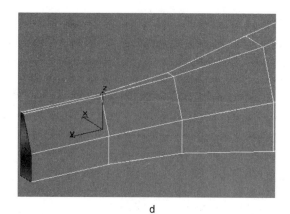

c                                         d

□ Stretch polygons in the rear end of the body and decrease them a little (fig. 2.5, a, b):

Right-click menu → Bevel Polygon

Select the polygons and deform them while holding the <Ctrl> key pressed.

**NOTE** When using the Right-click menu for **Editable Mesh**, you don't often need to enter the sub-object editing mode. Try to get accustomed to this method.

e                **Fig. 2.5, c, d, e.** The sequence of steps while editing the tail

Repeat the procedure described above a number of times to make the tail longer (fig. 2.5, c, d).

**NOTE** Make sure that the polygons don't overlap.

Edit the vertices in order to achieve the proper shape of the tail.

□ Press <L> to enter the **Left** viewport.

□ Enter the mode for editing the vertices:

Right-click menu → Sub-objects → Vertex

□ Select the vertical groups of tail vertices, move them and change their relative sizes:

Right-click menu → Move

Right-click menu → Scale

□ Press <T> to enter the **Top** viewport.

❏ Switch the grid on. To do so, press <G>.

❏ Select the horizontal groups of tail vertices and move them to the symmetry axis (fig. 2.5, e):

During the tail stretching, a number of unnecessary polygons appeared (fig. 2.6). Select and delete them.

> **TIP** Set the **Ignore Backfacing** checkbox in case you accidentally select the polygons on the other side.

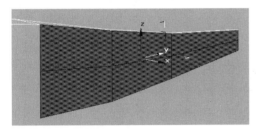

Now shape the ribs.

❏ Press <L> to enter the **Left** viewport:

❏ Cut the polygon which will have ribs (fig. 2.7, a) with four tilted lines:

Right-click menu → Cut Edge

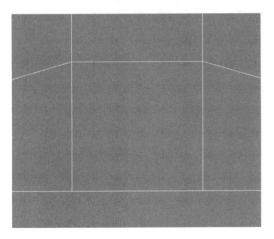

After moving the mouse pointer to the upper edge of the polygon, press the left mouse button and draw a line to the lower edge.

Press the right mouse button to end creating the rib.

Repeat the procedure described above, cutting the polygon as shown in fig. 2.7, b.

**Fig. 2.6.** The unnecessary polygons

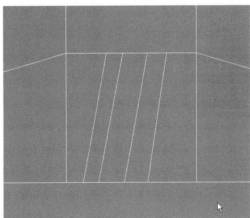

a

b

**Fig. 2.7.** The initial polygon, the cut polygon

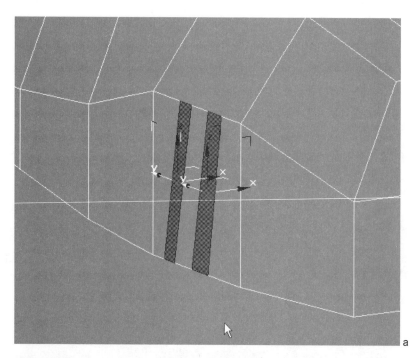

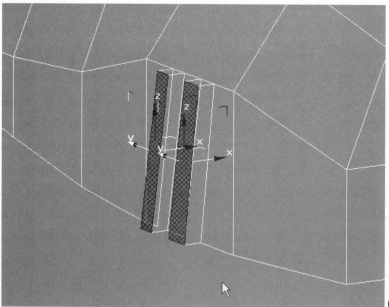

**Fig. 2.8.** Extruding polygons

❐ In the **Perspective** viewport, select the newly created polygons (fig. 2.8, a), and extrude them slightly (fig. 2.8, b):

    Right-click menu → Extrude Polygon

Now it's necessary to shape the crest and the neck.

❏ Rotate the viewport for convenience and cut the polygons along the crest (fig. 2.9, a).

    Right-click menu → Cut Edge

❏ Select the edges or the vertices of the back and move them upward (fig. 2.9, b).

Make the crest gradually disappear towards the tail (fig. 2.9, c).

❏ Select the vertices and collapse them.

    Right-click menu → Sub-objects → Vertex

    Control panel → **Edit Geometry** rollout → **Collapse** button     [ Collapse ]

❏ Keep on working with the crest until it satisfies you.

Now shape the neck.

❐ Select the polygons on the front end of the body. By stretching, rotating them, and changing their size, create an image like the one shown in fig. 2.10.

    Right-click menu → Extrude Polygon, Bevel Polygon, Rotate, Scale

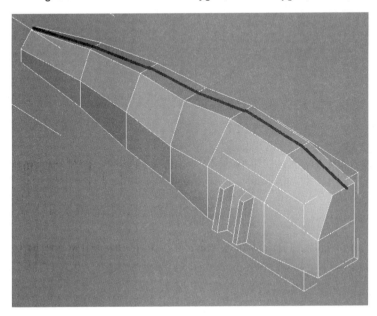

**Fig. 2.9, a.** Shaping the crest

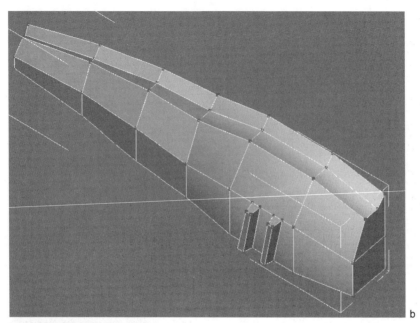

b

❏ Press <Del> to delete the selected polygons.

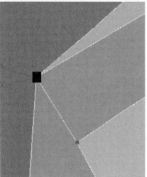

c    **Fig. 2.9, b, c.** Shaping the crest

A draft of the body is complete!

Let's proceed with the limbs.

Begin with creating a forelimb. Extrude, resize, and rotate the polygons to obtain the best result (see fig. 2.11).

To make the finders, proceed as follows:

❑ Cut the butt-end polygon of the paw into three parts (see fig. 2.12, a).

     Right-click menu → Cut Edge

❑ Move the edges so that the paw forms an arc (see fig. 2.12, b).

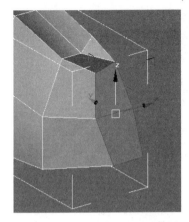

**Fig. 2.10.** Shaping the neck

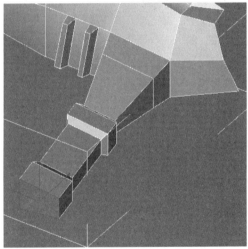

a

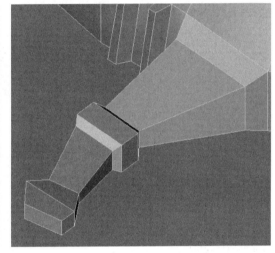

b

**Fig. 2.11.** Shaping the forelimb

❑ Extrude the fingers, having set the **Extrusion Type** radio button to **By Polygon**.

Control panel → **Edit Geometry** rollout

❑ Edit the fingers as shown in fig. 2.12, c.

❑ To sharpen the claws select the butt-end polygons and collapse their vertices (see fig. 2.12d).

Control panel → **Edit Geometry** rollout → **Collapse** button

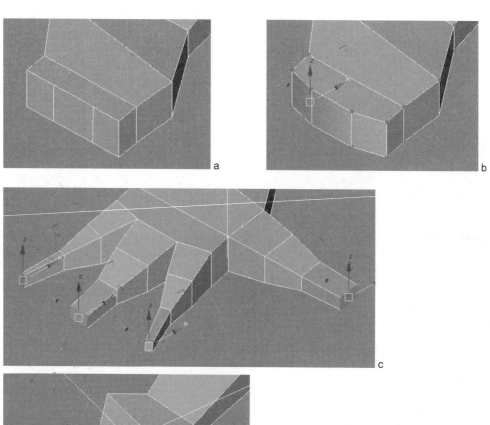

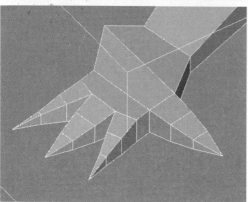

d    **Fig. 2.12.** Shaping the fingers

Create the hind limb.

❑ Select all the polygons of the forelimb and copy them as a whole, that is, drag-and-drop them while holding the <Shift> key (see fig. 2.13, a).

❑ Delete the polygon in the rear part and weld the corresponding vertices.

Right-click menu → Target Weld

❑ Select the vertices of the limb and move them to their corresponding vertices on the body (see fig. 2.13, b).

❑ Finish the hind limb, keeping in mind that it should look more powerful than the fore-limb (see fig. 2.13, c).

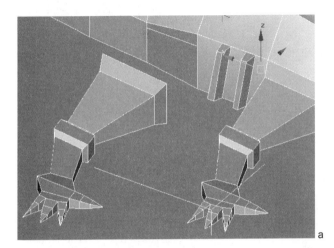

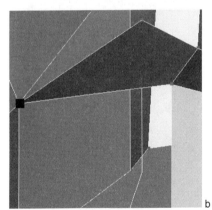
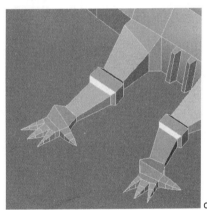

**Fig. 2.13.** The sequence of steps while shaping the hind limb

Assemble the crocodile's body.

❐ Enter the mode for editing the whole object:

Right-click menu → Sub-objects → Top-level

- Mirror the object about the X-axis while copying it:

  Menu Bar → TOOLS → Mirror

- Attach the initial object to the one you just obtained:

  Right-click menu → Attach List

  Select the Box02 object and click **OK**.

- Enter the vertex-editing mode:

  Right-click menu → Sub-objects → Vertex

- Clear the **Ignore Backfacing** checkbox.
- Select the vertices along the symmetry axis in the **Front** viewport.

Examine the selection by rotating the object in the viewport.

- Weld the vertices together:

  Control panel → **Edit Geometry** rollout → **Weld** group → **Selected** button

It's not unlikely that you'll fail at your first attempt. In order for the task to be fulfilled, increase the value of the **Selected** parameter in the **Weld** group.

You've just welded the two halves of the body together (fig. 2.14).

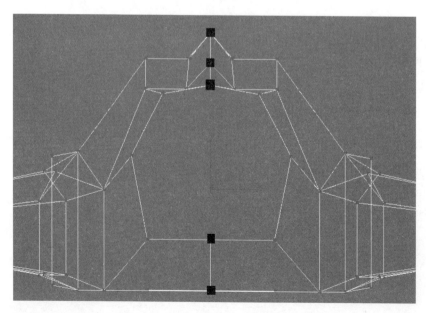

**Fig. 2.14.** Welding the halves of the body

# Modeling the Head

Modeling the head is similar to modeling the body.

☐ Select the body and press the <6> key to freeze it.

☐ Press <T> to enter the **Top** viewport.

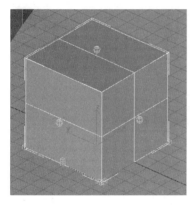

☐ Create a cube with a side of 60 units and place it where the head should be (fig. 2.15):

<Ctrl> + Right-click menu → Box

Control Panel → **Creation Method** rollout → Cube

☐ Set the Segs parameters as follows: **Length** to 1, **Width** to 2, and **Height** to 2.

☐ Convert the cube to Editable Poly:

Right-click menu → Convert To: → Convert to Editable Poly

**Fig. 2.15.** A dummy for the head

Extrude the muzzle on the head.

☐ Select the polygons as shown in fig. 2.16, a, and stretch them slightly (fig. 2.16, b).

Right-click menu → Extrude Polygon

☐ Decrease the Z-sizes of the polygons:

Right-click menu → Scale

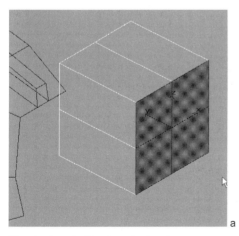

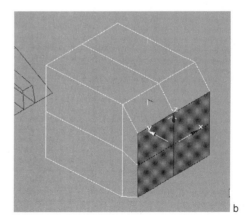

**Fig. 2.16, a, b.** Shaping the head

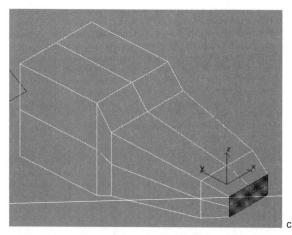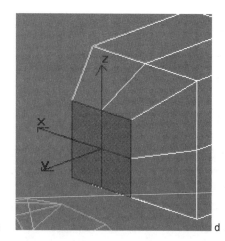

**Fig. 2.16, c, d.** Shaping the head

❐ Move the polygons down the Z-axis:

Right-click menu → Move

❐ Stretch the polygons, changing their sizes. Repeat this as shown in fig. 2.16, c:

Right-click menu → Bevel Polygon

❐ Stretch the polygons that form the occiput (fig. 2.16, d):

Shape the nostrils, the eye-sockets, and the jaws.

❐ Press <T> to enter the **Top** viewport.

❐ Select the right polygons and delete them:

Right-click menu → Sub-objects → Polygon

*TIP* There are two methods for selection. You select either with a window or with crossing. In the former case, the elements completely covered by the selection area are selected; in the latter case, the elements which are at least partially covered by the selection area are selected. You 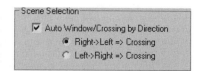 can toggle between the modes with the **Crossing/Window Selection** button in the Status bar. In the latest version of 3ds max 4 a feature appeared that allows you to specify the direction of selecting with crossing. Make use of this feature.

Main menu → Customize → Preferences... → **General** tab→ **Scene Selection** group

❐ Select the polygon on the nose (fig. 2.17, a).

❐ Stretch it upwards, changing its size:

Right-click menu → Bevel Polygon

❒ Rotate the selected polygon about the Y-axis (fig. 2.17, b):

Right-click menu → Rotate

❒ Select the polygon corresponding to the nostril.

❒ Stretch it inwards, changing its size.

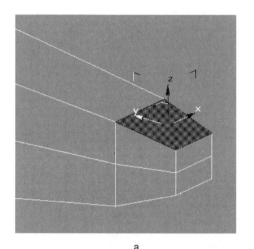

a

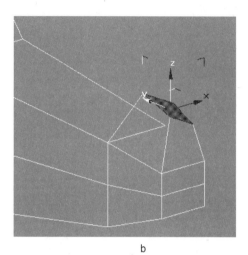

b

❒ Stretch it inwards, changing its size once more, and then rotate and move it as shown in fig. 2.17, c

❒ Press the <Del> key to delete the polygon.

❒ Select the edge on the head where the eye needs to be:

Right-click menu → Sub-objects → Edge

c

**Fig. 2.17.** The steps of shaping the nostril

❒ Move it upwards along the Z-axis and decrease its Y-size (fig. 2.18, a):

Right-click menu → Move, Scale

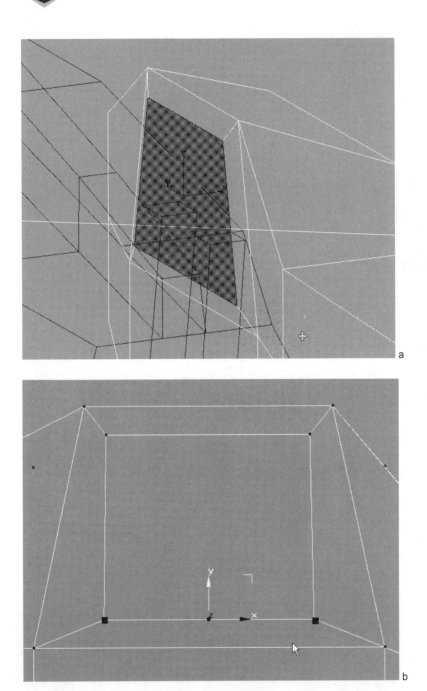

**Fig. 2.18, a, b.** The steps of shaping the eye-socket

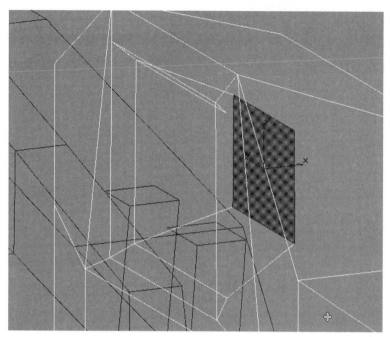

**Fig. 2.18, c.** The steps of shaping the eye-socket

❏ Select the polygon corresponding to the eye-socket and stretch it outwards, changing its size (fig. 2.18, b):

Right-click menu → Bevel Polygon

❏ Press <L> to enter the **Left** viewport.

❏ Enter the vertex selecting mode:

Right-click menu → Sub-objects → Vertex

❏ Select the vertices belonging to the lower edge of the polygon that corresponds to the eye-socket:

❏ Changing its size and position, turn the polygon into a square (fig. 2.18, b):

Right-click menu → Scale, Move

❏ Stretch the polygon of the eye-socket inwards, decreasing its size.

❏ Again, stretch the polygon inwards, decreasing its size (fig. 2.18, c):

Right-click menu → Bevel Polygon

Shape the jaws.

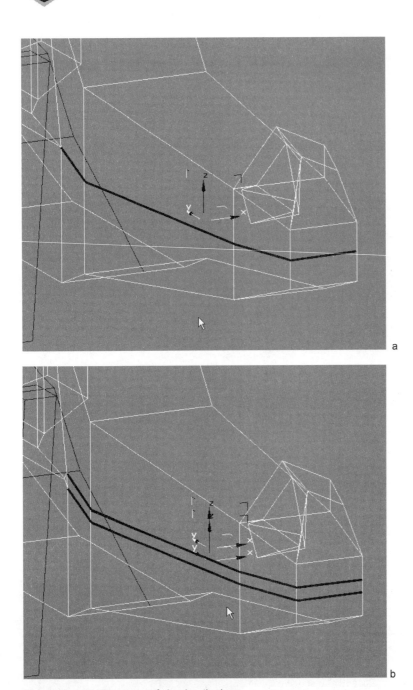

**Fig. 2.19, a, b.** The steps of shaping the jaws

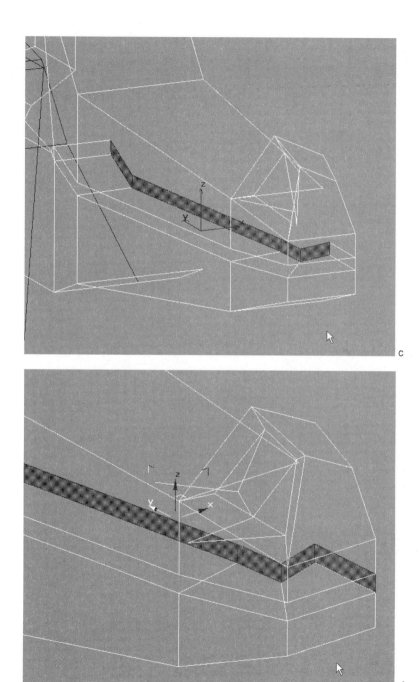

**Fig. 2.19, c, d.** The steps of shaping the jaws

❏ Select the edges corresponding to the jaws (fig. 2.19, a) and make a chamfer of these edges (fig. 2.19, b):

Right-click menu → Chamfer Edge

❏ Select the resulting polygons and stretch them inwards, using the local normals (fig. 2.19, c):

Right-click menu → Sub-objects → Polygon

Control panel → ... → **Edit Geometry** rollout → **Normal Local** checkbox

Right-click menu → Extrude → Polygon

❏ The polygon obtained after extruding (fig. 2.19, d) needs to be added to the selected polygons. Then delete the polygons with <Del> key.

Narrow the lower part of the head.

❏ Select the vertices that correspond to the lower part of the head and move them along the X-axis to the symmetry axis (fig. 2.20, a).

❏ Move the lower jaw forward.

❏ Select the vertices that correspond to the front part of the lower jaw and move them forward along the Y-axis (fig. 2.20, b).

Assemble the head.

❏ Press <T> to enter the **Top** viewport.

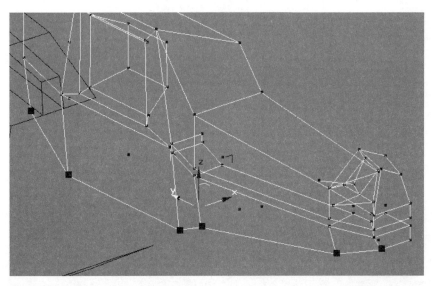

**Fig. 2.20, a.** Shaping the lower jaw

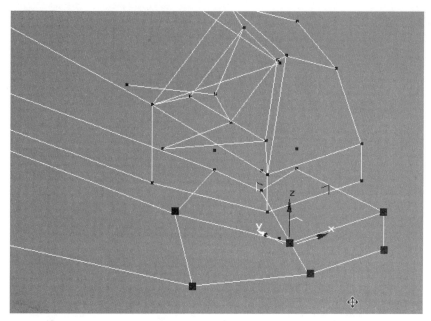

**Fig. 2.20, b.** Shaping the lower jaw

❒ Enter the mode for editing the whole object:

Right-click menu → Sub-objects → Top-level

❒ Mirror the object about the X-axis by copying it:

Menu Bar → Mirror

❒ Attach the object you just obtained to the initial one:

Right-click menu → Attach List

❒ Enter the vertex-editing mode:

Right-click menu → Sub-objects → Vertex

❒ Select the vertices along the symmetry axis. Examine the selection by rotating the object in the viewport.

❒ Weld the vertices together:

Control Panel → ... → **Weld Selected** button

You've now welded the two halves of the head of your animal together (fig. 2.21).

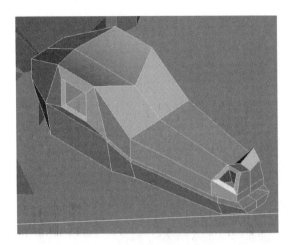

**Fig. 2.21.** The head of our crocodile

***Self-study*** Work on the geometry of the head by yourself. Try to make it look more interesting.

❑ Select and then delete the polygons that will be used while shaping the neck (fig. 2.22).

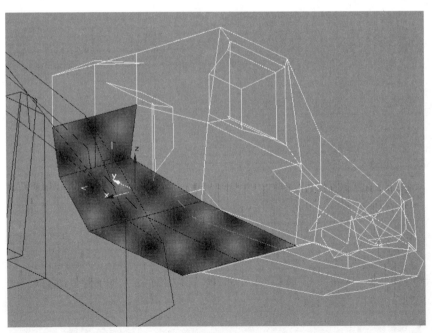

**Fig. 2.22.** The selected polygons of the neck

# Joining the Head
# and the Body Together

To join the head and the body together, we'll use an interesting method; namely, creating a Connect object.

❏ Press the <7> key to unfreeze all the objects.

❏ Press <L> to enter the **Left** viewport.

❏ Select the body.

❏ Create a Connect object, the body being the first operand and the head being the second:

Tab panel → Compounds → Connect Compound Object

Control panel → **Pick Operand** button

The result is shown in fig. 2.23.

The head seems a little too small. Enlarge it.

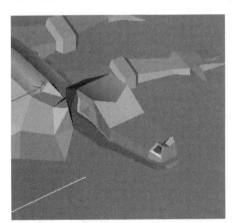

❏ Select the operand-editing mode:

Right-click menu → Sub-objects → Operands

❏ Select the head.

❏ Enter the Uniform Scale mode:

Main Toolbar → left-click the **Select and Non Uniform Scale** button and, while keeping the left mouse button pressed, select the **Select and Uniform Scale** icon

**Fig. 2.23.** Joining the head and the body together

❏ Increase the head size by a factor of about 1.5 and move it, as shown in fig. 2.24. Notice how the neck reacts to this procedure.

❏ Convert the object to Editable Poly:

Right-click menu → Convert To: → Convert to Editable Poly

❏ Create a sac on the neck.

❏ Select vertices on the crocodile's neck as shown in fig. 2.25, a, and delete them.

❏ Cut the neck lengthwise as shown in fig. 2.25, b.

Right-click menu → Cut Edges

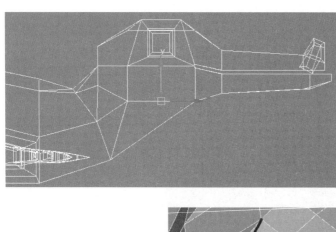

**Fig. 2.24.** The result of scaling and moving the head

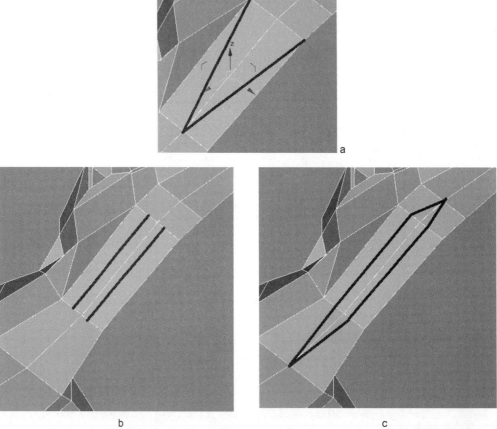

**Fig. 2.25, a, b, c.** Creating a sac on the crocodile's neck

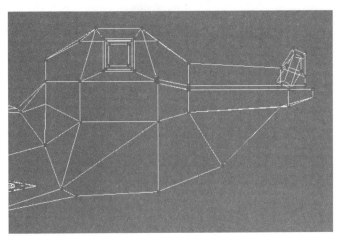

**Fig. 2.25, d.** Creating a sac on the crocodile's neck

❑ Create new edges (fig. 2.25, c).

Control Panel → **Edit Geometry** rollout → Create

❑ Select the vertices and move them to create the sack (fig. 2.25, d).

The body is finished! Rename the object "Body".

# Correcting Geometry

We've just made the model. Now let's correct its geometry.

❑ Apply the MeshSmooth modifier to the object:

Tab panel → Modifiers List → MeshSmooth

❑ Set the parameters of the modifier as shown in fig. 2.26.

> **NOTE**  Set the **NURMS** radio button. NURMS is a new type of MeshSmooth, which allows you to change the geometry by changing the weights of the vertices and edges.
>
> Set the **Apply to Whole Mesh** checkbox. Like many other modifiers, MeshSmooth allows you to modify a part of a model; or, to be more precise, its selected elements. By setting this checkbox you tell the modifier to ignore the selections.
>
> The **Subdivision Amount** parameters control mesh density and smoothness.
>
> Setting the **Display Control Mesh** checkbox results in emerging of a mesh that corresponds to the initial object.

Closely inspect the resulting model (fig. 2.27).

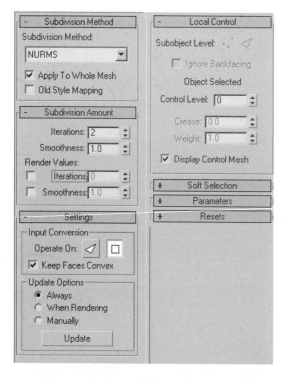

**Fig. 2.26.** The parameters of the MeshSmooth modifier

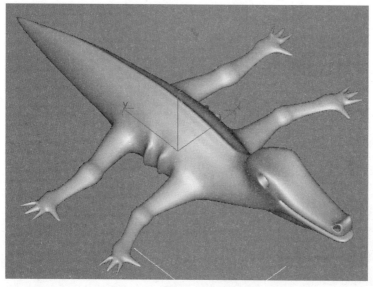

**Fig. 2.27.** The model after the MeshSmooth modifier has been applied

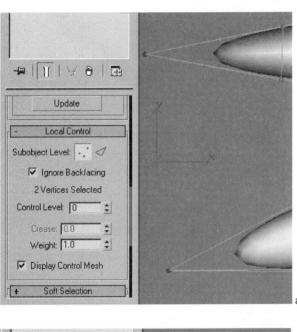

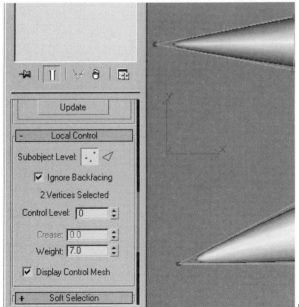

**Fig. 2.28.** The fingers before (a) and after (b) editing

The head is all right, but the limbs are far from perfect. And the ribs are simply ugly. So, let's remedy this.

The MeshSmooth modifier allows you to manipulate vertices and edges, that is, to move and resize them. I am sure you will be able to do the job without any difficulty. I am only going to give you some recommendations.

You can speed up the editing process by adjusting the **Iteration** parameter in the **Subdivision Amount** rollout.

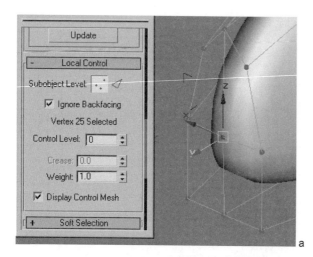
a

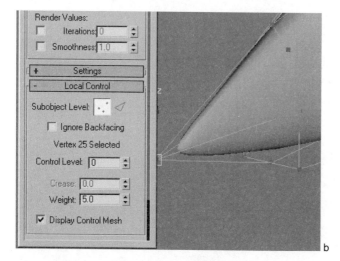
b

**Fig. 2.29.** The tail before (a) and after (b) editing

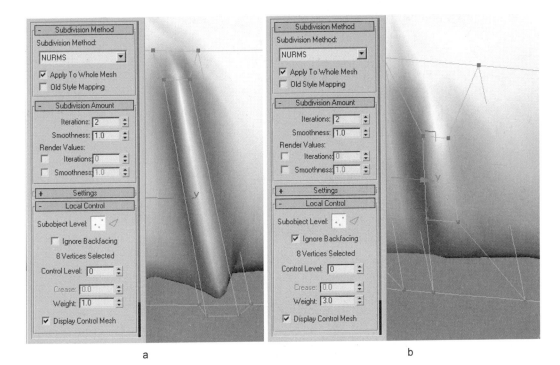

a                                    b

**Fig. 2.30.** The ribs before (a) and after (b) editing

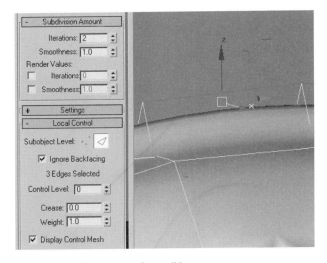

**Fig. 2.31, a.** The crest before editing

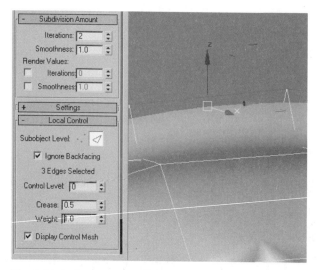

**Fig. 2.31, b.** The crest after editing

With the **Control Level** parameter in the **Local Control** rollout you can edit the vertices and edges of both the initial object (if the parameter's value is zero) and the objects obtained by applying the modifier.

By changing the values of parameters such as **Weight** and **Crease**, you can control the appearance of a surface.

The model elements before and after editing are shown in figs. 2.28 to 2.33.

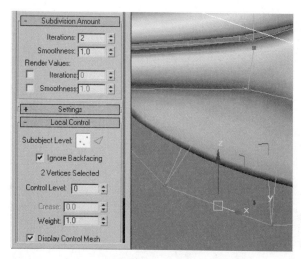

**Fig. 2.32, a.** The sac of the neck before editing

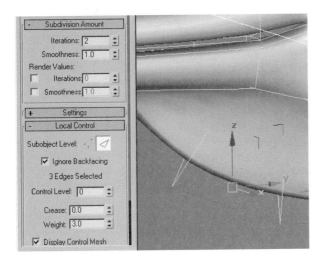

**Fig. 2.32, b.** The sac of the neck after editing

***Warning*** Jumping within the stack and adding/deleting any elements might cause unpredictable results!

The geometry is okay now. Let's proceed with creating materials.

❏ Save the file as Crock.max.

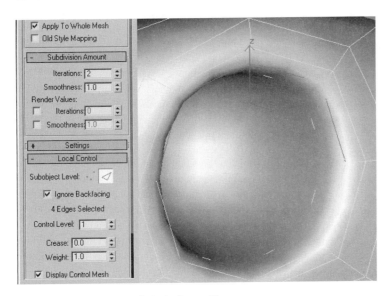

**Fig. 2.33, a.** The eye-sockets before editing

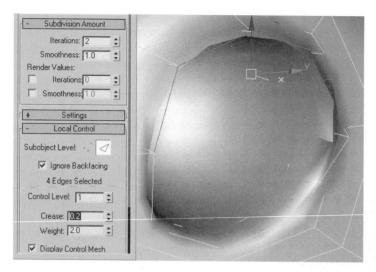

**Fig. 2.33, b.** The eye-sockets after editing

# Creating and Applying the Materials

Let's decide which materials and textures to use for our animal.

We'll need two main materials. The first is for skin on the back and the limbs. It should be coarse and glossy. We'll name it Skin_Top. The other material is the skin for the belly, which is softer and lighter. We'll name this Skin_Bottom.

Also, we need a smooth and glossy material for inner surfaces of the mouth, the eye-sockets, and the nostrils. (Gloss_Skin) and a material for claws (Claw) which will be black and glossy.

In total, four different materials.

Now we need to think about the material textures and the ways that they'll be applied.

Materials such as Claw and Gloss_Skin present no problems. They'll be applied to corresponding polygons through Material IDs. As for Skin_Top and Skin_Bottom, they need to have a smooth transition on their common boundary.

First of all, let's assign Material IDs to the corresponding polygons.

> **NOTE** Of course, you may assign materials with the drag-and-drop method.

❑ Jump through the stack to the mode for editing the initial object:

❑ Switch off the result displaying mode:

Control panel → the **Show end result on/off toggle** button

❑ Clear the **Ignore Backfacing** checkbox if it is checked.

❑ Press <T> to enter the **Top** viewport.

❑ Enter the polygon selecting mode:

Right-click menu → Sub-objects → Polygon

❑ Select all the polygons and set the **Material ID** parameter to 1:

Menu Bar → Edit → Select All

Control panel → ... → **Surface Properties** rollout → Material: ID

❑ Select the faces that correspond to the claws of one of the forelimbs (fig. 2.34).

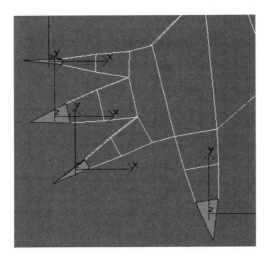

**Fig. 2.34.** The selected polygons corresponding to the claws

❑ Change the value of the **Material ID** parameter to 2.

❑ Repeat the steps described above with the other limbs.

Change Material ID for eye-sockets and nostrils.

❑ Select the polygons that correspond to the eye-sockets and the inner surfaces of the nostrils and the mouth (fig. 2.35).

**TIP** It is convenient to select the eyes and the nostrils in the **Left** viewport, having cleared the **Ignore Backfacing** checkbox. However, you will have to select the jaw's polygons, while rotating the viewport with the **Ignore Backfacing** checkbox set.

❑ Change the **Material ID** parameter for the selected polygons to 3.

❑ Enter the object editing mode:

Right-click menu → Sub-objects → Top-level

❑ Jump to the top of the modifier stack.

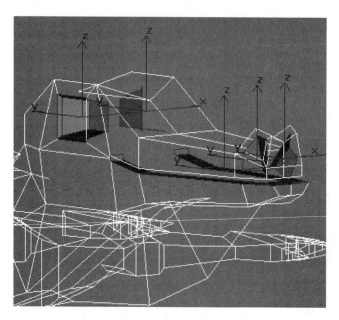

**Fig. 2.35.** The selected polygons of the eye-sockets, the nostrils, and the mouth

Start creating the materials.

❑ Press <M> to enter the Material Editor.

❑ Rename the material "Body".

❑ Change the material type to Multi/Sub Object:

Material Editor → **Standard** button

Material/Map Browser → Multi/Sub-object

❑ Change the number of sub-materials to 3:

Material Editor → Multi/Sub-object Basic Parameters → **Set Number** button

❑ Click the first sub-material button. You'll enter the editing mode for the material that will be applied to the polygons, since **Material ID** is 1 (the skin).

❑ Rename the material "Skin_Top".

❑ Change the diffuse color to dark green:

Material Editor → Shader Basic Parameters → Diffuse

Color selector → **Hue**: 77, **Sat**: 66, **Value**: 88

❑ Disable the connection between the diffuse color and the ambient color.

❏ Decrease the **Value** parameter of the ambient color:

Color selector → **Value**: 22

❏ Change the parameters **Specular Level**, **Glossiness**, and **Soften** to get a glossy material:

Material Editor → Blinn Basic Parameters → **Specular Level**: 88, **Glossiness**: 33, **Soften**: 0.6

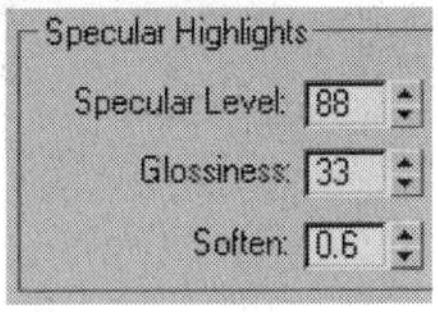

Now let's turn to the maps.

❏ Open the **Maps** rollout.

❏ Click the **None** button in the **Diffuse Color** line.

❏ Select the Cellular type of map.

❏ Set up the parameters as shown in fig. 2.36.

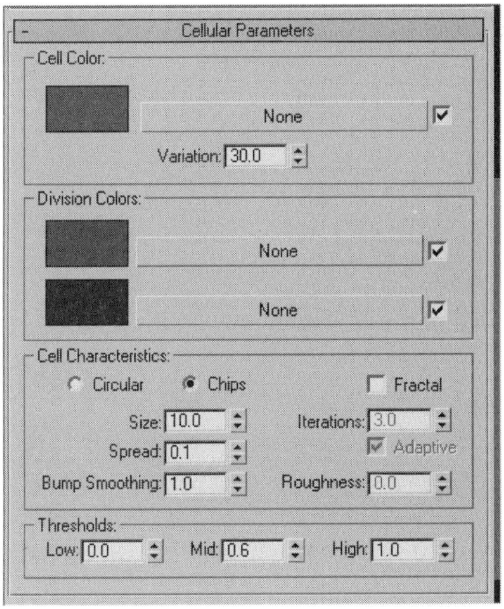

**NOTE**  Set the **Cell Color** parameter to the same value as the diffuse color, but change the **Hue** to get a brownish hue.

The **Variation** parameter controls how much the color of each cell differs from the base cell color (in percentage terms).

Set the **Division Colors** very dark, almost black.

The **Spread** parameter affects the "thickness" of the divisions.

Set the **Bump Smoothing** parameter to 1.

❏ Rename the map "Skin_Top_Map".

❏ Enter the mode for editing the Skin_Top material base parameters (click **Go to Parent**).

**Fig. 2.36.** The cellular parameters

❏ In the **Maps** panel, move the map from the **Diffuse Color** line to the **Bump** line using the Instance method. Set bump to 100.

The material is now ready. Assign it to your model.

❏ Select the model.

❏ In the Material Editor, click the **Assign Material to Selection** button .

❏ Run Active Shade

Main ToolBar → Active Shade Floater

For starters, the material looks quite decent. You might wish to adjust the color of the skin. As for me, I made it brownish. You'll finish it after inserting the model into the scene.

Now we need to create a material for the belly and the lower jaw.

❏ Select the second material slot in the Material Editor.

❏ Rename the map to "Skin_Bottom".

❏ Make the diffuse color light brown.

❏ Make the ambient color dark brown.

❏ Set **Soften** parameter to 1.

Don't change any other parameters.

❏ Apply the Noise map to the **Diffuse Color** channel.

❏ Leave the default values of the map parameters unchanged and set **Diffuse Color** to 20.

❏ Rename the map "Skin_Bottom_Diffuse".

❏ Apply the Noise map to the **Bump** channel, changing the **Size** to 2 in the map parameters.

❏ Rename the map "Skin_Bottom_Bump".

Now you have two materials that will be blended into one.

You've already learned how to create a Multi/Sub-Object material based on the **Material ID** parameter. Now we'll create a material based on blending.

❏ Select the Skin_Top material.

❏ Change its type to Blend, but save the initial material as one of the sub-materials:

Material Editor → **Standard** button

Material/Map Browser → Blend

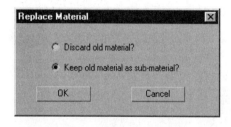

❏ In the **Replace Material** dialog box (fig. 2.37), set the **Keep old material as sub-material** radio button and click **OK**.

❏ Rename the material "Skin_Blend".

**Fig. 2.37.** The **Replace Material** dialog box

❑ Move the Skin_Bottom material from its material slot to the **Material 2** button, using the Instance method.

| Material 1: | Skin_Top ( Standard ) |
| Material 2: | Skin_Bottom ( Standard ) |
| Mask: | None |

You have the blend material at last. Let's examine it more closely.

You may have noticed the **Mask** button in the material parameters. Any map can be used as a mask, provided it defines how the materials are spread over the surface of a model. In our case, the darker areas of the map will correspond to the first sub-material, and the lighter areas will correspond to the second one.

Now we'll use one of the more exotic maps of 3ds max 4, Vertex Color.

❑ Click the **None** button in the **Mask** line and select the Vertex Color map.

This map doesn't have parameters; it's entirely described by the color of the vertices. Now we'll specify the colors for the corresponding vertices.

❑ Close the Material Editor.

❑ Select the model and jump through the stack to the mode for editing the initial object.

❑ Click (thus depressing) the **Show end result on/off toggle** button.

❑ Press <B> to enter the **Bottom** viewport.

❑ Enter the vertex selecting mode:

    Right-click menu → Sub-objects → Vertex

❑ Set the **Ignore Backfacing** checkbox.

❑ Select the vertices that will be covered by Skin_Bottom (fig. 2.38, a).

❑ Press <L> to enter the **Left** viewport.

❑ Uncheck the **Ignore Backfacing** checkbox.

❑ Clear any undesirable vertices (fig. 2.38, b). To do this, select them with a rectangle while keeping the <Alt> key pressed.

❑ Return to the **Bottom** viewport with the help of the <B> key or the <Shift>+<Z> combination.

❑ Change the color of the selected vertices to black:

| Edit Vertex Colors |
| Color: ▇ |
| Illumination: |
| Alpha: 100.0 |

    Control panel → ... → **Surface Properties** rollout → Vertex Colors: Edit Colors

Notice how the color of the area has changed (fig. 2.39, a).

❑ Click the **Show end result on/off toggle** button and perform test rendering (fig. 2.39, b).

Not a bad result, on the whole. However, it can be improved.

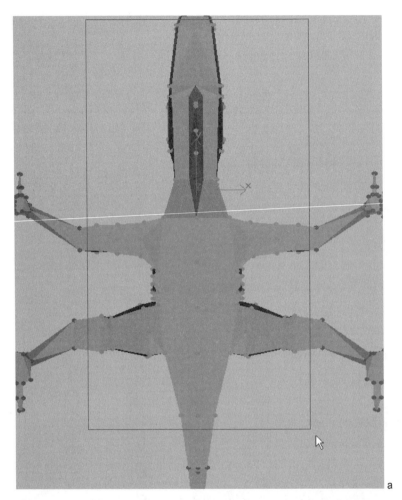

a

b

**Fig. 2.38.** Selecting the vertices in order to assign them colors

First, check the **Use Curve** checkbox among the parameters of the Skin_Blend material in the Material Editor. Set the **Upper** and **Lower** parameters to 1 and 0 respectively.

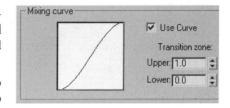

Second, change the color of the outline vertices to gray just to make the color transition smoother. To do this, use the Vertex Paint modifier.

**_NOTE_** The new version of the MeshSmooth modifier performs smooth color transitions automatically. Yet, this is sometimes insufficient.

❏ Press <B> to enter the **Bottom** viewport.

❏ Click (thus depressing) the **Show end result on/off toggle** button.

❏ Select all the black vertices:

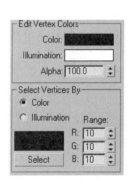

Drag the color from the **Edit Color** field to the **Existing Color** field and click the **Select** button

❏ Apply the Vertex Paint modifier:

Control panel → Modifier List → Vertex Paint

**_NOTE_** The Vertex Paint modifier must be lower than the MeshSmooth modifier in the modifier stack.

❏ Select the light gray color from the palette.

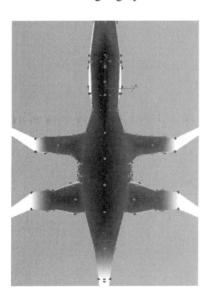

**Fig. 2.39, a.** Change in the color of the vertices

**Fig. 2.39, b.** The result of applying the Vertex Color mask

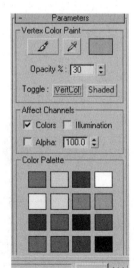

❏ By clicking the **VertCol** and **Shaded** buttons in the **Toggle** line, try to achieve a black-and-white map in the viewport.

❏ Click the button **Vertex Color Paint**, and then paint by moving the mouse pointer from one vertex to another while keeping the left mouse button pressed.

❏ Try to obtain a picture like the one shown in fig. 2.40.

❏ Click the **Show end result on/off toggle** button and perform test rendering.

Notice that the transition is smoother. This is what we hoped to achieve.

Now create the rest of the materials.

Create a material for the claws (Claw).

❏ Select an unused material slot.

❏ Make the diffuse color dark, almost black.

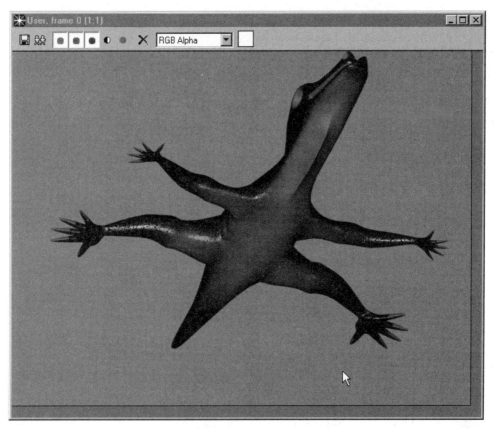

**Fig. 2.40.** The result of painting over the vertices

❏ Copy this color to the ambient color.

❏ Make the material glossy by setting both the **Specular Level** and **Glossiness** parameters to 60 and the **Soften** parameter to 0.5.

❏ Rename the material "Claw".

Create a material for the mucus membranes of the mouth, nostrils, and eye-sockets (Gloss_Skin).

❏ Copy the Claw material to any unused material slot.

❏ Rename the material "Gloss_Skin".

❏ Make the diffuse color claret and the specular color pink.

Now assemble all of these materials.

❏ Select the material slot of the Body material.

❏ Enter the uppermost material level, clicking the **Go to Parent** button if necessary.

❏ Using the Instance method, transfer the Claw and Gloss_Skin materials to the buttons corresponding to the sub-materials.

❏ Now you can convert the object to the Editable Poly type.

Right-click menu → Convert To: → Convert to Editable Poly

# Creating the Eyes and the Teeth

Each eye will consist of two parts: the eyeball and the eyelid.

❏ Press <L> to enter the **Left** viewport.

❏ For the eyeball, create a sphere with a 20 unit radius and 24 segments:

<Ctrl> + Right-click menu → Sphere

❏ Make sure to check the **Generate Mapping Coords** checkbox.

❏ Moving the sphere, place the eyeball in the eye-socket (fig. 2.41).

❏ Rename the sphere "EyeBall".

Create a material for the eyeball.

❏ Open the Material Editor (with the <M> key) and select an unused material slot.

❏ Change the shader to anisotropic:

Material Editor → Shader Basic Parameters

❏ Change the ambient, diffuse, and specular colors to dark gray, light gray, and white, respectively.

❏ Set the **Specular Level**, **Glossiness**, and **Anisotropy** parameters to 80, 80, and 65, respectively.

❏ Press the button in the **Diffuse** line and select a Gradient Ramp type of map.

❏ Apply the material to the EyeBall object and click the **Show Map in Viewport** button.

❏ Change the Gradient type to radial:

Material Editor → **Gradient Ramp Parameters** rollout → **Gradient Type** field

❏ Rotate the eye in the eye-socket about the X-axis so that the red spot (that is, the pupil) is directed toward you (fig. 2.42).

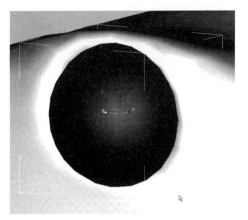

Fig. 2.41. The eye in the eye-socket

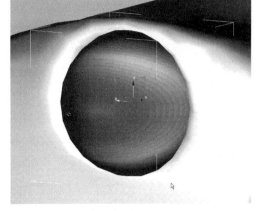

Fig. 2.42. The eyeball with the texture applied

Now we need to give the pupil the proper form.

❑ Change tiling along the U-axis to 2:

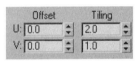

Material Editor → **Coordinates** rollout → U: Tiling

Now edit the gradient.

❑ Change the interpolation to custom:

Material Editor → **Gradient Ramp Parameters** rollout → **Interpolation** field

❑ Change the leftmost gradient color to pure black.

Double-click the leftmost slider with the left mouse button and set the color.

❑ Change the interpolation type for this color to Solid:

Right-click the leftmost slider and select the **Edit Parameters...** item

In the **Flag Properties** dialog box, select Solid

❑ Without closing the **Flag Properties** dialog box, proceed with editing the Flag#2 component.

❑ Change the color to dark claret.

❑ Move on to editing the Flag#3 component and change its color to white.

❑ Change the interpolation type to **Ease In**.

The eye looks like a real one.

**Self-study** You may have noticed the **Texture** button among the flag parameters. Try to apply some texture to the middle component of the gradient to obtain blood vessels on the white of the eye. A Marble-type texture would fit.

Create the eyelids. Again, use a sphere.

❏ Create a sphere of about a 22-unit radius and 12 segments.

❏ Position it so that the eyeball is inside the sphere. To achieve this, use the Align tool.

❏ Center the sphere in reference to the EyeBall object, using the Align tool:

Menu Bar → TOOLS → Align

Move the mouse pointer to the EyeBall object and left-click it.

In the dialog box that appears, check the X, Y, and Z check-boxes and click **OK**.

Make a cut for the eye.

> **TIP** To prevent other object from interfering, use Isolate Tool, new to 3ds max 4:
>
> Right-click menu → Isolate Tool
>
> To exit this mode, click the **Exit Isolate** button

❏ In the sphere parameters, check the **Slice On** checkbox and set the **Slice From** and **Slice To** parameters to 120 and 180 respectively.

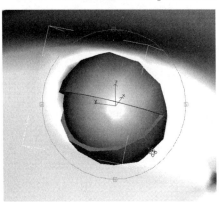

❏ Rotate the sphere so that the cut is in its proper place (see fig. 2.43)

❏ Convert the sphere to the Editable Mesh type and rename it "Eye_Out".

**Fig. 2.43.** The eyeball with the eyelids

Create a material for the eyelids.

❏ Use a Multi/Sub-Object type material with two sub-materials and name it Eye_Out.

❏ Use Skin_Top as one sub-material and Gloss_Skin as the other.

Define Material IDs for the materials.

> **TIP** When creating a primitive, 3ds max 4 usually assigns **Material ID** values to the primitive components. In this case, the **Material ID** values for the outer polygons of the sphere are equal

to 2. The values for the polygons, which appeared as the result of slicing, are 3 and 4. You can take advantage of this to select polygons and give new values to their Material IDs.

❏ Enter the polygon selecting mode:

Right-click menu → Sub-objects → Polygon

❏ Select the polygons whose **Material ID** parameters are 2:

Control panel → ... → **Surface Properties** rollout → Material: Select by ID

Enter 2 and click **OK**

❏ Change the **ID** of the selected polygons to 1.

❏ Invert the selection and change the **ID** of the selected polygons to 2:

Menu Bar → Edit → Select Invert

❏ Enter the object editing mode:

Right-click menu → Sub-objects → Top-level

❏ Apply the Eye_Out material to the Eye_Out object.

❏ Apply the MeshSmooth modifier to the object.

Rotate the eye so that it looks forward.

Now create the other eye.

❏ Change the viewport to Top.

❏ Select the EyeBall and Eye_Out objects and mirror them by copying about the X-axis.

❏ Place the new objects in their proper place.

Now the eyes are all right (fig. 2.44).

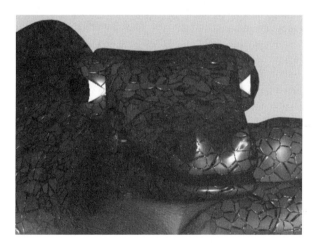

**Fig. 2.44.** The crocodile's head with the eyes

Now create the teeth.

There's no need to create each individual tooth. Instead, we'll choose another way.

❏ Create a jaw-like curve (fig. 2.45, a).

❏ In the parameters, set the number of steps to 24 and clear the **Optimize** checkbox.

❏ Apply the Extrude modifier to the curve and set the **Amount** parameter to 3.

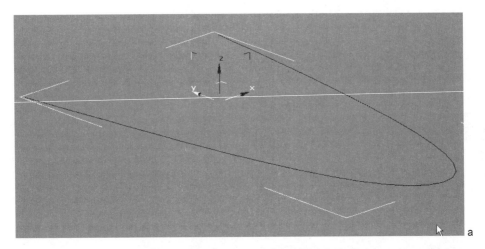

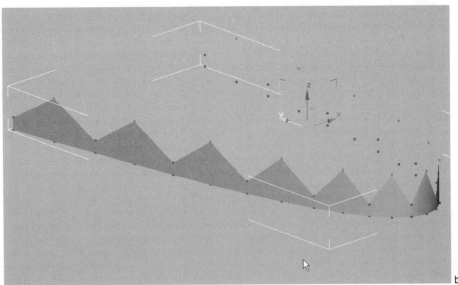

**Fig. 2.45, a, b.** The steps of creating the teeth

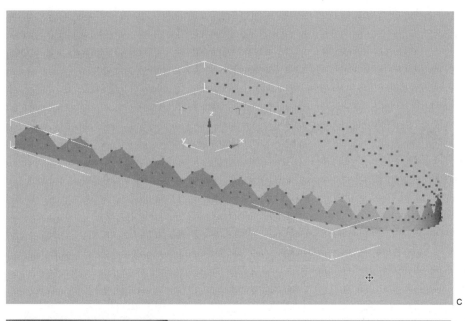

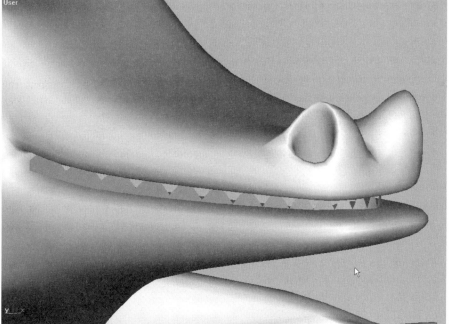

**Fig. 2.45, c, d.** The steps of creating the teeth

❏ Apply the Edit Mesh modifier:

Control panel → Modifier List → Edit Mesh

❏ Enter the vertex selecting mode and select alternate upper vertices.

❏ Move the selected vertices upwards (fig. 2.45, b).

❏ Apply the MeshSmooth modifier to the object.

❏ Clear the **Apply to Whole Mesh** checkbox in the modifier parameters.

The lower teeth are finished! (fig. 2.45, c).

**NOTE**  Even though this is a rough model, the teeth will suffice for our example.

❏ "Insert" the teeth into the mouth (fig. 2.45, d).

If required, change the shape of the initial curve. To do this, jump down the stack to the Line level and correct the types and the positions of the vertices.

❏ Rename the object as "Tooth".

❏ Create a material resembling white plastic; rename it "Tooth" and apply it to the teeth. Make sure it's 2-sided!

Now let's assemble our crocodile.

❏ Select the Body object.

❏ Using the **Attach List** command, attach all the objects in the scene to the body:

Right-click menu → Attach List

Select all the objects and click **OK**

❏ In the **Attach Options** dialog box, set the **Match Material ID to material** radio button, check the **Condense Material and ID** checkbox, and click the **OK** button.

Make sure the materials are all right.

❏ Open the Material Editor.

❏ Load the material in the scene into any material slot:

Material Editor → **Get Material** button

Material/Map Browser → Browse From: Scene

Select the material and double-click it with the left mouse button

❏ Rename the material "Crocodile".

❏ Save the file as Crock-complete.max.

# Creating and Setting the Environment

In this section, we'll actually create the scene where you'll put your model. As a background, a photo will be used that can be found on the accompanying CD-ROM in \Lessons\Lesson02\maps\coast.tif.

Inspect the photo. You can see stones in the foreground. Try to place your model on these stones as if the crocodile were climbing up the nearest one.

❏ Reset 3ds max.

❏ Press <T> to enter the **Top** viewport and maximize it with the <W> key.

❏ Create a camera as shown in fig. 2.46.

Tab panel → Lights & Cameras → Targeted Camera

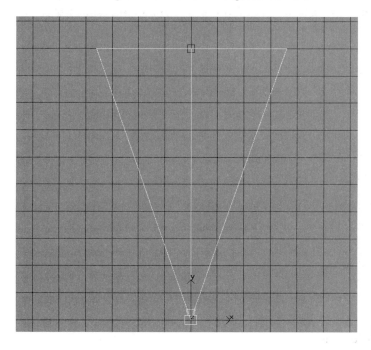

Fig. 2.46. Creating a camera

❏ Set the camera type to 50 mm in its parameters.

❏ Press <C> to enter the camera viewport.

❏ Set the background:

Menu Bar → Views → Viewport Backgrounds

In the dialog box, click the **Files** button and select the file coast.tif

Set up the **Aspect Ratio** parameter to **Match Aspect Ratio**

Set the **Display Background** checkbox and click **OK**

The background will appear in the Viewport.

❐ In the rendering parameters, set the image size to 640×480:

Menu Bar → Rendering → Render

Click the 640×480 button, then click **Close**

❐ Switch on the safe frame display in the viewport:

Right-click menu → set the **Show Safe Frame** checkbox

If you inspect the photo closely, you may notice that while shooting, the camera had been tiled down. Set up your camera in a similar way.

❐ Press <L> to enter the **Left** viewport.

❐ Select the camera and move it along the Y-axis upwards (fig. 2.47).

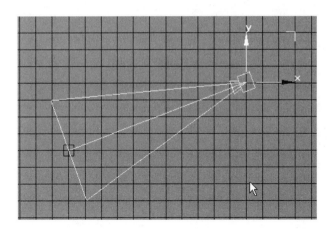

**Fig. 2.47.** Repositioning the camera in the scene

*TIP*    So you don't accidentally move the camera at a later time, proceed as follows. In the camera viewport:

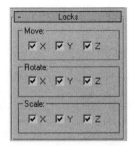

• Select the camera.

• Open the **Link Info** rollout:

Control panel → Hierarchy → Link Info

• Set all the checkboxes in the **Locks** rollout. By doing this, you'll disable any rotation or movement of the camera in any viewport.

Now create a surface on which the shadows will be cast.

❏ Press <T> to enter the **Top** viewport.

❏ Create a Quad Patch Grid object of 80×120 units, all the **Segs** (**Length**, **Width**, and **Height**) being equal to 6 (fig. 2.48).

Tab panel → Object → Quad Patch Object

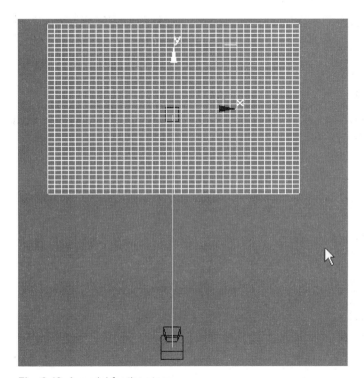

**Fig. 2.48.** A model for the stone

❏ Press <C> to enter the camera viewport.

❏ By moving the patch grid along all the axes and rotating it, try to make the object correspond to the stone in the foreground (fig. 2.49, a).

*TIP*   To make things easier, enter the Smooth+Highlights mode (the <F3> key), switch on the edge display mode (F4>) and the transparent object mode (<Alt>+<X>).

Now you need to edit the plane so that it matches the roughness of the stone.

❏ Use the Edit Patch modifier:

Control panel → Modifier List → Edit Patch

❏ Enter the vertex editing mode:

    Right-click menu → Sub-objects → Vertex

By moving the vertices and changing the curvature of the surface with the help of handles, try to make the patch fit the stone surface without going beyond it (fig. 2.49, b).

Now create a cleft corresponding to the one on the stone.

**Fig. 2.49.** Creating and editing a "stone"

❐ Use the Edit Mesh modifier:

Control panel → Modifier List → Edit Mesh

❐ Select the vertices along the cleft and move them downwards along the Z-axis (fig. 2.49, c):

Right-click menu → Sub-objects → Vertex

Right-click menu → Move

**TIP**  You probably will edit these vertices again. To ease selection of these very vertices next time, use the 3ds max 4 feature which allows you to name the selected elements of an object. Just enter a name into the **Named Selection Set** field, which is located in the **Main Toolbar**, and press <Enter>. In order to use this set, open the list in this field and select the desired element.

We've just finished the surface of the stone. Rename the object to Stone.

Now create a material for the stone.

❐ Press <M> to open the Material Editor.

❐ Select any unused material slot.

❐ Change the material type to Matte/Shadow, rename it "Stone", and apply it to the Stone object.

❐ In the material parameters, set the **Receive Shadows** checkbox.

**NOTE**  After a material of this type has been applied to an object, the object gains an interesting property. It can display shadows of other objects, while being invisible itself. (Moreover, in 3ds max 4, it can reflect objects.) It also overlaps the objects behind it without overlapping the background. It's just the property we need to use.

Perform a test rendering.

What a nuisance! You can't see the background photo. The background in the viewport and the background produced by the rendering aren't the same. The former is something more than a mere "back-drop" for the scene. It's possible to set an individual background in each viewport, and to keep it in line with scaling and moving the objects there. Thus, the background is a big help when modeling objects in various views.

Set the background for rendering.

❐ Open the window for setting up the environment:

Menu Bar → Rendering → Environment

❐ Click the **Environment Map** button and select the Bitmap type. Select the file coast.tif as a texture.

Repeat test rendering once more. That's all for right now!

*Self-study*   An environment map can be applied in a number of ways and has a great many parameters. To change their values, you first need to transfer the map to the Material Editor. This can be done in two ways. First, click the **Get Material** button in the Material Editor, set the **Scene** radio button in the **Browse From** group, and select it in the list. Second, move the map from the **Environment** dialog box with the Instance method. Try to change the parameters of the map on your own and watch the result.

Now you need to make certain that the Stone object is properly placed and to set up the parameters of the Stone material. To do this, create a simple object, for example a sphere, and position it over the Stone object.

Examine the photo once again to gain a better understanding of how the light source needs to be set. Judging by the shadows from the stones in the right part of the photo, the light is directed to us from the right with the source being high above the horizon. Your main light source needs to be positioned this way.

❐ Press <L> to enter the **Left** viewport.

❐ Create a directional light source (fig. 2.50, a):

    Tab panel → Lights & Cameras → Targeted Directional Light

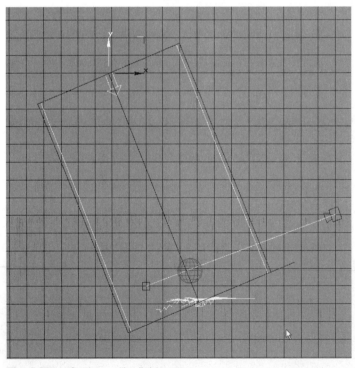

**Fig. 2.50, a.** Setting up the light source

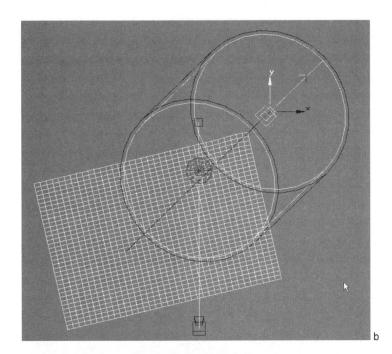

**Fig. 2.50, b, c.** Setting up the light source

☐ Press <T> to enter the **Top** viewport and move the light source to the right (fig. 2.50, b).

☐ Set the mode for casting shadows from this light source:

Right-click menu → Cast Shadows

☐ Perform test rendering, or start the process of interactive rendering (Active Shade) (see fig. 2.50, c).

Two drawbacks become evident. First, the shadow is too dark when compared to the shadows on the photo. Second, the cleft is in the wrong place.

The first one can be easily corrected. You can do one of the two things: either change the shadow brightness in the parameters of the Stone material, or change the density of the shadow in the parameters of the light source. Which method should we use? Let's inspect the photo again.

Notice that dense shadows can be viewed only on the bottom surfaces of the stones, so you can safely assume that the light is strongly scattered. This happens when particles of water are present in air, and the picture is proof of that. Besides, the stones themselves are secondary light sources strong enough to lighten shadows. Because of this, we'll change the shadow density in the light source parameters in case the shadows on your model will be too dark.

❏ Set the density parameter to 0.6 or 0.7:

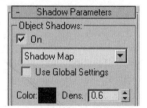

> Control panel → ... → **Shadow Parameters** rollout→ Dens

Perform test rendering.

Now correct the position of the cleft by moving the Stone object vertices and watching the changes in the **Active Shade** window.

**NOTE**  Active Shade was primarily designed to control changes in the parameters of materials and light sources. So, to refresh the screen, you have to select the **Initialize** item in the right-click menu of the **Active Shade** window. I hope that the developers of the application will correct this situation some day.

**TIP**  To speed up the process, select the **Draw Region** item in the same menu and outline the area to be rendered.

❏ Select the Stone object and enter the vertex-editing mode.

**NOTE**  If you unselected the vertices but, taking my advice, saved the named selection, you can restore the selection now. Just select the name in the corresponding list:

Main Toolbar → Named Selection Set

Otherwise, you'll have to select the related vertices again.

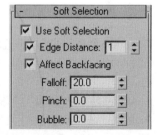

**TIP**  To make the task of moving the vertices to the desired places easier, use a soft selection. Its essence is that the selected elements of an object (more exactly, faces, polygons, etc) affect the adjacent elements with certain falling off. In 3ds max 4, the distance where soft selection is still in effect is measured in units set with the **Falloff** parameter. Besides, you can measure the distance by the number of edges (so-called "edge distance"). The **Pinch** and **Bubble** parameters allow you to control the influence on the vertices in a rather wide range. You can even make it so that, while moving a vertex, the adjacent ones move in the opposite direction. Selection of vertices can be monitored in the viewport by their color. Unfortunately, this is true only for vertices. You have to monitor other elements by eye.

❐ Open the **Soft Selection** rollout and set up the parameters as follows: check the **Use Soft Selection**, check the **Edge Distance**, and set the distance to 1. This means that only the vertices that are within a one-edge distance from the selected vertex will be affected.

❐ Move the vertices along the X- and Y- axes to place the shadow from the object correctly (fig. 2.51).

**Fig. 2.51.** The result of correcting the cleft position and shadow density

❐ Select and delete the sphere since you no longer need it.

Save the file as environ.max.

## Assembling the Scene

Now it's time to put our crocodile into the scene. In order to give the crocodile its desired shape, you need to use a method that shapes an object on the basis of a skeleton. This skeleton is made up of objects called Bones. In earlier versions of 3ds max, there was no built-in mechanism supporting bone systems. You had to use plug-ins, such as Character Studio or Bones Pro. In the previous version of 3ds max, the problem was partially solved by the Skin modifier, which was then further developed in the latest version. Moreover, you can use not only bones for a skeleton, but other objects, such as curves, as well.

❏ Open the environ.max file, select and freeze (key <6>) all the objects.

❏ Load the Body object from the Crock-complete.max file:

    Menu Bar → File → Merge

❏ Enter the **Top** viewport, scale the Body object, and move it so that it's on the stone (fig. 2.53).

    Right-click menu → Scale, Move

**Fig. 2.52.** The crocodile on the stone

***Caution***    Don't rotate the object about the vertical axis! If you do, you'll have problems creating the skeleton.

For proper editing of the object, you need to perform the Reset XForm operation for the object:

Control panel → Utilities → **Reset XForm** button→ **Reset Selected** button

**NOTE** This operation results in resetting the transformation matrix of the object. After that, the maps applied to the XYZ channel will be shown using new coordinates of the object. You can readily verify this with test rendering. To remedy the situation, decrease the **Size** parameters in the Top_Skin and Bottom_Skin materials maps approximately tenfold.

❏ Convert the object to Editable Poly:

Right-click menu → Convert To: → Convert to Editable Poly

The crocodile is now in the right place. We only need to give it the correct pose.

❏ Enter the **Left** viewport.

**TIP** You should freeze the object (key <6>) and switch to the **Fast View...** mode in the viewport:

Right-click menu → Configure...

**Set Fast View Nth Faces**

If you'd like to use Shaded rendering, make the object transparent (<Alt> + <X>) before you hide it. You should also enable default light sources in the menu where you set up the viewports.

Now create the skeleton.

The base object for the skeleton will be a box in the middle of the body (fig. 2.53, a).

❏ Create a box and name it Body_Box.

<Ctrl> + Right-click menu → Box

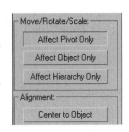

❏ Also, create a box for the head (fig. 2.53, b) and name it Head_Box. Move the pivot points of both objects to their centers.

Control Panel → Hierarchy → **Pivot** group → **Adjust Pivot** rollout → **Affect Pivot Only** button

**Alignment group** → **Center to Object** button

Now create the bones. In 3ds max 4, these have undergone radical changes. They are not just joints now — they are objects of full value.

❏ Enter the bone creating mode:

Main Menu → Animations → Create Bones

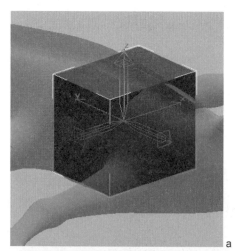

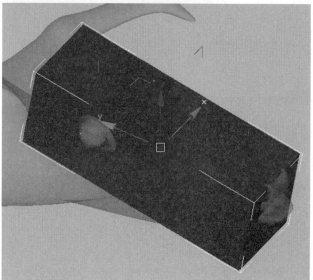

**Fig. 2.53.** Creating the base objects for the skeleton

❑ Don't check the **Assign To Children** checkbox in the parameters.

❑ Create a chain of bones from the Body_Box object to the tail (fig. 2.54, a). To terminate the chain creating process, click the right mouse button.

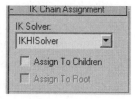

**TIP**   You should try to adjust the sizes of the bones and their geometry right now. It will re-duce  editing time in the future.

❑  Create a chain of bones from the Body_Box object to the head (fig. 2.54, b). Delete the little bone that appeared during the process, since you don't need it.

**NOTE**   It is very important that the chains don't branch. With this aim in mind, try to begin a chain some distance away from the bones of other chains.

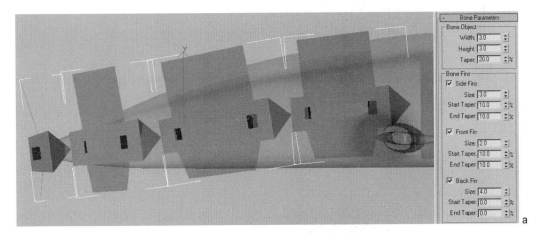

a

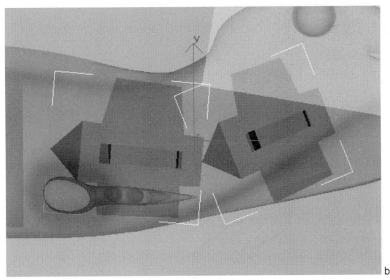

b

**Fig. 2.54, a, b.** The sequence of steps for creating a skeleton

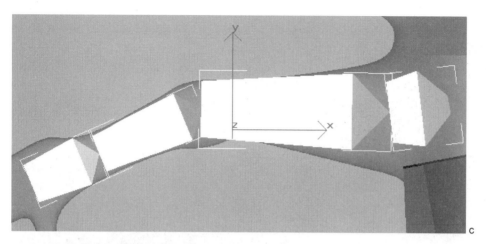

c

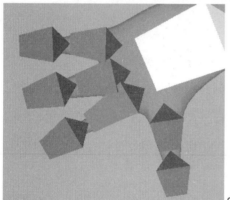

d

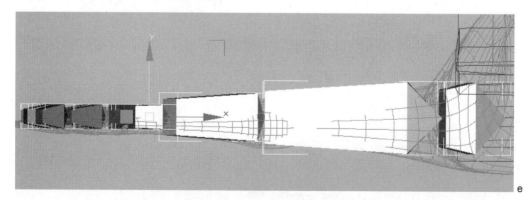

e

**Fig. 2.54, c, d. e.** The sequence of steps for creating a skeleton

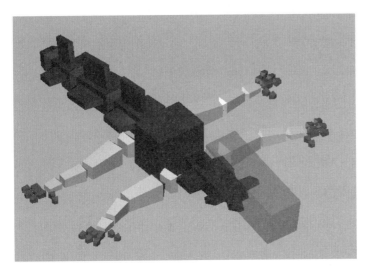

**Fig. 2.54, f.** The sequence of steps for creating a skeleton

❐ Create the bone chains for the forelimbs and the fingers.

❐ Press <T> to enter the **Top** viewport and create the bone chains (fig. 2.54, c and d).

❐ Press <F> to enter the **Front** viewport.

❐ Move the bones so that they're inside the model (fig. 2.54, e).

Adjust the parameters of the bones and their relative positions.

❐ Select the bones and make them independent.

    Control Panel → Hierarchy → **Pivot** group → **Adjust Transform** rollout → **Don't Affect Children** button

Create the bones of the hind limbs.

❐ Copy the bones of the forelimb by dragging them with the <Shift> key pressed.

❐ Adjust the sizes of the bones so that they fit the hind limb.

❐ Select all the bones of the limbs and mirror them with copying. This will create the bones for the opposite limbs (fig. 2.54, f)

Assemble the skeleton.

❐ Link the bones of the tail, the limbs, and the front to the Body_Box object (fig. 2.55, a).

    Main toolbar → Select and Link

❐ Link the head (Head_Box) to the nearest bone of the neck.

❐ Link the fingers to the corresponding bones of the paws (fig. 2.55, b).

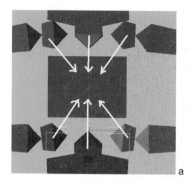 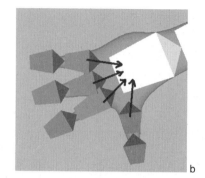

a

b

**Fig. 2.55.** Linking the elements of the skeleton

Test the suitability of your linking by selecting the Body_Box object and moving it. All the bones must move accordingly. Don't forget to return the object to its proper position!

The skeleton is ready.

Now create IK Chains. You are going to use them for the tail and the limbs. The fingers and the neck will follow the laws of direct kinematics.

The inverse kinematics (IK) of the previous versions of 3ds max was far from perfect. First of all, it was difficult to create and edit. In 3ds max 4, IK is much improved. Let's enjoy the innovations.

❏ Select the fore bone of the tail (fig. 2.56, a).

❏ Create the chain of the History Independent type (HI IK Solver).

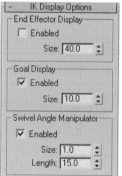

Main menu → Animation → IK Solvers → HI Solver

Click the end of the tail. A cross has appeared. You will be able to twist the tail after you select the cross (called "Goal") and move it.

*TIP* To resize the cross and the handle, adjust the parameters in the **Animation** group.

❏ In a similar fashion, create IK links between the limbs and the paws, as well as between the limbs and the shoulders (fig. 2.56, b).

Now the skeleton is finished. Associate it with the body.

❏ Unfreeze the Body object:

Control panel → Display → **Freeze** rollout → **Unfreeze by Name** button

❏ Select the Body object and apply the Skin modifier to it:

Tab panel → Modifiers → Skin

❏ Click the **Add Bone** button and select all the bones; that is, the objects whose names begin with "Bone".

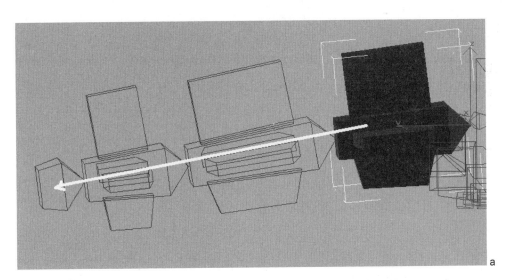

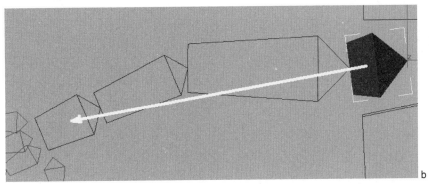

**Fig. 2.56.** Creating IK links

***TIP*** When selecting objects by names in 3ds max 4, you can enter the name in a special line. Objects with names beginning with the letter being entered will automatically be selected. You only need to click the **Select** button.

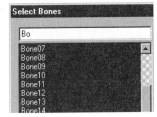

❑ Add the objects Body_Box and Body_Head.

Right-click menu → Add Bone

Now the bones are associated with the object. Take time to make sure this was done correctly.

❑ Enter the envelope mode:

Right-click menu → Edit Envelopes

Two curves will appear. The inner (red) curve defines an area where the bone affects the vertices by 100%. The outer (brown) curve defines the limits of this influence. The bone doesn't have an influence on vertices beyond this curve. The extent of this influence varies between the inner and outer envelopes in accordance with the falloff diagram you set in the Skin modifier parameters. As you go down the list of the bones, make sure that all of them affect the vertices adequately. In other words, make sure that the desired vertices are a color other than white. The red color indicates maximum influence, while blue indicates minimum. If you aren't satisfied with the extent of the influence of a bone, or some vertices fall outside the white area, change the shape of the envelope.

This can be simplified. Just move the Body_Box object. If no vertex remains in its place, everything is okay.

When I tried this, I achieved the desired result from the first attempt. If you choose the right sizes for the bones, you will also achieve success. I am going to leave you alone with the Skin modifier, since I am sure you'll be able to master it yourself. I must only mention that this tool is as powerful as the similar one from the kit Alias|Wavefront Maya, the recognized leader of animation.

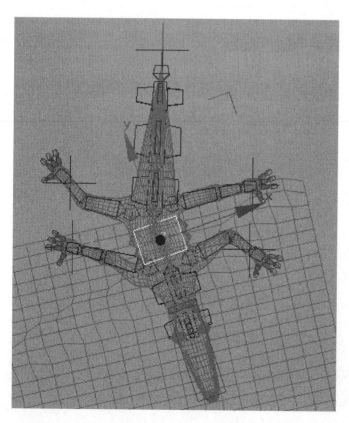

**Fig. 2.57.** The crocodile on the stone

Now let's turn to changing the crocodile's pose and shape.

☐ Show the hidden objects:

Control panel → Display → **Hide** rollout → **Unhide All** button

☐ Enter the **Top** viewport.

☐ Select the Body_Box object and move it to the edge of the stone so that the hind limbs are beyond the stone. Rotate the object as shown in fig. 2.57.

☐ Select and freeze all the objects but the bones (the <6> key).

Next, reshape the crocodile by selecting and moving the appropriate Goals of the IK chains. You can also enable the handles and rotate the chains. Moreover, you can move and rotate the bones not included in the IK chains, for example, the finger bones. Rotation should be performed in the local coordinates.

> **NOTE**   Be careful with the head! Don't move it. When you want to change its position, move the bones of the neck.

The result is shown in fig. 2.58.

**Fig. 2.58.** The final pose of the crocodile

Perform test rendering.

During my own experiments, it happened that the far edge of the stone didn't hide a hind limb. The solution was quite simple. I only had to select some of the stone vertices and correct their positions.

Make the objects Body_Box and Head_Box non-renderable.

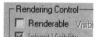

Right-click menu → Properties

## Setting up Lighting

There's only one light source in our scene, and it's obviously deficient.

❏ Let's use a very popular method of illumination, the so-called "Sky_Dome".

❏ Create a Target Spot light source and aim it at the center of the crocodile. The parameters of the source are shown in fig. 2.59.

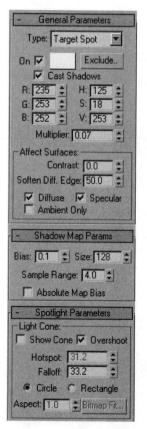

*TIP*  Assuming that there will be many sources, set a small value for the factor (say, 0.07). Select the light blue color. The shadow should not be sharp.

❏ Create two instances of the light source on the different levels above the horizon (fig. 2.60, a).

❏ Create a hemisphere of dependent sources so that they illuminate the crocodile (fig. 2.60, b). I created 21 sources.

❏ Adjust the sources. As for me, I made yellow illumination to come from below. This is to simulate reflected light (fig. 2.60, c). For this purpose I selected a group of sources, moved them, and made them independent of the others, though dependent on each other.

*TIP*  It is convenient to manipulate multiple light sources using Light Lister (fig. 2.61).

Tab panel → Lights & Cameras

**Fig. 2.59.** The parameters of the light source for creating a Sky Dome

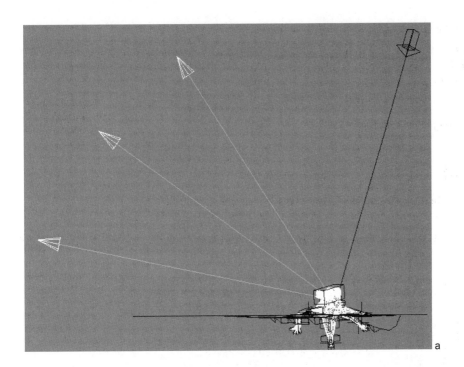

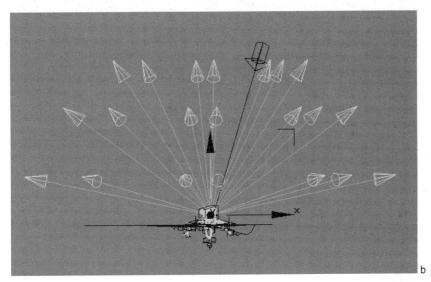

**Fig. 2.60, a, b.** Creating a Sky Dome

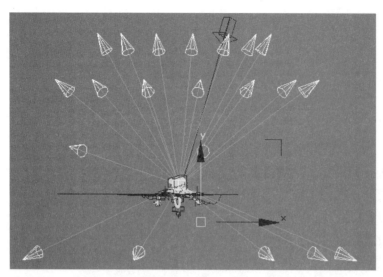

**Fig. 2.60, c.** Creating a Sky Dome

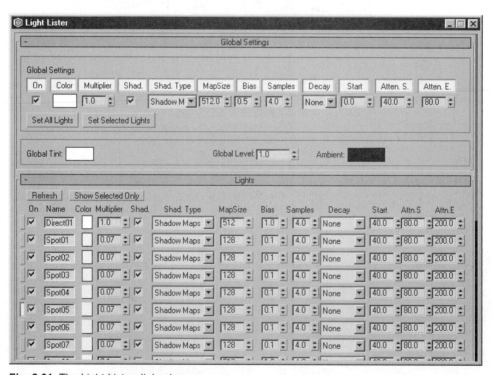

**Fig. 2.61.** The Light Lister dialog box

***Self-study***   Try to experiment with materials. For example, eliminate the crocodile's "Hollywood smile" by changing the diffuse color to gray  among the parameters of the Tooth material. You can also add some noise to the Bump channel of the Top_Skin material by changing the type of the map to Mix and by setting the blend to 50.

One finishing stroke. Let's make the crocodile's skin glow in the sun.

❏ Select the Body object and set the **Object Channel** value for **G-Buffer** equal to 10.

Right-click menu → Properties

❏ Add a Glow effect to the scene (**Lens Effect** rollout).

Main menu → Rendering → Effects

❏ Adjust the parameters to obtain some glow around the light areas of the skin.

The parameters that finally satisfied me are shown in fig. 2.62.

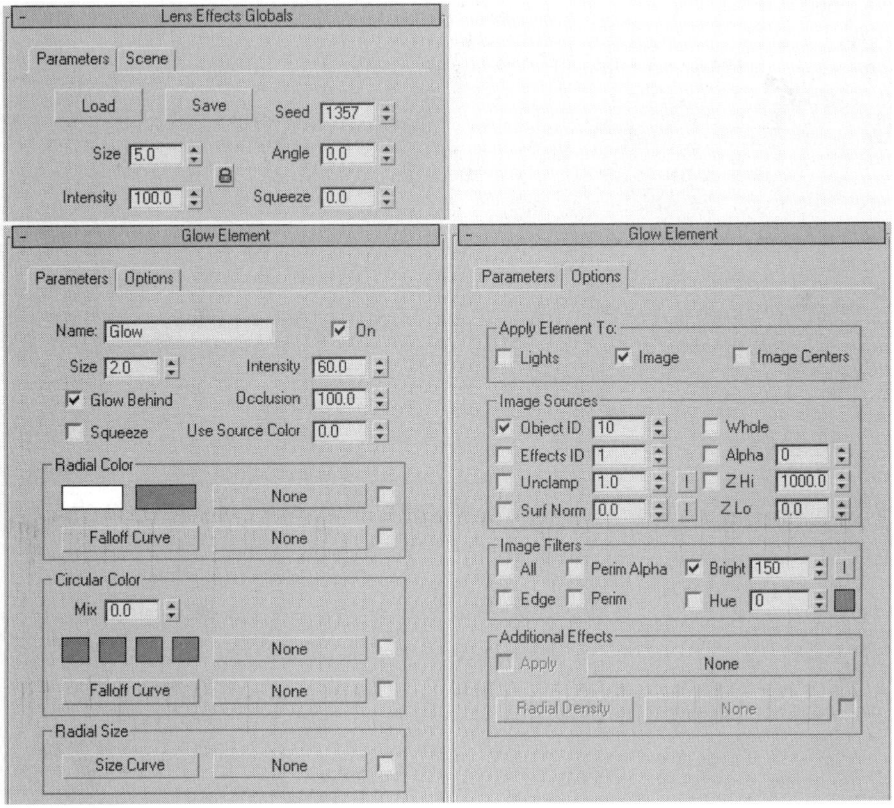

**Fig. 2.62.** The parameters of Glow

***TIP***   The **Object ID** parameter must correspond to the value set for the Body object.

The set **Bright** checkbox and the value 150 indicate that only those areas will glow which are lighter than 150 units (in the 1-to-255 range).

Adjust the sizes and intensity so that the glow is not too intense .

I recommend you to set the **Interactive** checkbox in the **Preview** group.

❑ Perform final rendering and save the resulting image on your hard disk.

❑ Save the project under the name of Lesson02.max.

# Summary

Now let's analyze our activities.

To begin with, the process of editing the crocodile wasn't the best. If we had chosen the correct sequence of steps, we could have avoided many of the side effects. Unfortunately, there are no "cut and dried" methods, so I hope you'll develop your own rational procedures for modeling. These will be *your procedures*, which you'll adhere to. Furthermore, as I stated in the *Introduction*, some flaws were made intentionally in order to show you different ways around the problem. Don't be upset when you fail. Remember, "He that never climbed, never fell".

You might notice that the crocodile's constitution is somewhat "unhealthy". The reason is that we didn't use certain features of the Skin modifier, specifically, simulation of muscle contraction. Try to correct the situation yourself.

To simplify manipulating the bones, we could create dummy objects and link them to the goals of the IK chains.

One last point: you may notice that the crocodile is somewhat "out of the photo", no matter how hard you've worked putting it in. The reason is that the quality of the photo (more precisely, the scanned picture) is far from perfect. That's why you have to intentionally deteriorate the quality of the rendered image down to that of the photo. Unfortunately, 3ds max 4 doesn't enable you to do this unless you use a plug-in from a third-party manufacturer. This is easily solved with Adobe PhotoShop or any other raster image editor. If, at a later time, you're able to mix 3D objects with real world pictures, try using your best quality picture as a background.

# Lesson 3

# Logo

In this lesson, we'll try to create a promotional movie of a hypothetical company called Triangle. You can view the logo of this company by opening the logo640.tif file in the \Lessons\Lesson03\Images on the companion CD. The movie itself resides in the same directory in the lesson03.avi file.

## Aims of This Lesson

After completing this lesson, you'll know how to:

❏ Create complex materials and assign them to the parts of the objects.

❏ Animate objects and modifier settings using key frame animation.

❏ Work with Video Post, create effects, and compose a simple video.

## Preliminary Notes

We won't be modeling complex objects in this lesson. The most important aspect of this lesson will be to learn the correct sequence of actions when creating and animating models and materials. 3ds max 4 allows you to return and add a necessary action at almost any stage of the project. However, this normally requires some additional work. Because of this, I did not separate the process of modeling, creating materials and animation. All of these actions will be performed in the order that's required for quickly and efficiently obtaining the final result. This simple movie can be created using various techniques. When preparing this lesson, I tried at least five different methods and selected the one that, in my opinion, is the easiest to understand and at the same time demonstrates all the power of 3ds max 4.

The result that you'll get when you complete this lesson can hardly be considered realistic. My aims were different. In the movie, I tried to illustrate the most interesting 3ds max 4 functionality related to object parameter animation and special effects.

## Scenario

Before starting anything, it's necessary to understand what do you want as a final result. Also, if you're doing the job for a customer rather then for yourself, it's important that the customer knows what he really wants.

Because of this, it's necessary to develop a scenario.

1. A blue laser beam hits the black backing. The beam starts moving, and burns out a furrow on the black backing surface. Scorching particles of the burning substance bounce apart and deposit at the edges of the furrow, which gradually cools down. At the same time, the camera begins to move after the beam in such a way that the whole furrow remains in the field of vision.

2. When the furrow reaches approximately half of its final length, the camera moves, allowing you to see that three different colored beams have burned out three furrows.

3. Finally the camera focuses on the spot where all three furrows form the logo.

4. The backing explodes with a flash, revealing the logo.

5. The logo remains on screen for a while and then gradually fades out.

Of course, this is just a general description of the scenario, but it helps you to understand what will take place.

# Specifying the Time Settings

Before starting the modeling process, you need to specify the time settings. The version of movie you'll be creating will be displayed on the monitor. Because of this, a frame rate equal to 15 frames per second will be sufficient. The running time of the whole movie is about 15 seconds, 10 seconds of which will be needed for active animation, making 150 frames. According to these assumptions, specify the time configuration settings.

❑ Reset 3ds max 4 to initial state:

Main menu → File → Reset

❑ Open the animation settings:

Time controls → **Time Configuration** button

❑ Set the frame rate to 15 FPS (Frames per Second) and duration about 8 seconds (fig. 3.1):

Time Configuration → Frame Rate: Custom

Time Configuration → Time Display: SMPTE

Time Configuration → Animation: End Time: 0:10:0

*NOTE*  You can also use a normal format with a simple frame numbering scheme. The SMPTE format, however, provides more a vivid presentation. It uses the following frame numbering scheme: minutes:seconds:frames. Thus, the frame that follows frame 00:00:14, is numbered 00:01:00 rather than 00:00:15 (the numeration starts from 0).

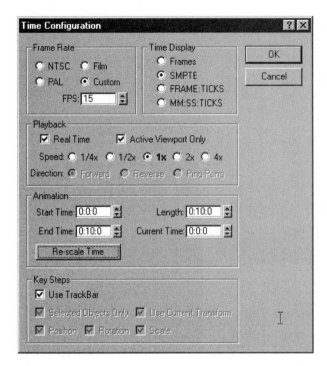

**Fig. 3.1.** Time configuration settings

# Creating the Backing Model

❏ Go the **Front** viewport by pressing the <F> key, and then press the <W> key to maximize the viewport.

❏ Specify the Logo320.tif file stored in the \Lessons\Lesson03\Maps directory on the companion CD as the viewport background:

Main menu → Views → Viewport Background

❏ Specify the background settings as shown in fig. 3.2.

*TIP* You can lock the background to the geometry by specifying the **Lock Zoom/Pan** checkbox.

❏ Create a new rectangle larger than the background picture (fig. 3.3):

Tab panel → Shapes → Rectangle

*TIP* Enable the snaps by pressing the <S> key.

❏ Rename the rectangle to "Plate".

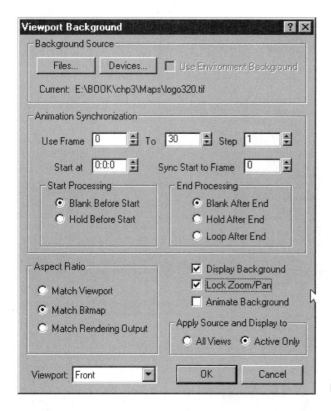

**Fig. 3.2.** The background settings

**Fig. 3.3.** Logo picture and backing dummy

❏ Create another rectangle to enclose the lower colored stripe of the logo.

❏ Create two clone copies of this rectangle. Rotate and move the new rectangles to follow the logo pattern, as shown in fig. 3.4:

Main menu → Edit → Clone

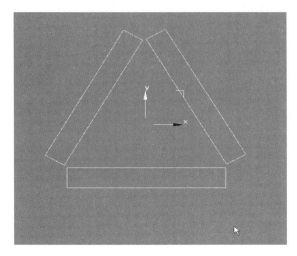

**Fig. 3.4.** Dummy object that corresponds to the logo pattern

Make sure that the edges forming the rectangles don't intersect.

*TIP* Turn the angle snap on by pressing the <A> key.

❏ Disable the background display:

Viewport right-click menu → clear the **Show Background** checkbox

❏ Select the **Plate** object and convert it to Editable Spline:

Right-click menu → Convert To: → Convert to Editable Spline

❏ Attach all of the remaining rectangles to this object:

Right-click menu → Attach

❏ Convert the resulting object to Editable Mesh:

Right-click menu → Convert To: → Convert to Editable Mesh

You've got the dummy object with slots (fig. 3.5).

Now it's necessary to "close" the slots. There are two methods of accomplishing this task. First, you can use the Cap Hole modifier. Second, you can manually create the missing polygons. Unfortunately, the first method isn't the easiest. The Cap Hole modifier closes all of the holes. Because this surface is single-sided, the other side of the object will also be considered as a hole. The Cap Hole modifier will try to correct this error by creating an unnecessary polygon. You'll need to delete this polygon, and you'll probably make several errors trying to get rid of it. Because of this, I recommend that you proceed as follows.

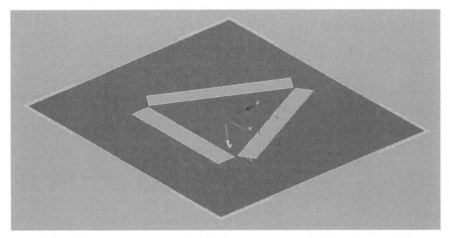

**Fig. 3.5.** The dummy object with slots

❐ Switch to the polygon object:

Right-click menu → Create → Polygon

❐ Select the vertex belonging to one of the slots and create a new polygon by clicking the mouse button sequentially on the hole vertices (in a counter-clockwise direction). Click the left mouse button on the first vertex to complete this operation. Be very careful! 3ds max 4 introduced the capability of creating polygons based not only on the existing vertices. Therefore, make sure that the mouse pointer turns into small filled cross rather than cross-hairs.

❐ Create polygons for each hole.

**NOTE** The direction selected for creating the polygons is very important. For example, the direction of normals for newly created polygons depends on this factor.

Now we have to prepare our object for further editing.

First of all, it's necessary to specify the **Material: ID** setting for each polygon. You'll need four materials: one material for the backing and one material per furrow.

❐ Select all of the polygons:

Right-click menu → Sub-objects → Polygon

Main menu → Edit → Select All

**NOTE** Default settings for 3ds max don't include a keyboard shortcut for this operation. Step by step instructions on assigning a keyboard shortcuts were provided in Lesson 1.

I, personally, selected the <Grey *> key.

For operations like **Select None** and **Select Invert**, it's easy to assign keyboard shortcuts, such as <Ctrl>+<Grey *> and <Alt>+<Grey *>, respectively. Be careful, though, when assigning new keyboard shortcuts, because they may already be in use by other commands!

❐ The **Material: ID** setting for each polygon should be set to 1:

Control panel → ... → **Surface Properties** rollout → Material: ID

❐ Select the polygons that correspond to the lower furrow and modify the **Material: ID** setting by specifying the 2 value.

Select the polygons sequentially (in a counter-clockwise direction) and modify the **Material: ID** setting as necessary (fig. 3.6).

❐ Select the polygons that correspond to the furrows.

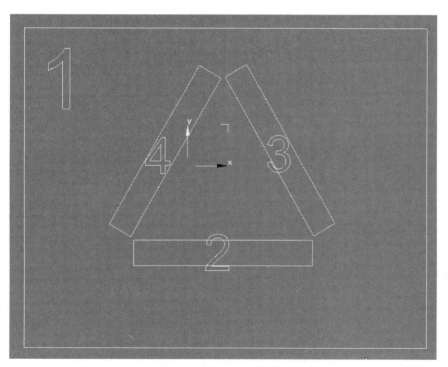

**Fig. 3.6.** The model. Digits shown in this figure are **Material: ID** values assigned to the polygons

❐ Split them to smaller polygons.(fig. 3.7):

Control panel → ... → **Edit Geometry** rollout → select the **by Edge** tessellation type and set the **Edge tension** value to 0

Click the **Tessellate** button four times

❐ The dummy object is ready.

To simplify the transition between subobjects, assign each group of polygons appropriate name.

❐ Select the polygons with the **Material ID** parameter equal to 1:

Control panel → **Surface Properties** rollout → **Material** group → Select By ID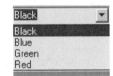

Enter 1 and click **OK**

❐ In the Main toolbar, go to the **Named Selection Set** list, enter the value Black, and press <Enter>.

❐ Select groups of polygons one by one and assign them the Red, Green, and Blue names, respectively.

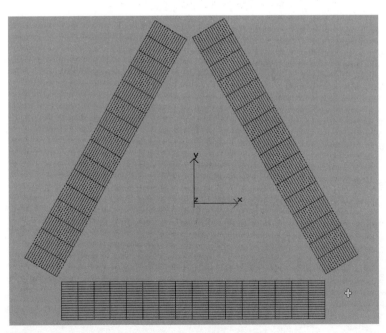

**Fig. 3.7.** The result of applying the Tessellate modifier

# Animating the Dummy

You need to animate two parameters. First, you need to animate UVW mapping to be able to correctly apply textures to the respective polygons. Second, you need to animate the vertex selection in order to reshape the polygons and get furrows.

❐ Switch to polygon mode and select the polygons that correspond to the lowest furrow (fig. 3.8):

Right-click menu → Sub-objects → Polygon

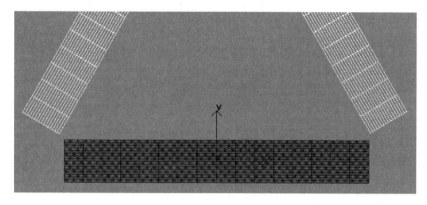

**Fig. 3.8.** Selected polygons corresponding to the lower furrow

❐ Apply the UVW Map modifier for the polygons:

Control panel → Modifier List → UVW Map

Don't modify the default modifier settings since they already meet our requirements.

❐ Switch to the Gizmo mode:

Right-click menu → Sub-objects → Gizmo

❐ Move the Gizmo to the leftmost position (fig. 3.9, a).

❐ Enable the mode for recording animation by pressing the <N> key. Go to the 0:8:0 frame (8 seconds) by moving the time slider, or by entering "8:0" into the current frame field in the time controls.

> **NOTE** You can also switch the animation recording on and off by pressing the **Animate** button. Select whichever method you prefer.

❐ Move the Gizmo to its final position (fig. 3.9, b). After doing this, set the animation key at frame 0:8:0.

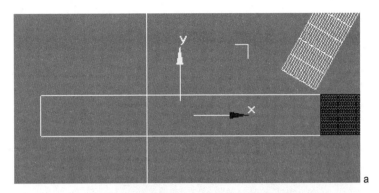

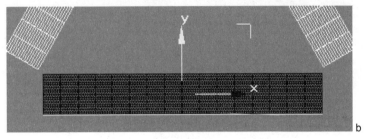

**Fig. 3.9.** Initial (a) and final (b) positions of the UVW Map Gizmo

❏ Switch the animation-recording mode off by pressing the <N> key. View the resulting animation:

Time controls → **Play Animation** button

As you can see, the Gizmo moves from left to right.

Now you need to apply mapping coordinates for all of the other furrows.

*TIP* The modifier stack will be quite large. To simplify navigation within the stack, 3ds max 4 allows you to rename the modifiers contained in the stack. To do so, open the right-click menu of the stack, select the **Rename** command, and enter the unique name. Because the elements of our logo have different colors, I recommend that you use names like "UVW Mapping Red".

❏ Apply the Mesh Select modifier and select the polygons of the right furrow:

Control panel → ... → Mesh Select

Control panel → ... → **Mesh Select Parameters** rollout → **Polygon** button

Select by **Material ID** – enter "3" into the ID: field and click the **Select** button

You can do the same thing using another method — named selections.

❐ In the Modifier stack, return to Editable Mesh.

❐ Copy the Green set of polygons.

    Control panel → **Selection** rollout → **Copy** button

    Select the Green set and click **OK**

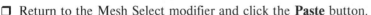

❐ Return to the Mesh Select modifier and click the **Paste** button.

In our case it is more convenient to use the first method, because different sets have different Material IDs.

Let us continue editing.

❐ Rename the modifier to Mesh Select Green, it you wish.

❐ Select the UVW Mapping Red and Mesh Select Green modifiers. To do so, press and hold the <Ctrl> key and copy them to the top of the stack by simply dragging with the pressed <Shift> key.

❐ Rename the modifiers to UVW Mapping Green and Mesh Select Blue.

❐ Copy the UVW Mapping Green modifier to the top of the stack and rename it to UVW Mapping Blue.

❐ The stack now will look as shown in fig. 3.10.

**Fig. 3.10.** The Modifier stack

Now you need to specify the modifier parameters.

❐ Go to the UVW Mapping Green modifier.

❐ Change the map channel:

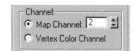

    Control panel → ...→ Channel: "2"

❐ Switch to the Gizmo mode and rotate the gizmo around the Z-axis 120° in a counter-clockwise direction. Don't forget to enable the angle snap by pressing the <A> key:

    Right-click menu → Rotate

Specify the gizmo animation settings.

❐ Go to frame 0:0:0 and move the Gizmo, as shown in fig. 3.11, a.

❐ Switch to the animation-recording mode by pressing the <N> key.

❐ Go to frame 0:8:0 and move the Gizmo to the final position, as shown in fig. 3.11, b.

❐ Switch the animation-recording mode off and view the resulting animation.

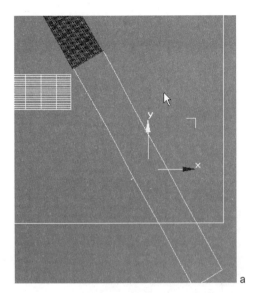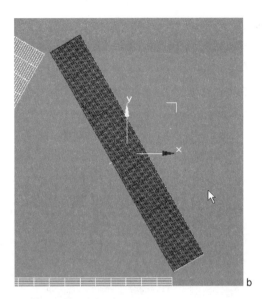

**Fig. 3.11.** Initial (a) and final (b) positions of the UVW Mapping Green Gizmo

*TIP* You can use the <.> (period) and <,> (comma) for moving along the time axis. These keys can work in two modes, set by the **Key Mode Toggle** button. If the key mode isn't enabled (the **Key Mode Toggle** button isn't depressed), then pressing the <.> and <,> keys moves you along the time axis one frame forward and backward, respectively. If you enable the key mode by pressing this button, you'll jump ahead or backwards to the keyframes where you've set animation keys.

Now you just have to edit the settings for the last, blue furrow.

❑ Return to the new Mesh Select modifier and select the polygons where the **Material: ID** parameter is set to 4.

❑ Edit the UVW Mapping Blue settings and its animation. Set the **Map Channel** setting to 3, rotate the gizmo counter-clockwise 120° and specify the direction of the gizmo movement from top to bottom.

*Warning* Unfortunately, 3ds max 4 doesn't allow you to group modifiers within the stack or protect their settings from accidental modifications. You can move upwards or downwards along the stack, but remember that any modification of the modifier settings can lead to undesirable results which are sometimes hard to eliminate.

Now you need to select the vertices that will be used to form the furrows. Use the Vol. Select and XForm modifiers.

❑ Apply the Vol. Select modifier:

Control panel → Modifier List → Vol. Select

❏ Specify the following parameters for this modifier: **Stack Selection Level: Vertex** and **Selection Method: Replace** (fig. 3.12).

❏ Go to the Gizmo mode:

Right-click menu → Sub-objects → Gizmo

❏ Modify the size and location of the gizmo, as shown in fig. 3.13.

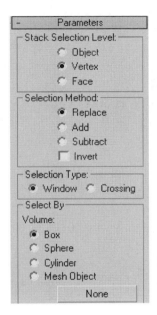

**Fig. 3.12.** Settings specified for the Vol. Select modifier

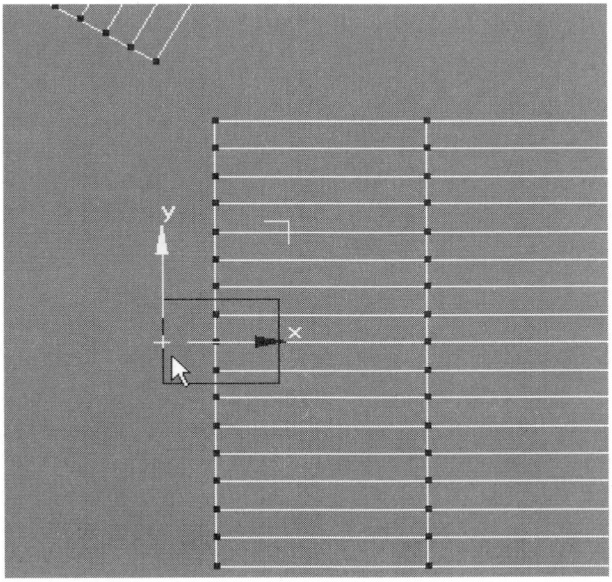

**Fig. 3.13.** Starting position of the Vol. Select modifier gizmo. Notice position of the gizmo center

❏ Start editing the center of the gizmo:

Right-click menu → Sub-objects → Center

❏ Move the center to the leftmost position (fig. 3.13).

Specify Soft Selection to make the furrow shapes realistic.

❏ Enable the Soft Selection mode:

Control panel → ... → **Soft Selection** rollout → set the **Use Soft Selection** checkbox

❏ Set the **Falloff** setting to make the vertices furthest from the Gizmo blue.

*NOTE* Selection doesn't affect these vertices. All other vertices are affected by the selection according to the falloff curve. The color of each vertex reflects the extent to which that vertex is affected.

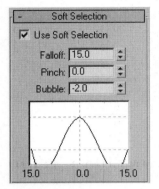

□ Set the **Bubble** setting to –2. Notice the change in the shape of the curve (fig. 3.14).

*NOTE* The shape of the curve defines the extent to which the vertices react to the transformations applied to them. If the vertex falls in a range of positive values (above the axis), then the transformations applied to it are direct. Vertices that fall in a range of negative values are subject to reversed transformations.

**Fig. 3.14.** Changes in the shape of the curve

□ Apply the XForm modifier:

Control panel → Modifier List → Xform

□ Change to the isometric user view by pressing the <U> key, enable the rendering mode by pressing the <F3> key and move the XForm gizmo along the Y-axis to produce the furrow.

You'll certainly be far from happy with this result (fig. 3.15, a). Now let's correct it.

□ In the modifier stack, return to the Vol. Select modifier.

□ Decrease the **Falloff** setting to make the result look better (fig. 3.15, b).

Now everything's all right.

*NOTE* Don't pay any attention to the fact that the furrow has sharp edges. This will be corrected later.

Now animate the Vol.Select gizmo.

□ Go to the **Front** viewport by pressing the <F> key. Enable rendering mode in the **Wireframe** viewport by pressing the <F3> key.

□ Start editing the Vol. Select gizmo.

□ Switch to the Non-Uniform Scale mode:

Main Toolbar → the **Select and Uniform Scale** button

Press this button, and drag the mouse to the **Select and Non-Uniform Scale** option

□ Enable the animation mode by pressing the <N> key, then go to the 0:8:0 frame.

□ Change the gizmo size along the X-axis as shown in fig. 3.16.

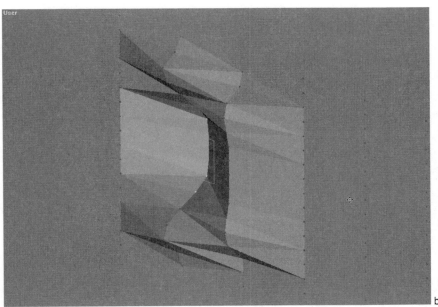

**Fig. 3.15.** The results of applying the XForm modifier after editing the **Falloff** parameter of the Vol. Select modifier

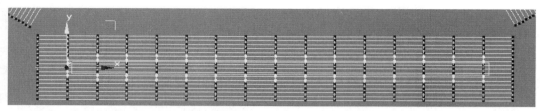

**Fig. 3.16.** The Vol. Select gizmo in the 0:8:0 frame

❏ Rename the Vol. Select modifier to "Vol. Select Red".

❏ Copy the Vol. Select Red modifier by moving it *under* the Xform modifier, and rename the copy as "Vol. Select Green".

❏ Edit the Vol. Select Green gizmo by rotating it counterclockwise 120° and move it, as shown in fig. 3.17, a.

❏ Enable the animation, go to the 0:8:0 frame and reposition the gizmo (fig. 3.17, b).

❏ Toggle the animation mode by pressing the <N> key.

❏ Set the **Add** option from the **Selection Method** group for the Vol.Select Green modifier. Instruct the modifier to add a new vertex selection to the previous one.

❏ Copy the Vol. Select Green modifier, edit its gizmo and rename it to "Vol. Select Blue".

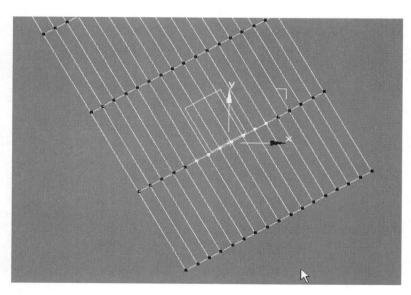

**Fig. 3.17, a.** Animation of the Vol. Select Green Gizmo

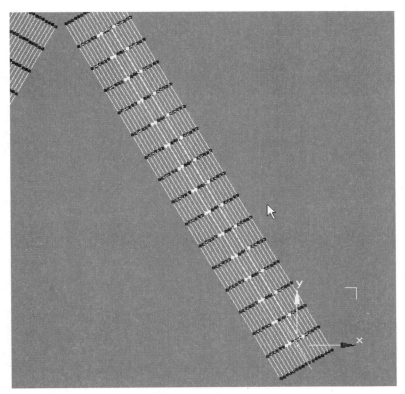

**Fig. 3.17, b.** Animation of the Vol. Select Green Gizmo

Add some chaos to the form of the furrows.

❑ Go to the top of the stack.

❑ Apply the Noise modifier:

    Control panel → Modifier List → Noise

❑ Set the parameters as shown in fig. 3.18.

Make the furrows smooth.

❑ Apply the Mesh Select modifier and select the polygons belonging to the furrows:

    Control panel → Modifier List → Mesh Select

❑ Switch to the polygon selection mode and select the polygons where the **Material: ID** parameters are set to 1:

    Invert selection → Main menu → Edit → Select Invert

❏ Apply the Smooth modifier and assign any smoothing group to the selected polygons; for example, 8:

Control panel → Modifier List → Smooth

The Modifier stack will now look as shown in fig. 3.19.

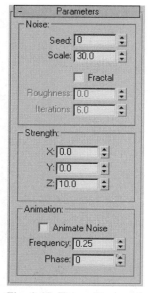

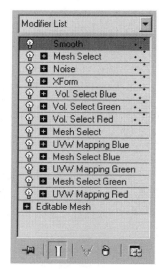

**Fig. 3.18.** The settings of the Noise modifier      **Fig. 3.19.** Final view of the Modifier stack

Thus, the geometry is ready.

# Creating and Assigning Materials

The settings for all the necessary materials can vary widely. The most important thing is to make the materials shiny. All of these materials will be composed from four basic ones.

❏ Open the material editor (the <M> key).

❏ Select the first sample slot.

❏ Set the Ambient and Diffuse colors to black, and the Specular color to white.

❏ Set the **Specular Level**, **Glossiness**, and **Soften** parameters to 120, 60, and 0.5, respectively.

❏ Rename this material to "Black".

❏ Copy the material three times to different sample slots.

*TIP* To simplify the process of creating the materials, increase the number of preview windows displayed at a time. Right-click any sample slot displayed by the material editor and select the **5×3 Sample Windows** option from the context menu.

❏ Rename the new materials to "Red", "Green", and "Blue", respectively.

❏ For each of the newly created materials, change the Diffuse and Ambient colors to red, green, and blue, respectively.

*TIP* You can modify the color by entering the value to the respective channel. For example, if you need to get red, enter 255 into the **Red** channel.

❏ Unlock the Diffuse and Ambient colors and make the Ambient color darker.

❏ Apply the Noise map to the Self-Illumination channel. Specify the following values for the settings — dark gray and white — Fractal map, size — 5, **Threshold High** and **Low** values — 1.0 and 0.5, respectively (fig. 3.20).

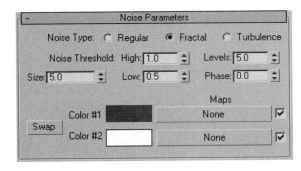

**Fig. 3.20.** Parameters of the Noise map for creating non-uniform self-illumination of materials

❏ Clear the **Color** checkbox in the settings of the self-illumination channel.

*NOTE* I wish to admit, that I myself adjusted the settings for this map after everything was ready, in the course of the test rendering.

*TIP* It is convenient to proceed as follows. First adjust the map for one of materials, move it to the free material slot using the Instance method, and then assign to appropriate materials buttons.

❏ Select the free sample slot and change the material type to Multi/Sub-Object:

Material editor → the **Type** button

❏ Change the number of sub-materials to 4:

Material editor → **Multi/Sub-objects Basic Parameters** rollout → **Set Number** button

❐ Move the Black material to the first button in the list of sub-materials using the Instance method.

❐ Rename the composite material to "Plate".

Now let's discuss how our materials should behave during animation.

First, as the beams that burn out the furrows move, the area of respective color has to appear at the place where the beam hits the plate. As the beam moves, the furrow gradually cools down, changing its color to black. Second, the area of scorching material must smoothly give way to black on both sides of the furrow.

It's implementation of these effects that required the time you spent applying and animating the texture coordinates.

For each sub-material, you need to create two Blend materials using two masks.

❐ Select the second sub-material and change its type to Blend.

❐ Rename the material to "Black+Blend Red".

❐ Select the Black material as the first sub-material by dragging it from the sample slot using the Instance method.

❐ Select gradient texture as a mask. Click the **Mask** button and select the **Gradient** option

❐ Rename this texture to "Red Mask 1".

❐ Return one level upward by clicking the **Go to Parent** button.

❐ Select the second sub-material and change its type to Blend.

❐ Rename this material to "Blend Red".

❐ Select the Black material as the first sub-material, and Red as the second sub-material. Copy these materials from their respective sample slots using the Instance method.

❐ Select gradient texture as a mask.

❐ Rename the texture to "Red Mask 2".

❐ Assign the Plate material to the Plate object by dragging it from the sample slot to the Plate object.

Now specify the settings for gradient textures.

*TIP* Use the Material/Map Navigator to simplify the process of navigating materials and switch between material elements (fig. 3.21).

❐ Go to frame 0:4:0.

❐ Start editing the Red Mask 2 texture and enable the texture display in the viewport.

❐ Modify the texture settings to look like those shown in fig. 3.22, a:

Gradient colors (Color #1, #2 and #3) should be set to white, gray, and black, respectively. Set the Color 2 Position setting to 0.2

Disable tiling (Tile) for the U coordinate and enable mirroring (Mirror) for the V axis.

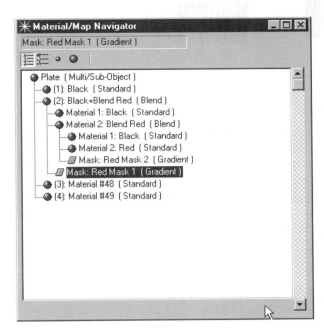

**Fig. 3.21.** The **Material/Map Navigator** window

☐ Start editing the Red Mask 1 texture and enable the texture display in the viewport.

☐ Modify the texture settings to make them look like the ones shown in fig. 3.22, b.

☐ Gradient colors (Color #1, #2 and #3) should be set to black, white, and black, respectively. The **Position** setting for Color#2 should be set to 0.9.

☐ Specify the noise settings as follows: **Amount:** — 0.5, **Size:** — 0.5, and select **Fractal** type.

☐ Disable tiling for the U and V coordinates. Rotate the texture by 90° in relation to the W axis (simply specify the 90 in the **Angle W** field).

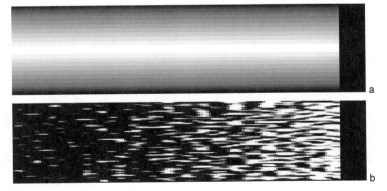

**Fig. 3.22.** Texture editing

Animate the noise parameters.

❏ Without exiting the material editor, go to the last frame (0:10:0) and press the <N> key to enable the animation.

❏ Enter 20 into the **Phase** field.

You've just specified the settings for one sub-material. Now create all the other sub-materials.

❏ Using Material/Map Navigator, go to the Plate material.

❏ Create the third and the fourth sub-materials by copying the second (Black+Blend Red) sub-material.

**NOTE** Notice that it's the copying method that should be used to create these sub-materials, since you'll later need to edit these sub-materials and modify most of their settings.

The Plate material tree now looks like the one shown in fig. 3.23, a.

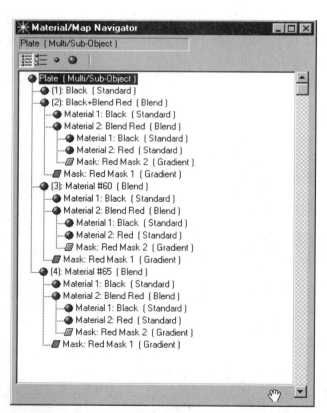

**Fig. 3.23, a.** Sub-material tree for the Plate material (before editing)

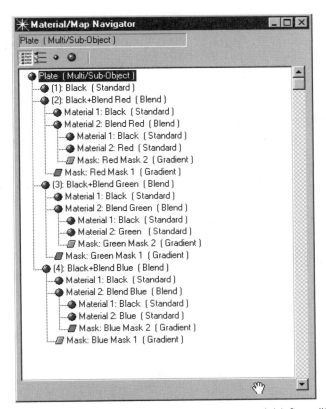

**Fig. 3.23, b.** Sub-material tree for the Plate material (after editing)

Follow this tree to change the material settings (don't forget to rename the materials after editing). The resulting tree is shown in fig. 3.23, b.

**TIP** First, drag the Green and Blue materials to their appropriate positions by using the Instance method.

Next, modify the **Map Channel** setting in the texture settings for Green Mask # and Blue Mask # textures. Set the value to 2 and 3, respectively, to map them to the UVW Mapping Green and UVW Mapping Blue modifiers.

**NOTE** The most difficult aspect in this lesson is material editing. If you understand that, you can learn to create materials of any level of complication. The important point here is to assign the materials and textures unique and meaningful names.

Finally, I'd like to point out that no one is insured against natural human errors. Members of the production team who prepared this book (including myself) are no exception. Thus, if you proceed exactly as described here, but aren't happy with the results, try to achieve the desired result using another method.

***TIP***   3ds max has another capability of representing the objects and materials tree – the Schematic View. It's possible that this representation will be easier for you. No wonder that in most 3D or video-editing programs, this method of representing the project is the primary one!

To complete the process of creating and editing materials for the plate, and to proceed further with scene editing, two additional operations need to be done. First, it's necessary to correct the coordinate mapping. Next, we need to prepare the Green, Red, and Blue materials before applying special effects to them.

Go to any frame (0:4:0, for example) and perform test rendering. You'll notice that the front of material doesn't match the form of the furrow. Correct this situation.

❏ Select the Plate object and begin editing it:

   Control panel → Modify

❏ Expand the modifier stack and go to the UVW Mapping Red modifier.

❏ Modify the **Width** setting so that the modifier's gizmo will enclose the front of the furrow.

Perform the same operations for UVW Mapping Green and Blue modifiers.

❏ Open the material editor.

❏ Set the Material Effects Channel to 15 for Red, Green, and Blue materials.

Now everything's correct!

# Creating and Animating Laser Beams

Direct Light and Volume Light are the most convenient for creating laser beams.

❏ Go to the **Top** viewport by pressing the <T> key.

❏ Create new Direct Light as shown in fig. 3.24. The source of light needs to be placed far enough from the plate:

   Tab panel → Lights & Cameras → Target Directional Light

❏ Enable editing mode for the light:

   Control panel → Modify

❏ Change the color to bright red.

**Fig. 3.24.** The light-imitating laser beams

❑ Go to the front viewport by pressing the <F> key. Edit the light setting, including the bright spot and attenuation, to get a beam with a diameter equal to half the width of the furrows:

Control panel → ... → **Directional Parameters** rollout

❑ Set the **Hotspot** and **Falloff** settings equal to 5 and 7, respectively.

❑ Rename the light to "Laser Red".

❑ Select the object named Laser Red.Target and move it to the new position, as shown in fig. 3.25, a.

❑ Go to frame 0:8:0, and enable animation by pressing the <N> key and repositioning the Laser Red.Target object, as shown in fig. 3.25, b. When finished, disable the animation by pressing the <N> key.

Now let's create the laser beam.

❑ Select the Laser Red light and begin editing its settings.

❑ Open the **Atmospheres & Effects** rollout (fig. 3.26) and press the **Add** button to add the Volume Light effect.

❑ Select the Volume Light effect and press the **Setup** button.

❑ Specify the settings as shown in fig. 3.27.

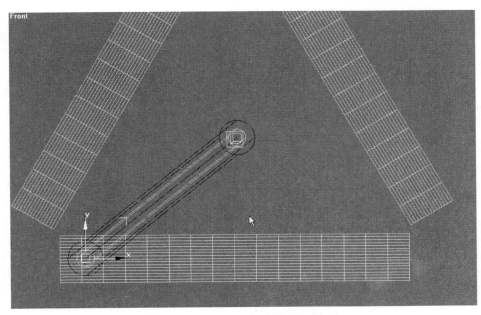

**Fig. 3.25, a.** The starting position for the Laser Red.Target object

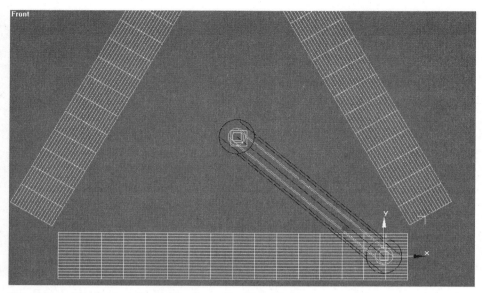

**Fig. 3.25, b.** The final position of the Laser Red.Target object

**Fig. 3.26.** The **Atmospheres & Effects** rollout

***NOTE*** Rename the effect to "Laser Red". Set the **Fog Color** setting to white. The problem, though, is that the color resulting after applying the Volume Light effect combines the light color and fog color using logical multiplication. Thus, if the fog color specified in the **Volume Light Parameters** is white, then the resulting beam will be the same color as the light.

Select the **Noise** option to imitate noise, and specify the noise parameters.

To check the settings, it's necessary to perform test rendering. 3ds max 4 renders all atmospheric effects only in the **Camera** or **Perspective** windows. Because of this, you need to go to the **Perspective** window (press the <P> key).

***Self-study*** Modify the settings for this effect to obtain a better result (according to your own tastes). For example, you can increase the density (the **Density** setting), and at the same time decrease the **Hotspot** setting for the light.

Now try to imitate the wind effect for the "fog".

❑ Enable the animation by pressing the <N> key, then go the last frame and change the **Phase** setting to 20.

❑ Disable the animation and set the direction and velocity of the "wind".

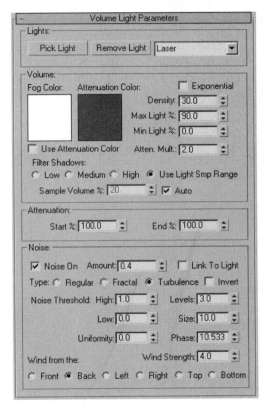

◄ **Fig. 3.27.** Settings for the Volume Light effect applied to laser beams

Now create green and blue laser beams.

Copy the Laser Red light twice and assign the copies the names "Laser Green" and "Laser Blue". Then change the color of the light and edit the targeted animation for each laser (fig. 3.28).

We also need to create auxiliary objects, which will help to create an illusion of the laser beam rather than a simple beam of light.

❑ Go to the **Left** viewport by pressing the <L> key.

❑ Create a line starting at the point corresponding to the light source, and ending at the point defined by the Laser Red.Target object:

Tab panel → Shapes → Line

❑ Rename this line to "Laser Red Beam".

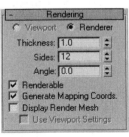

❑ Concerning the line properties, set the **Renderable** checkbox and set the **Thickness** setting to 1.

> ***NOTE*** Notice that 3ds max 4 introduces the capability of adjusting parameters of the renderable curves. Moreover, you can make the curves visible in the viewports.

❑ Start editing vertices:

Right-click menu → Sub-objects → Vertex

❑ Select the vertex that corresponds to the end of the beam and move it to the point corresponding to the Laser Red.Target object (fig. 3.29).

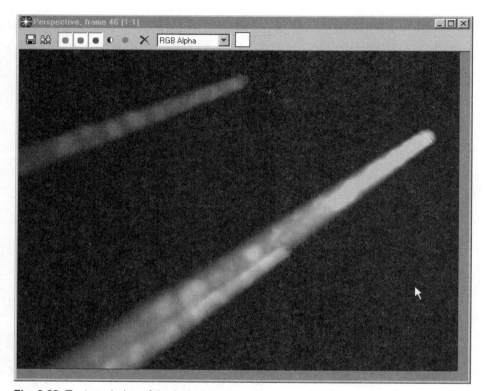

**Fig. 3.28.** Test rendering of the laser beams

❑ Apply the Linked XForm modifier to the selected vertex:

Control panel → Modifier List → Linked XForm

❑ Select the Laser Red Target object as the control object by clicking the **Pick Control Object** button.

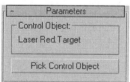

> **TIP** Sometimes it may be easier to select an object from the list. To do so, press the <H> key and select the object.

Create the Laser Blue Beam and Laser Green Beam objects by copying the Laser Red Beam object twice. Then correct the position of the vertices and pick a control object for each of them.

> **NOTE** Obviously, you understand that all of these manipulations need to be performed in frame 0:0:0.

Now we're going to assign the appropriate materials to the beams we've just created.

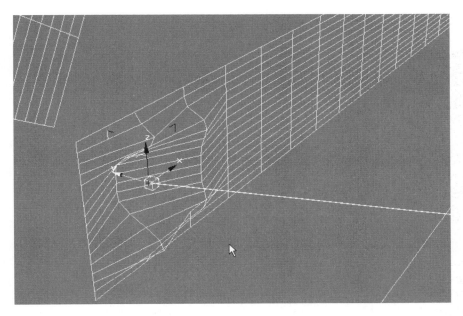

**Fig. 3.29.** Starting position of the laser beam

❏ Press the <M> key to open the material editor.

❏ Copy the Red, Blue, and Green materials by dragging them to unoccupied sample slots.

❏ Rename these materials to "Red Beam", "Green Beam", and "Blue Beam", respectively.

❏ In the material settings rollout, specify the **Self-Illumination** parameter to 100 and clear the **Color** checkbox

❏ The **Material Effect Channel** for these materials should be set to 14.

❏ Assign these materials to the appropriate objects.

> **NOTE** Material editor in 3ds max 4 supports Drag-and-Drop. Because of this, you can assign materials by simply dragging them from the material editor to the appropriate objects.

❏ Perform test rendering. Go to the **Perspective** viewport (by pressing the <P> key) and select the viewpoint.

# Creating and Animating Additional Lights

We need to create three additional lights, which are intended to model the scorching material.

❏ Create the directional light:

Tab panel → Lights & Cameras → Directional Light

❑ Place this light near the red furrow and turn it to make the light hit the furrow at a slant (fig. 3.30, a, b).

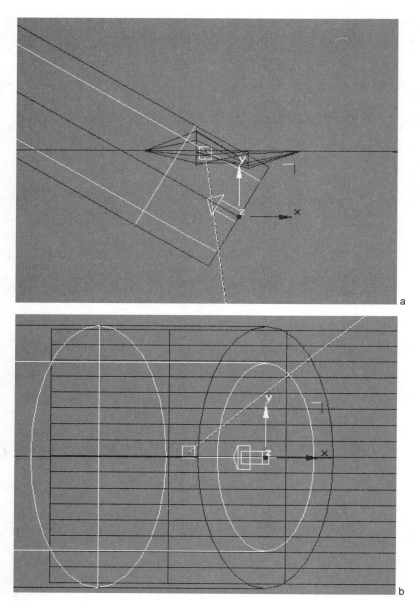

a

b

**Fig. 3.30, a, b.** Creating and positioning additional light

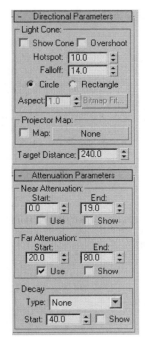

**Fig. 3.30, c.** Specifying the settings for additional light

❐ Set the falloff parameters to smooth the edges of the light spot (fig. 3.30, c).

❐ Apply the Linked XForm modifier to the light. Select the Laser Red Target object as a control object.

Create two copies of the light, and appropriately place them for the green and blue furrows. Apply the Linked XForm modifier to each of these lights and change control objects as needed.

# Creating and Animating the Camera

Now it's time to create and animate the camera. Why is that necessary now? As was mentioned before, many 3ds max 4 effects are renderable only in the **Camera** or **Perspective** viewports, and the **Camera** window provides the easiest method of controlling the process of applying special effects.

❐ Go to the **Front** viewport by pressing the <F> key.

❐ Go to frame 0:0:0.

❐ Create the camera (fig. 3.31):

Tab panel → Lights & Cameras → Targeted Cameras

❐ Switch to the editing mode and position the camera, as shown in fig. 3.32, a, by moving both the camera and its target.

*TIP*  The position of the Camera01.Target object needs to match the position of the Laser Blue.Target object in the front viewport, and be located to the right in the left viewport.

❐ Switch to the animation mode and go to frame 0:4:0.

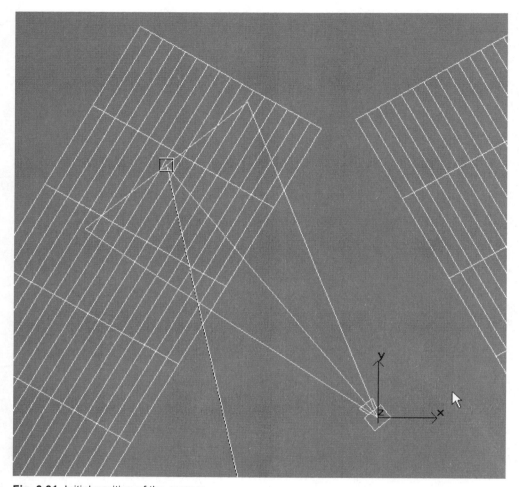

**Fig. 3.31.** Initial position of the camera

❑ In this frame, move the Camera01.Target object in such a way as to follow the Laser Blue.Target object (fig. 3.32, b).

❑ Go to frame 0:7:0 without toggling the animation mode.

❑ Move both the camera and its target so that the display in the camera viewport corresponds to the logo (fig. 3.32, c).

*TIP* It may be useful, sometimes, to enable the background display in the viewport. In the background properties, disable the **Lock Zoom/Pan** checkbox!

☑ Display Background
☐ Lock Zoom/Pan

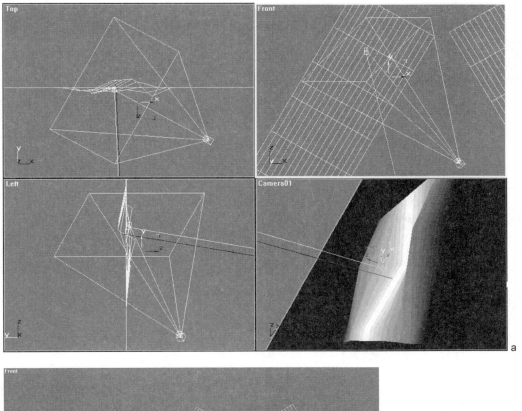

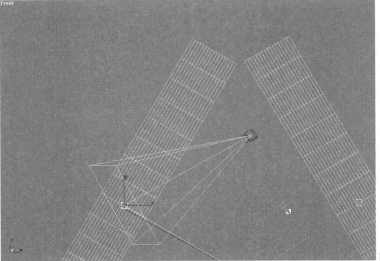

**Fig. 3.32, a, b.** Sequence of recording animation of the camera and its target

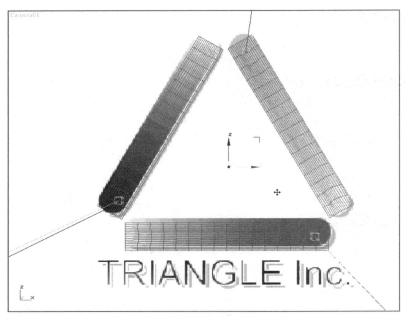

**Fig. 3.32, c.** Sequence of recording animation of the camera and its target

# Creating Special Effects

As you remember, we specified the **Effect Material Channel** parameter for materials. Now it is time to use this parameter.

You have already used special effects in the second lesson. In this lesson, we will use the Video Post module for applying special effects.

❏ Open the **Video Post** dialog:

    Main menu → Rendering → Video Post...

❏ Add the scene event to the event list: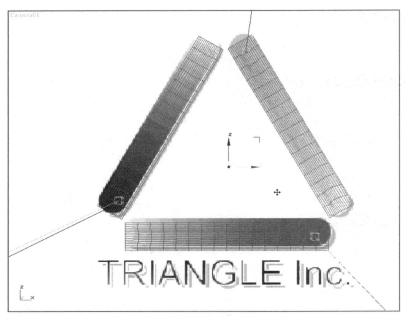

    Video Post → Add Scene Event

❏ Specify the settings as shown in fig. 3.33.

Now let's apply the special effects. We need to add several glow effects and tune each of them to obtain the effects of burning material, fog, and a laser beam.

❏ Add the Lens Effect Glow:

    Video Post → Add Image Filter Event

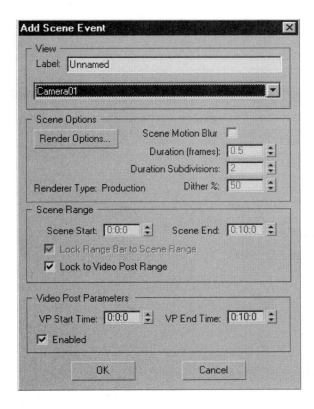

**Fig. 3.33.** The Scene Event settings

☐ Select the **Lens Effect Glow** item from the list of effects and click the **Setup** button.

☐ Specify the settings as shown in fig. 3.34.

> *TIP* Set the **Effects ID** checkbox and specify a value of 15 for the ID setting. Thus, you'll instruct the program to influence only the part of display obtained as a result of rendering the object with material that has the effects channel set to 15.
>
> If the **All** checkbox in the **Filter** tab is set, the effect will influence all the pixels that correspond to the selected channel.
>
> The **Size** setting in the **Effect** option group in the **Preferences** tab specifies the size of the glow area.
>
> The **Pixel** radio button in the **Color** option group specifies that the glow will be based on the material color.

☐ Rename the effect to "Glow Material".

☐ Click the **Execute Sequence** button to test the rendering. The **Execute Video Post** dialog will appear. Specify the rendering settings as shown in fig. 3.35.

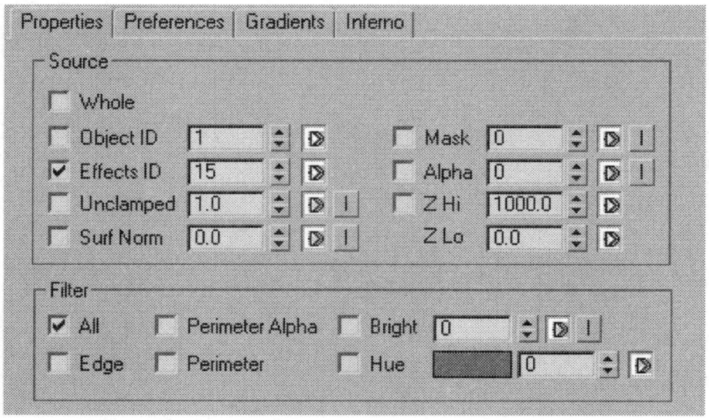


a

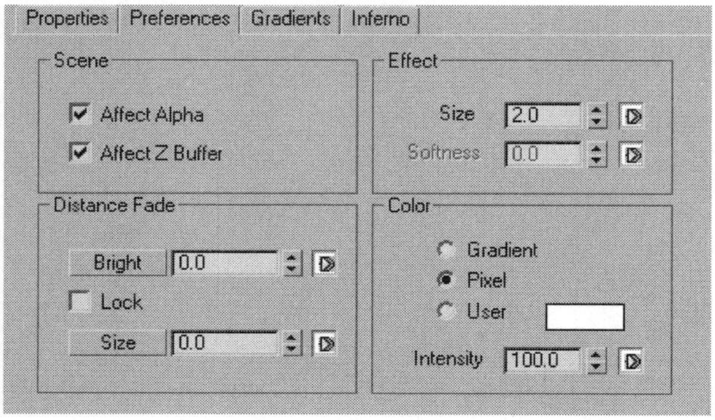


b

**Fig. 3.34.** Initial settings for the Glow Material effect

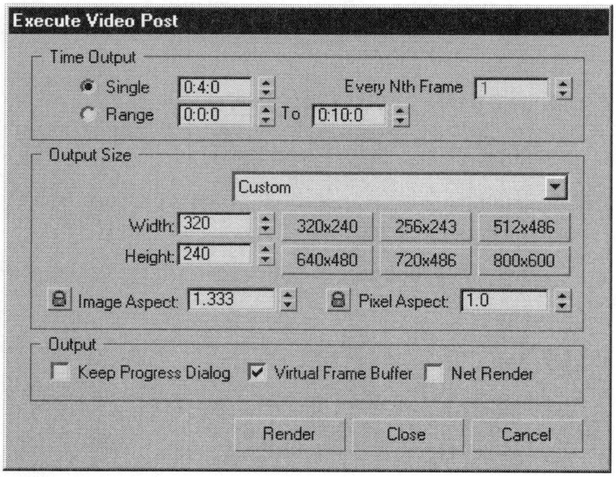


**Fig. 3.35.** Test rendering settings

Try to get a better result by modifying the effect parameters. I obtained the best result by setting the **Size** value to 2.

❑ Add one more Glow effect and rename it to "Glow Smoke". Specify the parameters for this effect, as shown in fig. 3.36 (a, b, c).

To get a better understanding, experiment with the settings.

> ***TIP*** To produce the smoke effect, go to the **Inferno** tab and set the **Red**, **Green**, and **Blue** checkboxes.

❑ Finally, we need to add one more Glow effect for the laser beams. Create the Glow effect and rename it to "Glow Beam". Specify the parameters for this effect as shown in fig. 3.37 (a, b).

> ***TIP*** Set the **ID** value to 14. Thus, the effect will match the materials of the laser beams.

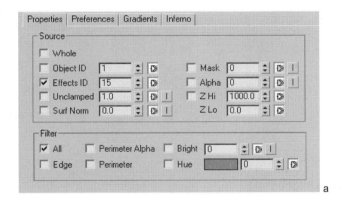

a

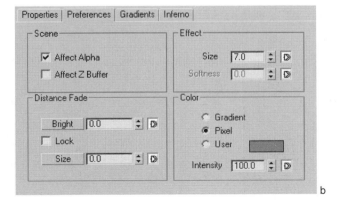

b

**Fig. 3.36, a, b.** Settings for the Glow Smoke effect

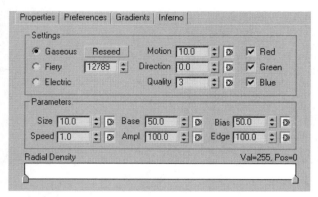

**Fig. 3.36, c.** Settings for the Glow Smoke effect

a

b

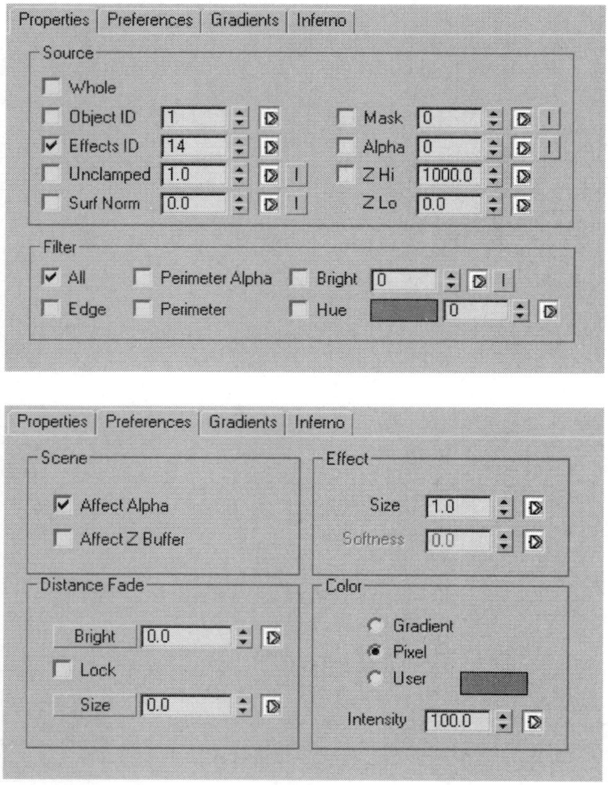

**Fig. 3.37.** Settings for the Glow Beam effect

As a result, the **Video Post** dialog will contain the structure shown in fig. 3.38.

**Self-study**   Render several frames and select the settings you like the best. You can also animate various parameters of the Glow effects.

**Fig. 3.38.** Stack of events in the **Video Post** dialog

# Creating and Animating Sparks

To create the sparks, let's use a simple built-in particle system — Spray.

☐ Go to the **Front** viewport by pressing the <F> key.

☐ Create the Spray particle system (fig. 3.39):

Tab panel → Particles → Spray Particle System

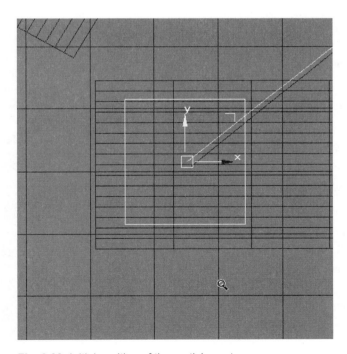

**Fig. 3.39.** Initial position of the particle system

*TIP* Set the **AutoGrid** checkbox to place the particle system on the logo surface

❑ Rename the new object to "Red Sparks".

❑ Switch to the editing mode and specify the settings, as shown in fig. 3.40.

*TIP* Set the particle size to 0.1. The particles will be used as a base for your effect, so the value shouldn't be large.

Specify a negative value for the particle velocity to change the direction from which the particles leave their source. To reverse the direction, you can also turn the particle source by 180°.

Now we need to edit the behavior of the particles. To do this, apply the Gravity and Wind space warps to the particles.

❑ First, create the Gravity space warp, and place it anywhere in the scene:

Tab panel → SpaceWarps → Gravity Space Warp

❑ Rotate the object to make its direction arrow point downwards.

❑ Bind the Gravity01 and Red Sparks objects:

Tab panel → Main Toolbar → **Bind to Space Warp** button

❑ Select the Red Sparks object and drag it to the Gravity object (fig. 3.41).

❑ Set the gravity strength (the **Strength** setting from the **Force** option group) to 0.4.

Now you need to create vortices in the flow of particles. Use the Wind space warp to do this.

❑ Create the Wind space warp near the Red Sparks particle system (fig. 3.42):

Tab panel → SpaceWarps → Wind Space Warp

❑ Bind it to the particle system (proceed the same way you did when binding the Gravity space warp).

❑ Change the type of the wind to spherical and specify the settings to produce the vortex.

*TIP* The best way of controlling the effect of the space warp on the particle system is to go to an intermediate frame (for example, go to frame 0:2:0).

❑ Select the Red Sparks particle system and change the channel number for the object to 1. You'll need to assign the sparks effect to the particles:

Right-click menu → Properties → **G-Buffer: Object Channel** rollout

◀ **Fig. 3.40.** Settings for the Red Sparks particle system

☐ Select the particle system and Wind space warp and group them under the name RSparks:

Main menu → Group → Group

☐ Assign the Read Beam material to the Red Sparks particle system by dragging the material from the sample slot in the material editor window to the object.

☐ Create two copies of the RSparks object and rename the new groups to "GSparks" and "BSparks".

☐ Assign the Green Beam and Blue Beam materials to their respective particle systems.

☐ Go to frame 0:0:0 and position the particle groups in the points where the laser beams hit the plate.

☐ Link each group to the appropriate object (for example, Laser Red.Target).

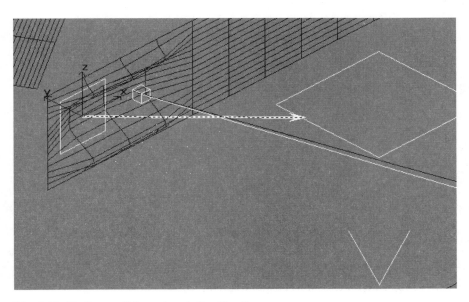

**Fig. 3.41.** Binding particle system to the Gravity space warp

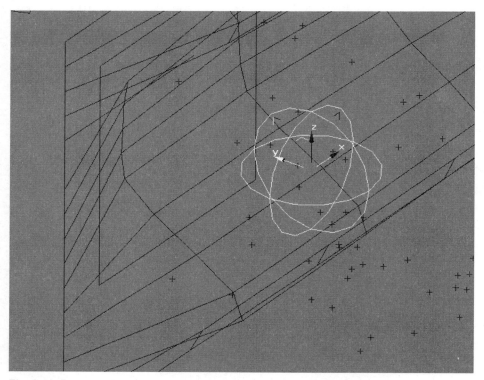

**Fig. 3.42.** Position of the Wind space warp in relation to the particle system

**_NOTE_** Unfortunately, we can't use the Linked Xform modifier in this case. A detailed explanation for this is provided in 3ds max 4 User Manual.

❑ Select the RSparks group:

Tab panel → Main Toolbar → Select and Link

❑ Open the **Select by name** window by pressing the <H> key and select the Laser Red.Target object.

Now let's add the sparks effect and assign it to the particle system.

❑ Open the **Video Post** dialog and add Lens Effect Highlight:

Main menu → Render → VideoPost

Video Post → Add Image Filter Event

❑ Specify the settings for this effect as shown in fig. 3.43 (a, b, c).

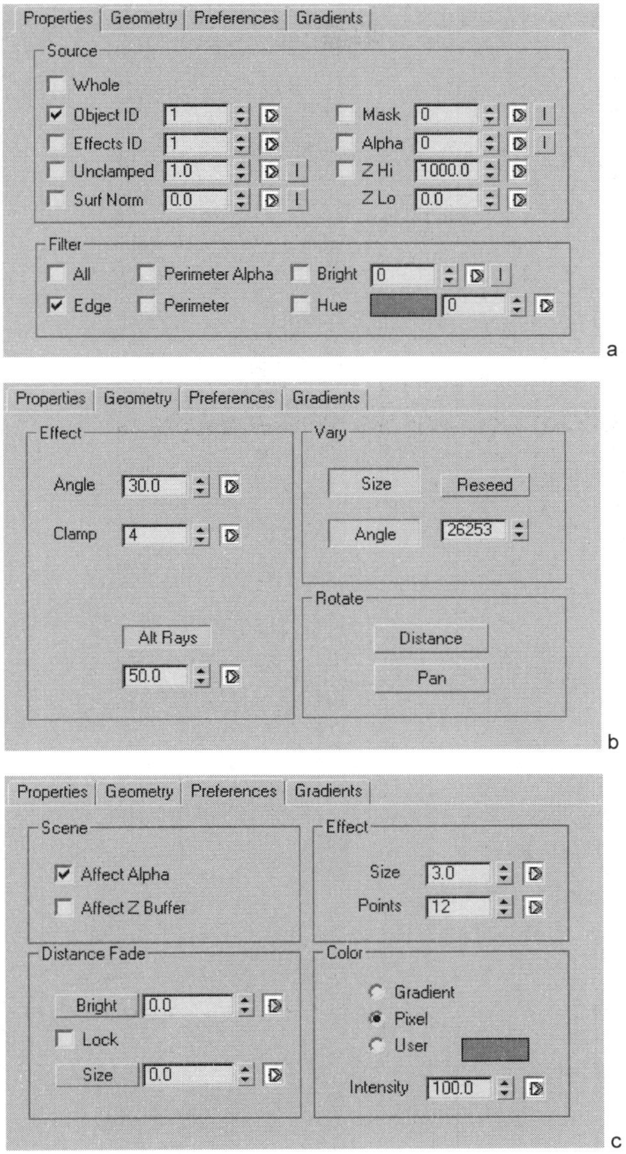

**Fig. 3.43.** Settings for the Lens Effect Highlight

**TIP** We've specified channel 1 for the particle system. Because of this, the sparks will be created only for the particles.

The **Size** and **Angle** buttons in the **Geometry/Vary** rollout allow changing the size and rotation angle of the beams during animation by an arbitrary amount.

The **Alt Rays** button will also increase the chaos of the sparks geometry.

You certainly can experiment with the settings to produce better results.

# Creating the Effects of Explosion and Object Disappearance

To create the effect of an explosion, use the Bomb space warp. This space warp can't be recommended for creating realistic explosions, but in our project it provides the simplest (and most efficient) solution.

❏ Create the Bomb space warp and place it behind the Plate object (fig. 3.44, a):

Tab panel → Space Warps → Bomb Space Warps

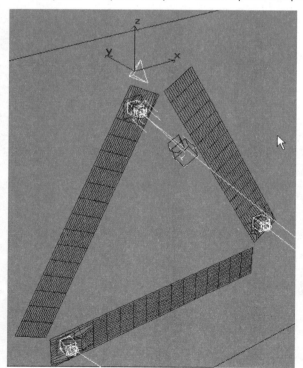

❏ Bind it to the Plate object:

Main Toolbar → Bind to Space Warp

❏ Specify the Bomb settings as shown in fig. 3.44, b.

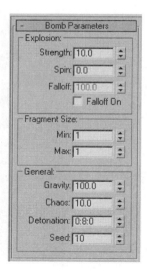

a                                                       b

**Fig. 3.44.** Positioning (a) and settings (b) for the Bomb modifier

*NOTE* Set the explosion time (Detonation) to 0:8:0 so that explosion takes place when the animation of the laser beams is completed.

*Self-study* Try to experiment with the settings. Probably, you'll find many more interesting settings for an explosion.

Now let's create the effect of gradually disappearing objects.

☐ Select all the objects within the scene, and group them.

☐ Go to frame 0:8:5, enable the animation (by pressing the <N> key or clicking the animation button) and go to the group settings:

Right-click menu → Properties

☐ Set the **Visibility** parameter to 0.

☐ Click **OK**, go to frame 0:8:0 and open the group settings.

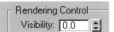

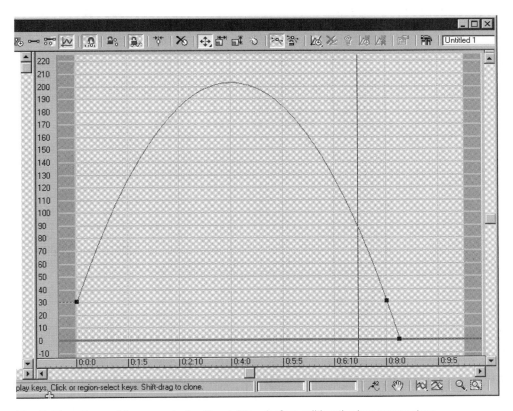

**Fig. 3.45, a.** Form of the curve in the **Track View** before editing the key parameters

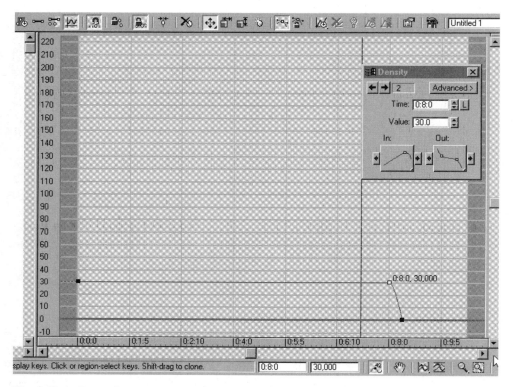

**Fig. 3.45, b.** Form of the curve in the **Track View** after editing the key parameters

❏ Set the **Visibility** parameter to 1.

❏ Disable the animation mode by pressing the <N> key.

Now you need to "turn off" the lasers.

❏ Open the environment settings and switch to editing the Laser Red atmospheric effect:

Main menu → Rendering → Environment → **Atmosphere** rollout

❏ Go to frame 0:8:5 and enable animation.

❏ Set the density setting to 0.

❏ Go to frame 0:8:0 and set the **Density** setting to 30.

❏ Disable the animation.

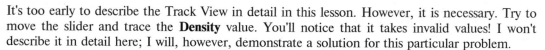

It's too early to describe the Track View in detail in this lesson. However, it is necessary. Try to move the slider and trace the **Density** value. You'll notice that it takes invalid values! I won't describe it in detail here; I will, however, demonstrate a solution for this particular problem.

❑ Open the Track View:

    Main menu → Track View → Open Track View

❑ In the tree to the left, find the Environment track. Expand it to the lowest level by right-clicking it and selecting the **Expand Tracks** menu item.

❑ Find and select the Laser Red/Density track and modify the key presentation in this track:

    Track View → **Function Curves** button ⟋⟍

Notice what the curve looks like (fig. 3.45, a).

❑ Right-click the vertex corresponding to frame 0:8:0. The dialog will open to where you need to set the **In** curve, as shown in fig. 3.45, b.

❑ To perform the final correction of the curve, click the left-arrow button near the **In** field. Notice that the curve has been reshaped.

❑ Close the Track View.

# Rendering the Scene

Final rendering of the scene will be done using Video Post.

❑ Open Video Post. The stack of events needs to look like what's shown in fig. 3.46, a.

    **NOTE**   In Video Post, the events are executed sequentially from right to left, from the "bottom" event (in our case, this is the **Camera01** viewport rendering) to the top (Lens Effect Highlight) and then from top to bottom. To add a new event to the queue, you need to select at least one event. Adding events to the bottom of the stack isn't determined by the selection of any events.

First, you need to edit the final frame of the rendering sequence.

❑ Select all the events and move the right end points to the position corresponding to frame 0:8:5. Control the correct position according to the Video Post status bar.

Add the new event — the White.tif file, which will imitate the bright flash.

❑ Make sure that no event in the queue has been selected, and add the White.tif file located on the companion CD in the \Lessons\lesson03\maps directory, to the end of the stack:

    Video Post → Add Image Input Event 🔲

❑ Set the starting and final settings to 0:8:0 and 0:8:5 frames by moving the left (Start Point) and right (End Point) points to their respective positions.

❑ Select Lens Effect Highlight and White.tif events.

❏ Notice that the **Add Image Layer Event** button became available in the Video Post toolbar. **Click** this button and select the **Cross Fade Transition** option. Set the start and end points to frames 0:8:0 and 0:8:5.

The stack will look like the one shown in fig. 3.46, b.

❏ Add another White.tif file to the bottom of the stack (don't forget to deselect all the events within the stack):

Video Post → Video Post → Add Image Input Event

❏ Set the start and end points for it to 0:8:6 and 0:9:0. Now add the logo320.tif file to the stack bottom.

❏ Start and end points should be set to frames 0:8:6 and 0:12:0.

❏ Select the logo320.tif and white.tif events.

❏ Click the **Add Image Layer Event** button and select the **Cross Fade Transition** option.

❏ Set the start and end points for this event to 0:8:6 and 0:9:0 (fig. 3.46, c).

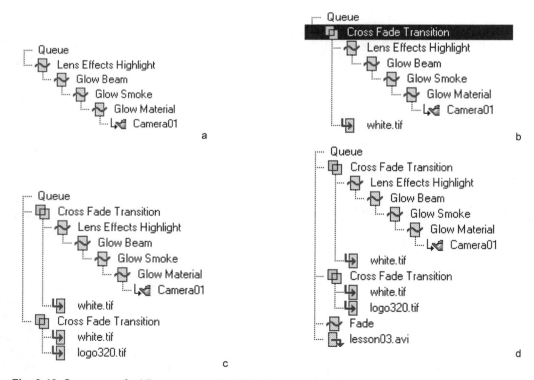

**Fig. 3.46.** Sequence of adding events to the Video Post stack

❏ Add the Fade Out effect to the bottom of the stack:

Video Post → Add Image Filter Event → Fade

❏ Click the **Setup** button. The **Fade Image Control** window will open (fig. 3.47). Select the **Out** radio button.

❏ Set the start and end points to 0:10:8 and 0:12:0.

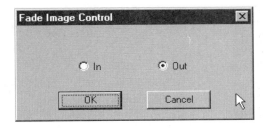

**Fig. 3.47.** The **Fade Image Control** window

❏ Finally, add the Image Output event (fig. 3.46, d):

Video Post → Add Image Output Event

❏ Select the file output for this event and specify the file name (lesson03.avi, in our example).

❏ In the codec settings, select the compression type (fig. 3.48) and specify its settings.

**NOTE** You may use any codec installed in your system.

❏ Save the scene in lesson03.max file.

**NOTE** Don't forget to save the scene! The rendering process may take several hours, and anything could happen during this time. Certainly, you'll feel hurt, if the results of all your efforts are lost!

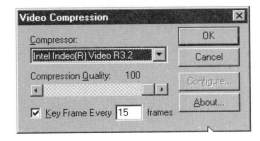

**Fig. 3.48.** The **Video Compression** dialog

❏ Start the calculation of the project by clicking the **Execute Sequence** button in Video Post. Specify the settings as shown in fig. 3.49, and click the **Render** button.

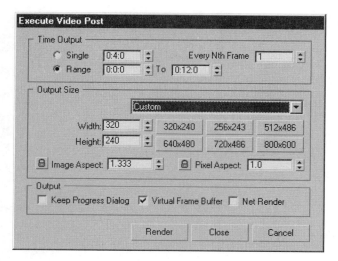

**Fig. 3.49.** Settings for the final rendering

# Summary

If you complete this lesson and calculate the project, you'll notice some differences between your results and the results shown on the companion CD. I modified some of the settings and added extra lights and effects to emphasize the explosion. I recommend that you carefully study the Lesson03.max file, which is located on the companion CD in the \Lessons\Lesson03\Scenes directory.

In general, you should always look at your projects from a critical point of view. If you have a feeling that something's wrong, always try to correct the situation. Sometimes you'll need to completely redo an almost completed project. Don't let this bother you, though, because it's the only way to acquire the necessary experience — experience that will later allow you to avoid errors.

# Lesson 4

# Puppet Fireman

I n this lesson, we'll create a small movie, where a puppet fireman will suppress a realistic fire in the puppet city. You can view the results by opening the following file: \Lessons\Lesson04\Images\Lesson04.avi.

## Aims of This Lesson

After completing this lesson, you'll know how to:

❏ Model simple organic objects by combining Patch modeling and Polygon modeling.

❏ Use interesting functions of the particle systems.

❏ Apply new materials and object types.

❏ Animate characters by implementing the bones system using the new capabilities of the inverse kinematics.

## Preliminary Notes

Both the face and the body of our fireman are stylized. That's why I decided to use the "puppet" fireman and place him in the puppet town.

For creating the fire I used the standard Fire Effect plug-in module. This effect, previously known as Combustion, is built into 3ds max since release 1.1. Since that time, this standard plug-in did not change significantly. However, this plug-in module has bad reputation among 3D artists, mostly because its default settings produce only very approximate imitation of fire. However, a skilful artist can produce quite an impressive result even with this plug-in.

I'd like to mention that fire and other pyrotechnic effects always were and still remain very popular among developers of the plug-ins for 3ds max 4 and other software packages. Sometimes, these plug-ins are quite expensive. However, there are several freeware plug-ins for 3ds max 4, such as Blur Fire from the Blur or plug-in library based on the Combustion algorithm, developed by Peter Watje, whom I mentioned in the first lesson. Unfortunately, for the moment of this writing these plug-ins were not recompiled for 3ds max 4. However, you can always find the latest versions at the home pages of their developers.

I'm not going to begin this lesson by describing the script or presenting any details. All we have to know is that we need to create a small part of an advertising movie, that it has to be completed tomorrow morning, and there's no time for a lot of planning.

# Modeling

## Modeling the Fireman's Body

To model the fireman's body, let's use some curves, which will later be used to create a patch Bezier surface.

To begin with, let's create a simple framework to rough out the shape of the fireman's leg.

❑ Create a circle with a radius equal to approximately 10 units (fig. 4.1, a):

   <Ctrl>+Right-click menu → Circle

❑ Create multiple copies of this circle. Hold down <Shift> and drag the source circle to move a clone of the selection away from the original (fig. 4.1, b).

❑ Select the bottom circle and attach all the other circles to it, working your way up the outside of the object:

   Right-click menu → Convert To: → Convert to Editable Spline

   Right-click menu → Attach

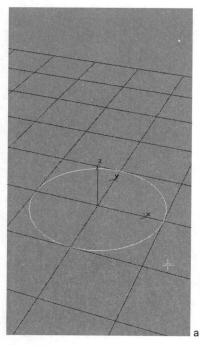
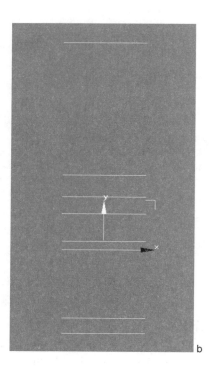

**Fig. 4.1, a, b.** Creating framework for the leg

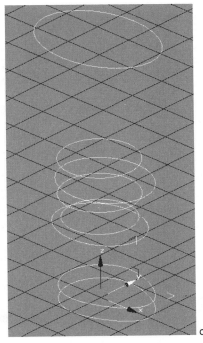
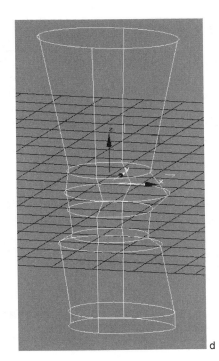

**Fig. 4.1, c, d.** Creating framework for the leg

> ***NOTE*** The order in which you attach splines is very important!

❑ Move the vertices and splines to make the sections look like the shape of a leg clothed in trousers and with a jackboot on it (fig. 4.1, c):

Right-click menu → Sub-objects → Vertex, Spline

Right-click menu → Move, Scale

Main toolbar → **Use Selection Center** button

❑ Apply the CrossSection modifier:

<Ctrl>+Right-click menu → Modifiers → CrossSection

❑ Select the **Linear** radio button in the **Spline Options** group. These options determine what type of curve will be used through the spline vertices.

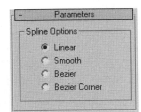

The result you get is totally different from what we'd like it to be (fig. 4.1, d). So, let's proceed with further editing.

❐ Convert the object to Editable Spline:

Right-click menu → Convert To: → Convert to Editable Spline

❐ Add one extra vertex per generatrix at the points corresponding to the boot instep (fig. 4.2, a):

Right-click menu → Refine

❐ Select the bottom spline and Shift-Move it close to the position corresponding to the new vertices (fig. 4.2, b).

❐ Resize the spline.

❐ Fuse the generatrix vertices to the appropriate vertices of the new spline (fig. 4.2, c):

Right-click menu → Sub-objects → Vertex

❐ Click the **Fuse** button on the Control Panel, click a point and drag it to another point without releasing the mouse button.

*NOTE*    The **Fuse** operation for Bezier curves is different from the Fuse operation for NURBS. In NURBS, fused points behave as a single point until you unfuse them. In Bezier curves, each of the fused vertices remains independent. To move these vertices, you need to select them all or use the **Area Selection** checkbox allowing to select several vertices at a time, positioned within the limit specified by the **Threshold** value.

❐ Work with the vertices and splines to get the result you need (fig. 4.2, d).

❐ Now you need to edit the shape of longitudinal curves. To make this process faster, select all cross-sections and hide them:

Right-click menu → Sub-objects → Spline

Right-click menu → Hide → Spline

❐ Besides, you can use the new selection method. Select longitudinal splines. Start selecting vertices by clicking the **Select By** button, then the **Spline** button.

❐ Select the vertices one by one; then change their type and edit them:

Right-click menu → Bezier, Bezier Corner...

*TIP*    This task is very easy to do. Simply turn off the TRANSFORM Gizmo temporarily (by pressing the <X> key) and select the coordinates in the Main Toolbar or using the <F5> — <F8> keys.

*Warning*    Don't move the vertices!

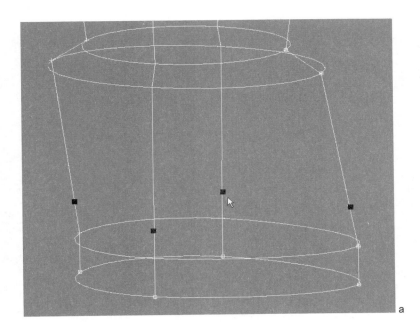

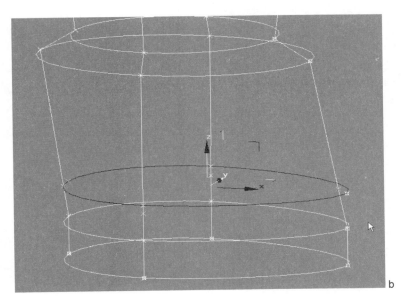

**Fig. 4.2, a, b.** Editing the leg framework

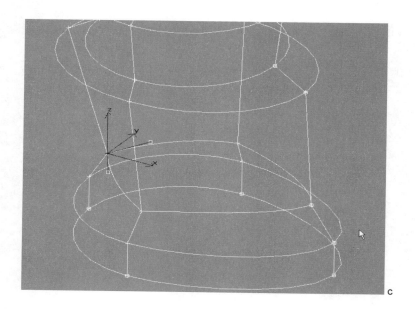

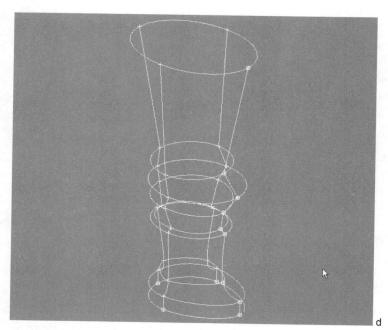

**Fig. 4.2, c, d.** Editing the leg framework

**NOTE** You may find the capability of editing a number of nodes corresponding to the highlighted vertices very useful. To do so, click the **Lock Handles** button in Control panel.

☐ After editing all the vertices of each longitudinal section, unhide all the splines (if they were invisible):

Right-click menu → Unhide All → Spline

Work with the vertices and try to get a satisfactory result.

Clone the first leg and mirror it about appropriate axis (fig. 4.3):

Main toolbar → Mirror Selected Objects

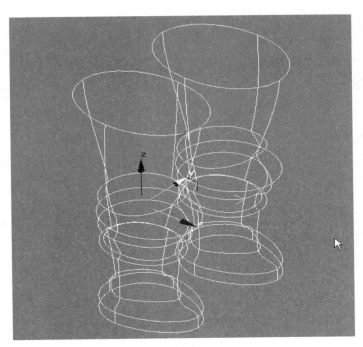

**Fig. 4.3.** Copying and mirroring the leg

In my opinion, it isn't necessary to provide a detailed description of the whole process of creating the body and hands. These procedures are very similar to the procedure of creating the legs (fig. 4.4).

Now assemble the fireman's body.

☐ Select the fireman's torso and convert it to editable spline, if this hasn't been done already. Then attach all the other elements to it.

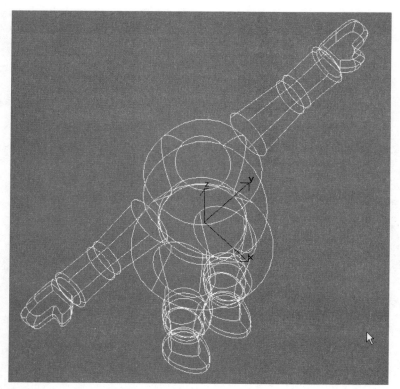

**Fig. 4.4.** The framework of the fireman's body

Try to apply the Surface modifier to the object (fig. 4.5).

> <Ctrl>+Right-click menu → Modifiers → Surface

You see that the surface normals are pointing in different directions. This may be related to the fact that you copied the splines using mirroring. To solve this problem, go back to the stack bottom and change the orientation of the splines by selecting each spline and clicking the **Reverse** button. [ Reverse ]

Another problem is that all of the parts that form the fireman's body are now independent from each other. To clarify the actions that you need to perform, I'll provide a brief explanation of the working principles of the Surface module. This module creates Bezier patch surfaces, based on three or four spline segments bound by vertices. In an ideal case, the vertex coordinates should coincide. In most cases, this result is hard to obtain. However, there is the **Threshold** parameter, which fuses spline vertices based on their proximity. As long as the spline vertices are close enough for the **Threshold** parameter in the Surface modifier to weld them together, a surface will be generated.

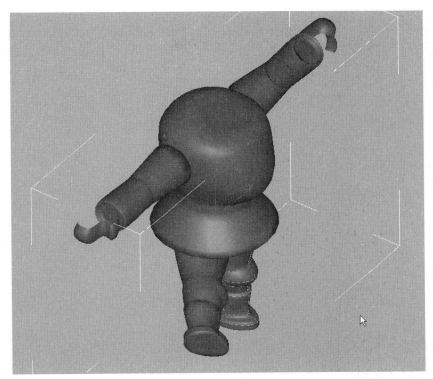

**Fig. 4.5.** The results of applying the Surface modifier

Thus, to complete the generation of our surface, it's necessary to refine the splines.

☐ Delete the Surface modifier from the stack:

Right-click menu of the Modifier stack → Delete

☐ Add the missing segments for welding the legs and torso (fig. 4.6, a).

**NOTE** This can be accomplished using the two methods. First, you can connect vertices, previously breaking the splines to which they belong:

Control panel → **Geometry** rollout → Break, Connect

The second method is more elegant. You can create new lines (sections of the straight line), and adjust the snap settings as shown in fig. 4.7. You can open this dialog by clicking the right mouse button at the snap panel. Don't forget to enable the snaps by pressing the <S> button.

Besides, you can temporarily (for one operation) redefine the snap type:

<Shift>+Right-click menu, then select **Vertex** (fig. 4.8)

Make sure that you are creating straight sections by simply clicking at the starting and ending points of the section. This is important, because if you drag the line, you'll automatically switch to the mesh plane, and your line will turn to a curve, different from the needed one.

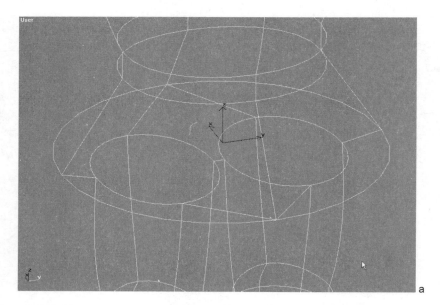

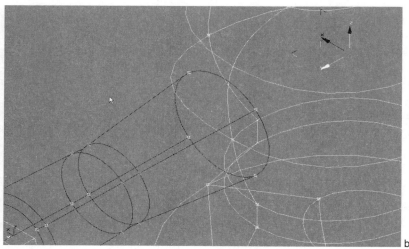

**Fig. 4.6, a, b.** Editing the wireframe of the fireman's body

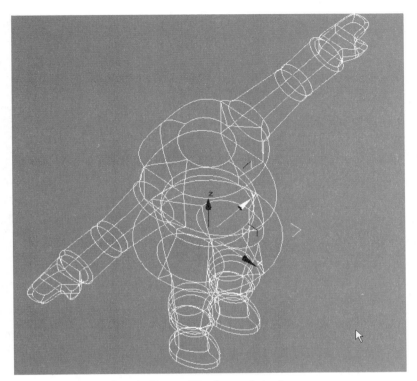

**Fig. 4.6, c.** Editing the wireframe of the fireman's body

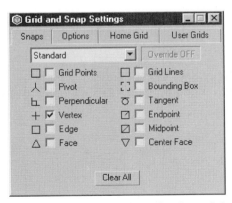

**Fig. 4.7.** The **Grid and Snap Settings** dialog

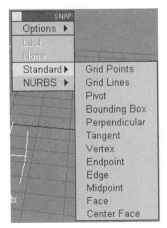

**Fig. 4.8.** Snaps right-click menu

Welding the hands to the torso is slightly more difficult. You'll need to break the torso segments at random points, then delete any unnecessary segments and connect the newly created vertices to the hand vertices.

*TIP* I recommend that you select all of the hand splines and rotate them by 45° about the longitudinal axis (fig. 4.6, b) This will greatly simplify the process of editing the geometry. Hide all the splines that shouldn't be affected by your editing.

One other recommendation: Edit the region where one of the hands is connected to both the torso and the glove, then delete the segments of the other hand and create a mirrored copy of this object. All you need to do, then, is to connect the newly created object to the torso.

*NOTE* I've omitted the process of editing the gloves, because I think that by now, you'll be able to complete this task without any additional instructions.

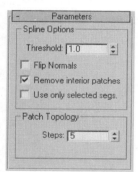

Now you've created the semi-finished object for fireman's body (fig. 4.6, c).

Apply the Surface modifier to the object, whose settings are shown in fig. 4.9. More than likely, you'll see that some normals point in the wrong direction. By now, though, you already know how to correct the problem.

**Fig. 4.9.** Parameters of the Surface modifier for the fireman's torso

*NOTE* Generally speaking, for the moment it is not necessary to correct the flipped normals. This problem may be solved when working with patches by using the two-sided material. However, I recommend you to correct the geometry already at this stage.

Thus, the fireman's body is ready. Transform it to Editable Patches:

Right-click menu → Convert To: → Convert to Editable Patches

*Self-study* Edit the fireman's body to produce the desirable proportions.

Notice that patches have undergone significant modernization in the new release 3ds max 4. For example, now it is possible to create patches by vertices, work with normals, copy the patches within an object. Generally speaking, the new release provides quite a lot of capabilities for working with patches.

# Fireman's Head

To create the fireman's head, you need to use the Bezier patch method. Later, you'll refine it using polygon modeling.

**NOTE**  Polygon modeling has become increasingly popular, gradually displacing NURBS and patch modeling. Both the patch and NURBS methods have one main shortcoming: to achieve the required level of model precision, you need to make the mesh significantly more detailed. This is an especially important factor when using "pure" NURBS. It's the main reason why several 3ds max 4 plug-in modules were developed. These plug-ins are mainly used to eliminate NURBS and patch modeling drawbacks. You've probably heard about H-Splines or the DaVinci module. Vendors of these plug-ins are never too tired to praise their products, and usually these praises are well grounded. However, polygon modeling in 3ds max 4 became truly efficient only with the development of NURMS (Nonuniformly Rational MeshSmooth) technology. The new release introduces new type of objects — Editable PolyMesh — and improved Editable Mesh makes this process fast and easy to use. The main advantage of this method is the ability of controlling any surface up to the polygon. The capability to set different weights for each control vertex allows minimizing additional elements of the source model.

Polygon modeling of complicated organic objects from scratch requires a certain amount of experience. Because of this, I recommend that you prepare a patch object first, and then refine it by converting it to editable mesh.

Now let's start modeling the head.

❏ Create a contour of the head on the left viewport (fig. 4.10, a):

<Ctrl>+Right-click menu → Line

❏ Convert the final curve to Editable Spline:

Right-click menu → Convert To: → Convert to Editable Spline

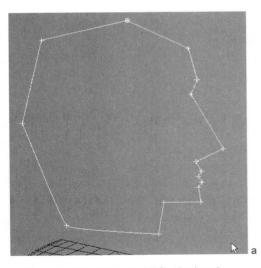

**Fig. 4.10, a, b.** Creating a model for the head

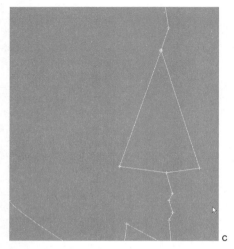

**Fig. 4.10, c, d.** Creating a model for the head

❏ Hide any unnecessary objects:

&lt;Ctrl&gt;+ Right-click menu → Isolate Tool

❏ Now let's model the nose.

❏ In the snap settings, specify **Snap to the vertices** and turn on the 3D Snaps by pressing the &lt;S&gt; key:

Snaps panel → Right-click the **Snap** button

Set the **Vertex** checkbox and clear all the other checkboxes

❏ Create a new line as shown in fig. 4.10, b. Remember that this has to be a straight section.

Right-click menu → Create Line

❏ Add a new vertex to the new line at the level of the tip of the nose:

Right-click menu → Refine

❏ Move the newly created vertex as shown in fig. 4.10, c.

**NOTE**  I have a habit of working with a single viewport. However, you may find it easier to control the mode in several viewports simultaneously.

❏ Connect the vertex you just moved to the nose tip with the line.

❏ Now create the lips using the same technique as for the nose (fig. 4.10, d).

**NOTE**  The **Fuse** operation may prove to be very helpful.

*TIP*   Even at this early stage, I recommend that you use the Surface modifier to control the geometry.

❏  Create half of the head frame by adding lines and vertices (fig. 4.11, a, b, c, d, e).

*TIP*   The new 3ds max 4 version introduces many interesting new functions for curve editing. For example, the **Refine** command now includes several options that simplify the modeling process. Try setting the **Connect** checkbox, add several new vertices sequentially, and

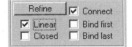

then click the right mouse button. When you finish adding the vertices with **Refine, Connect** makes a separate copy of each new vertex and then connects all of the copies with a new spline.

The **CrossInsert** command adds vertices to the two splines belonging to the same spline object at their intersection.

The **Fillet** and **Chamfer** commands let you round corners where the segments meet, and bevel shape corners. There are two techniques for working with these commands. First, you can enter the values from the keyboard (this is the parametric method) for the previously selected vertices. You can also use an interactive method by selecting the vertices and dragging the mouse cursor in the viewport.

Most of these new commands are present in the right-click menu. Normally, they don't require that you select the sub-object beforehand.

Try experimenting with these commands.

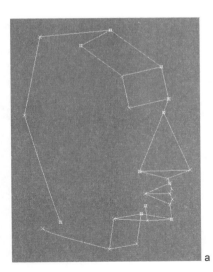
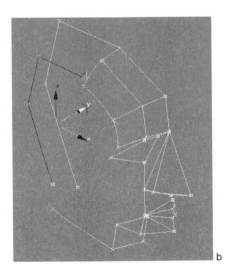

**Fig. 4.11, a, b.** The sequence of editing the head frame

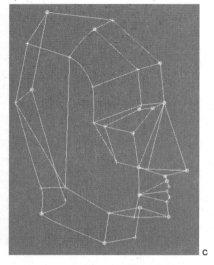

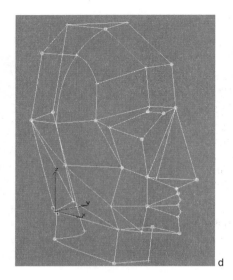

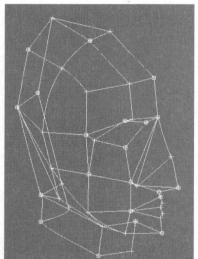

***Self-study*** Try to create the ears. I won't describe how to do this, because they'll be hidden under the helmet anyway. Don't forget that everything needs to be ready by tomorrow morning!

❏ Apply the Surface modifier to the frame you just created:

&lt;Ctrl&gt;+Right-click menu → Modifiers → Surface

❏ Set the **Patch Topology** value in the modifier settings to the value of 1.

**Fig. 4.11, c, d, e.** The sequence of editing the head frame

❏ Apply Edit Mesh and MeshSmooth modifiers:

Tab Panel → Modeling → Edit Mesh Modifier

Tab Panel → Modeling → Mesh Smooth Modifier

The settings for the checkboxes and radio buttons of the **Parameters** rollout are shown in fig. 4.12.

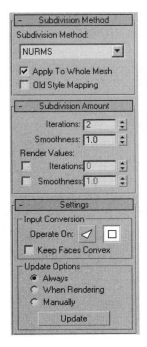

◄ **Fig. 4.12.** Parameters of the MeshSmooth modifier

These results may not satisfy you. If this is so, go back to the bottom of the stack and work with the vertices and segments of the source curve.

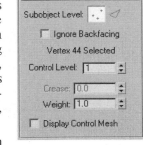

After that, you can work with the vertices and polygons in the Mesh Smooth. The new release 3ds max 4 makes the Mesh Smooth modifier full-featured modeling tool. Now you can move the vertices, change the weight factors of the vertices and edges to achieve additional smoothness of the surface. On the other hand, you can also sharpen the angles if desired.

Furthermore, instead of the Mesh Smooth modifier, you can apply the HSDS modifier, which was covered in the second lesson.

In general, the result is quite satisfactory.

**NOTE**   The result of our work is certainly amateurish, but that's what my project looks like. I hope that you understood the principle behind this. That's the main thing, and any further results from you depend on your endeavor, patience, and power of observation.

Now connect the two halves to produce the head.

❏ Create the mirror copy of the object.

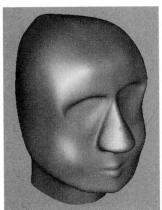

   ❏ Convert the original object to Editable Mesh.

   ❏ Attach the mirror copy to the source object.

   ❏ Select and weld the vertices placed on the axis of symmetry.

Of course, the result is far from perfect (fig. 4.13). However, being short of time, you can't afford to start from scratch. So let's hide the flaws.

First of all, let's create the helmet.

You can create the helmet by using the same method we used to create the fireman's head and body (fig. 4.14, a, b, c).

**Fig. 4.13.** The final look of the head

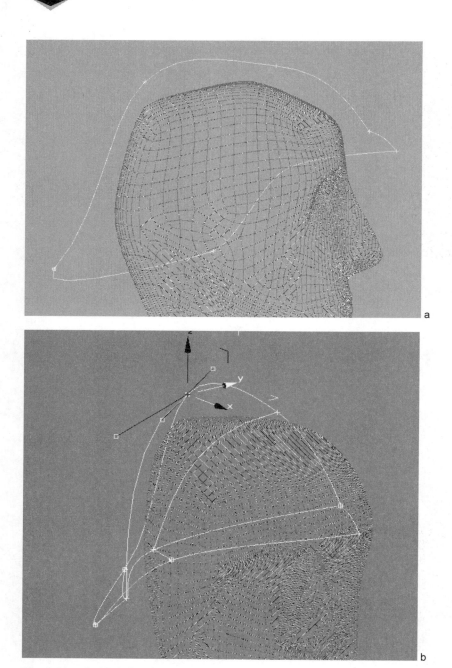

**Fig. 4.14, a, b.** Modeling the helmet

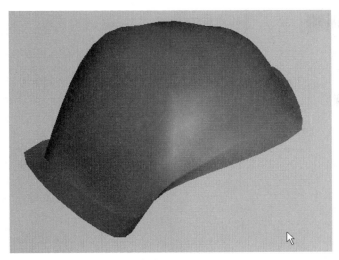

**Fig. 4.14, c.** Modeling the helmet

Now let's create the protective goggles. I don't think this will be a problem for you. (fig. 4.15).

Next, we'll create the straps for the helmet.

The final result is shown in fig. 4.16.

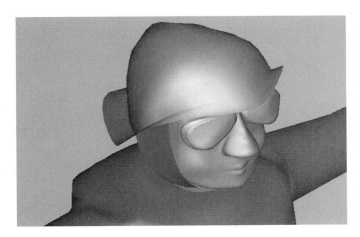

**Fig. 4.15.** Protective goggles

◄ **Fig. 4.16.** "Assembled" head of the fireman

Don't assemble the objects just yet. Select all the objects that form the head, and move them to the required position.

# Supplementary Objects

Now we need to create the source of the fire, and, of course, the things used by the fireman to suppress the fire. We'll also need to create the surface where we'll place the objects, including cubes, cylinders, pyramids, and other primitives, which we'll paint in various colors.

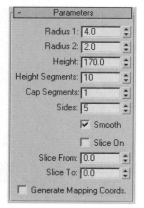

I have decided that the Christmas tree will be the source of fire. Of course, it'll be long before the Christmas Eve comes, but let us prepare everything beforehand. Certainly, in the Puppet City the Christmas trees must also be toys. So, let's proceed as follows.

❏ Create a cone and set its parameters as shown in fig. 4.17. This will be the trunk of our Christmas tree (fig. 4.18, a):

   Tab panel → Objects → Cone

**Fig. 4.17.** Parameters of the trunk of the Christmas-tree

❏ Specify the **Height Segments** value to be large enough since we need the Christmas tree to melt naturally during subsequent animation.

❏ Go to the **Top** viewport and create the curve to correspond to the lowest branch (fig. 4.18, b):

   <Ctrl>+Right-click menu → Line

❏ Create a plate from this curve by applying Extrude or Bevel modifiers.

❏ Copy the branch by rotating it around the trunk in the **Top** viewport (fig. 4.18, c):

   Right-click menu → Rotate

   Tab panel → Main Toolbar → Reference Coordinate System → ... → Pick. Select the trunk (Cone01)

   Tab panel → Main Toolbar → the **Use TRANSFORM Coordinate Center** button

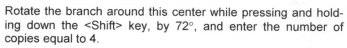

   Rotate the branch around this center while pressing and holding down the <Shift> key, by 72°, and enter the number of copies equal to 4.

❏ Convert one branch to editable mesh and join the branches:

   Right-click menu → Convert To: → Convert to Editable Mesh

   Right-click menu → Attach

Create all the other branches (fig. 4.18, d).

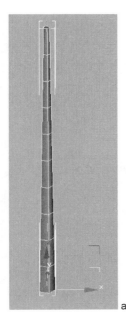

❐ Press the <N> key to enable animation and go the last frame.

**NOTE** Don't worry that the animation settings aren't established yet. You're creating objects that don't depend on these settings.

❐ Move the branches in a vertical direction then rotate and resize them.

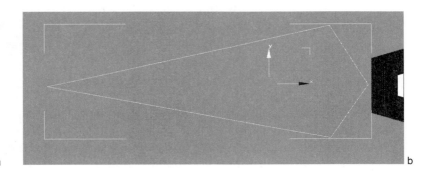

a                                            b

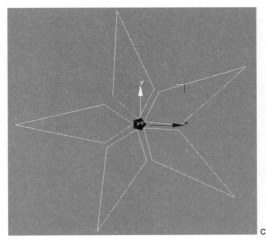

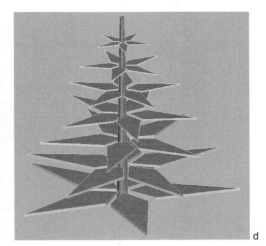

c                                           d

**Fig. 4.18.** Modeling the Christmas-tree

❐ Create copies of the branches using the Snapshot tool with the settings shown in fig. 4.19:

Main menu → TOOLS → Snapshot

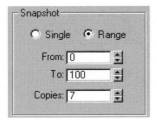

☐ Delete the source branches, since you no longer need them.

☐ Select the trunk of the Christmas tree, convert it to editable mesh and attach all the branches to it.

**Fig. 4.19.** Snapshot settings for creating copies of the branches

I doubt that you'll have any problems creating the fire-plug. It can be created using any technique. For example, you can base it on a curve and apply the Lathe modifier to it.

For the fire-hose, I recommend that you create it using the new object, which, by the way, happens to have the same name — Hose.

☐ Create the object of the Hose type:

Main menu → Create → Extended Primitives → Hose

☐ Specify its diameter equal to the inlet of the fire plug.

☐ Somewhere in the scene, create a dummy object, to which you'll bind one of the ends of your hose.

Tab panel → Helpers → Dummy Object

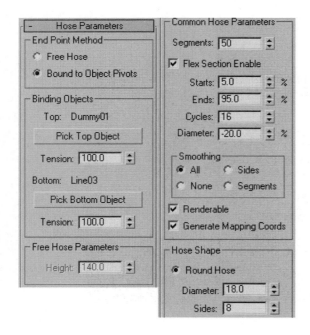

**Fig. 4.20.** Parameters of the Hose object

❑ In the parameters of the Hose01 object set the **Bound to Object Pivots** radio button.

❑ Select the fire plug as the first object, and Dummy01 as the second object.

❑ Most probably, you'll need to correct the pivot point of the fire plug. Do this by rotating and moving the pivot point:

Control panel → Hierarchy → Pivot → Affect Pivot Only

❑ Set the hose parameters (fig. 4.20).

❑ I have achieved the result shown in fig. 4.21.

Try to move the fire plug, and notice that the hose follows its movements.

Create all the remaining objects yourself. The Plane primitive is convenient for creating the surface. You can find the other primitives in the **Objects** tab panel (fig. 4.22).

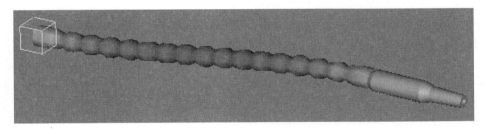

**Fig. 4.21.** Hose with the fire plug

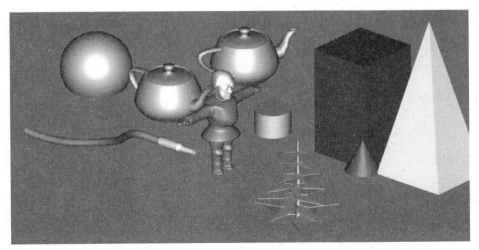

**Fig. 4.22.** The final scene

# Creating Materials

Nearly all of the materials in this scene will be based on a type of the shader — Strauss. This type of the shader is recommended for imitating metallic surfaces. However, you can use it for other surface types as well. The main difference between the Strauss shader and other types of shaders is the presence of a single color in the basic parameters, which corresponds to the diffuse color. Ambient and highlight colors are calculated based on the diffuse color.

The material used for the fireman's body will be the single complex material in this scene.

❑ Open the material editor and select any sample slot.

❑ Change the shader type to Strauss.

❑ Specify the material settings as shown in fig. 4.23.

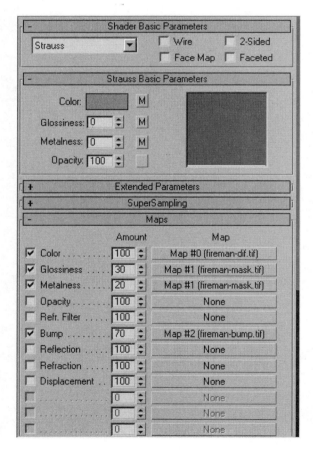

**Fig. 4.23.** Settings for the material of the fireman's body

**NOTE** Apply Bitmap textures for the Color, Glossiness, Metalness, and Bump channels by selecting the appropriate files from the \Lessons\Lesson04\maps directory on the companion CD.

Set the **Amount** values for these textures.

In the texture parameters rollout for the Color channel, enable texture display in the viewport (by clicking the **Show Map in Viewport** button).

☐ Now select the fireman's body and assign this material to it.

Finally, we need to adjust the mapping coordinates of the texture to the fireman's body.

☐ Convert the fireman's body to Editable Patch:

Right-click menu → Convert To: → Convert to Editable Patch

☐ Select the patches corresponding to the fireman's torso (fig. 4.24, a).

☐ Apply the UVW Map modifier to the selected patches and specify the cylindrical mapping type.

The texture will appear in the viewport window. However, you'll notice that the result is different from the one we expected. Let's proceed with further editing.

☐ Rotate the UVW Map Gizmo around the vertical axis to place the belt clasp to the desired position.

☐ Apply the Unwrap UVW modifier:

Tab panel → Modifiers → Unwrap UVW

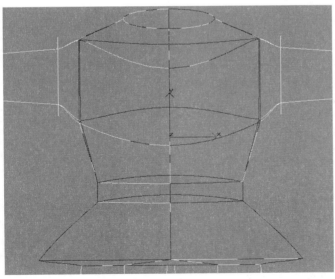

**Fig. 4.24, a.** Adjusting the map placement to the fireman's body

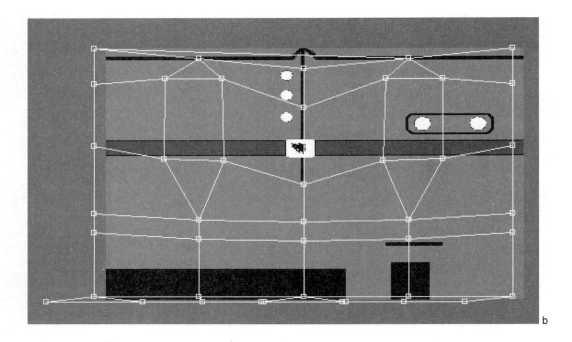

b

c

❏ Go to the edit window (fig. 4.24, b).

❏ Correct the texture mapping by selecting and moving the vertices and adjusting the handles as necessary. Control the process in the viewport window.

❏ Close the UVW Coordinate editor.

❏ Apply the Edit Patch modifier.

❏ Proceed with editing patches:

Right-click menu → Sub-objects → Patch

**Fig. 4.24, b, c.** Adjusting the map placement to the fireman's body

❏ Select the patches that correspond to the fireman's legs.

❏ Apply the UVW Map modifier and set its parameters using the same method as in the previous case.

❏ Apply the Unwrap UVW modifier and edit the vertices.

Use the same method for editing the fireman's arms. The only difference, in this case, is that you'll need to edit each arm separately.

*TIP*   You can use the capability of copying modifiers within modifier stack.

You've finally produced the final result (fig. 4.24, c). In my opinion, you won't have any trouble at all creating the other materials for this scene. For the helmet and fire-plug, create materials similar to copper or brass. You can use material with reflection for the helmet and goggles. For certain objects, you'll need to use two-sided materials.

The results I managed to produce are stored in the Materials.tif file on the companion CD in the \Lessons\Lesson04\Images directory.

# Animation

## Creating the Bones System, Completing the Model, and Positioning the Fireman

❑ Convert the fireman's body to Editable Patch:

Right-click menu → Convert To: → Convert to Editable Patch

*NOTE*   Carefully think everything over before making this step. This conversion will make map editing very difficult and embarrassing.

❑ Convert any element of the fireman's head to Editable Mesh and attach all the other elements to it, including the helmet and goggles. 3ds max 4 will automatically assemble all the materials into one if you set the **Match Material IDs to Material** in the **Attach Options** dialog.

You can change the fireman's attitude using the bone objects.

First of all, let's create the bones system (a skeleton).

Detailed description of the process of creation of the bones system can be found in the second lesson. Therefore, here I will limit myself to a brief listing of the required steps.

❑ Select the head and torso, and make them transparent by pressing <Alt>+<X> keyboard combination. After this, freeze the head and torso.

❑ Create the Point object at the waist level:

Tab panel → Helpers → Point Object

❑ Start the chain of bones at the side view, in the immediate vicinity of the central point. Finish it in the center of the head by clicking the right mouse button (fig. 4.25, a):

Main menu → Animation → Create Bones

Clear the **Assign To Children** checkbox in Control Panel

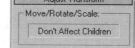

❑ Delete the small bone that appears after clicking the right mouse button, because you won't need it.

❑ Create the bones for the fireman's legs by creating one independent chain at the side view. Copy this chain (fig. 4.25, b). Don't delete the small bones, because you may need them for subsequent creation of the hierarchical links.

❑ Model the bones for hands. Create another independent chain, then create its mirror copy (fig. 4.25, c).

Now it is necessary to adjust as precisely as possible the position of pivot points, size, and mutual position of the bones according to the fireman's body. The more carefully you do this work now, the less problems will arise later.

❑ Start editing hierarchical links and disable mutual influence of the objects making up the hierarchy:

Control panel → Hierarchy → **Pivot** tab → **Adjust Transform** rollout → click the **Don't Affect Children** button.

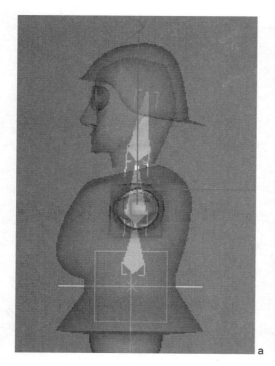
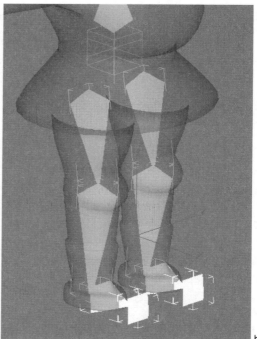

**Fig. 4.25, a, b.** The sequence of creating the bones system

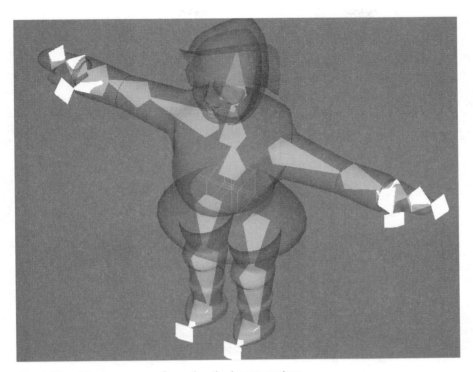

**Fig. 4.25, c.** The sequence of creating the bones system

Now you'll be able to move the bones independently from one another.

In contrast to the previous releases, in 3ds max 4 the bones are fully-functional. Navigate to Control panel and edit parameters of the bones (an example is presented in fig. 4.26).

❑ Link the chains of torso and legs to the central point. Then link the hands to the neck vertebra:

Main toolbar → **Select and Link** button

❑ Select the main bone, which is positioned at the belly level, and drag it to the central point.

Now let us create the systems of inverse kinematics (IK Solvers). In the second lesson we used the History Independent type (HI Solver). For a change, now let us use the IK Limb Solver type, which serves for creating a simple link between two bones.

❑ Select the thigh of one of the legs.

❑ Create the link of the IK Limb Solver type to the foot of the same leg:

Main menu → Animation → IK Solvers → IK Limb Solver

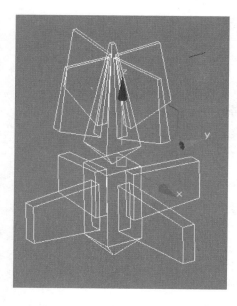

◄ **Fig. 4.26.** The result of editing the bones system

❏ Connect the thigh and the foot with a line.

❏ The bones will probably "twist" around the vertical axis. If this happens, reposition them using the manipulator (fig. 4.27):

Right-click menu → Manipulate

❏ Do the same operations in relation to the other leg.

❏ For the hands, create links from shoulder to hand. Bear in mind that IK Limb works only with the chains comprising two bones!

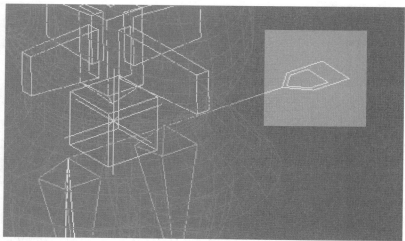

**Fig. 4.27.** Correcting the twisted bones using manipulator for rotating the IK Limb plane

❏ For other bones you don't need to create IK Solvers. You will use forward kinematics to animate them.

**NOTE** Strictly speaking, we have created a very primitive model, which also is not very convenient. However, it works, and this is the main thing for the moment!

❏ Apply the Skin modifier to the fireman's body and add all the bones:

<Ctrl>+Right-click menu → Modifiers → Skin

Control panel → ... → Add Bone

> **_NOTE_**  You can select the **Add Bone** command from the right-click menu of the Skin modifier. Unfortunately, it is inconvenient, because you'll need to add bones one by one.

Let's tune the influence of the bones to the object. In the first approximation, the bone system may be tested by selecting the main element of the hierarchical system (in our case, this will be the bone placed at the level of the breast) and moving it along any coordinate. You'll notice that some parts of the body remain in their previous position or undergo undesirable deformations.

❏ Start editing envelopes of the bones. Go through the list and edit each envelope. I recommend that you do it in the viewport using the Smooth mode. This is convenient, because you'll be able to control bones influence by their color.

> **_NOTE_**  The Skin modifier allows you to adjust the surface deformation of the bones with a high level of precision, including individual vertices. This topic has been covered in detail both in the documentaion supplied with the 3ds max and in the online Help system.

❏ Link the fireman's head with the upper central bone of the skeleton (neck).

Now it's time to give the fire-plug to our fireman. Before proceeding with this operation, turn the fire-plug to point at the Christmas tree.

❏ Select the central point and move it to the fire-plug, turning the body as needed (fig. 4.28). Notice that end effectors remained in their positions and stretched hands and legs. Correct the situation by moving them to appropriate position in the top view. You can also avoid this situation by selecting them together with the central point and moving everything together.

> **_TIP_**  Freeze both the head and the body of the fireman. Starting from now, all manipulations will be done with the bones. For better viewing of the events that take place on the screen, disable the **Show Frozen in Grey** mode before freezing object. To do so, clear appropriate checkbox in the object properties (Right-click menu → Properties). Don't forget about this manipulation and don't panic if you can't select an object!

Now we can start specifying the attitude. The fireman needs to hold the fire-plug with both hands.

> **_TIP_**  Hide all unnecessary objects.

❏ Select all the bones and make them transparent. Thus, the bones will not interfere with your controlling the process. To do so, click the <Alt>+<X> keyboard combination.

❏ Move end effectors, rotate and move the bones ruled by forward kinematics in order to appropriately position the fireman (fig. 4.29).

**Fig. 4.28.** Starting position of the fireman

**NOTES** I did not succeed when trying to position the glove on the left hand as required using the bones. Instead of this, I simply detached respective patches, turned the glove and then linked it to appropriate bone. Perhaps, our bone system proved to be too simplistic and primitive, after all.

New implementation of the bones and IK systems represent a significant progress as compared to that available in previous releases of 3ds max. Before their arrival, one had to make significant efforts to implement something using bones. This was due to the fact that in earlier releases of 3ds max the bones were implemented at a very low level. Notice that when I say "low level" I don't mean that the bones were implemented "poorly". Nothing of the sort! What I really mean, is that the developers of this module tried to make everything "just the same as in real life". When tuning the bones parameters you can adjust all links as you like. For example, you can specify the limits within which each bone can rotate around the specified axis. You can specify the level of influence of specific bone to all the other bones belonging to different levels of the hierarchy, both upper and lower. You can even specify the limits of the length deformation for the bones (notice that this is against all the laws of inverse kinematics). Using all these features provided by 3ds max 4, you can create any realistic or fantastic movements of any characters or machines. However, it usually requires a very long time. Of course, after animating a dozen of characters you will know various tricks, and certainly it will be much easier to animate each subsequent character. However, this task is very difficult and requires a hard work, if you are doing this for the first time... This is the reason why 3ds max 4 introduces new IK solvers, which simplify the animator's tasks and have very much in common with similar systems implemented in other 3D software packages.

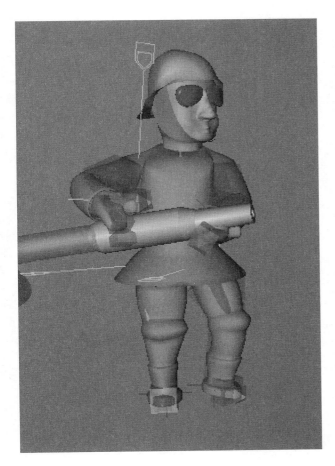

**Fig. 4.29.** The final position of the puppet fireman

☐ Turn the head and legs of the fireman to provide a more realistic attitude.

☐ Link the hand effectors to the fire-plug. After all, it's the fire-plug that will be animated!

    Main toolbar → Select and Link

Now try to move the fire-plug. You'll notice that the fireman's hand follows the motion of the fire-plug.

# The Liquid Jet

We'll need three objects to create the liquid jet. First of all, we'll need the Super Spray source of particles. Next, we'll need two space warps — Gravity and Deflector.

❏ Create the Super Spray particle system:

Tab panel → Particles → Super Spray Particles System

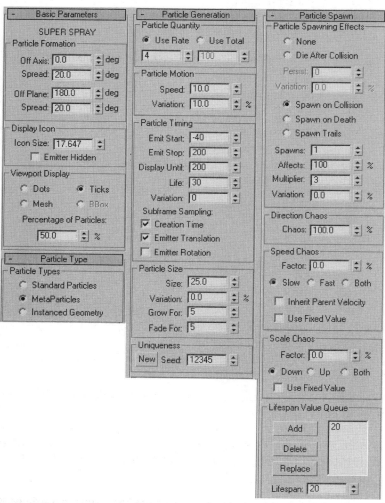

**Fig. 4.30.** Settings for the particle system imitating the liquid jet

❏ Move it to the fire-plug and direct it according to the current position of the fire-plug.

❏ Specify the particle system parameters as shown in fig. 4.30.

*TIP*  The **Basic Parameters** rollout. Specify the values of the **Spread** parameter so that the particle system resembles a jet.

The **Particle Generation** rollout. The number of particles generated by the source in each frame is defined by the **Use Rate** parameter. Specify a small value for this parameter. The starting time for particle emission (the **Emit Start** parameter) has to be negative because we need the particles to be present in frame 0:0:0.

Specify a large enough value for the particle size.

The **Particle Type** rollout. Select the **MetaParticles** option. Uses **Metaball particles**. These are particle systems in which the individual particles blend together in blobs or streams.

The **Particle Spawn** rollout. Select the **Spawn on Collision** radio button. Set the number of spawns to 1. The number of particles generated by one particle should be set to 3.

The **Direction Chaos** parameter should be set to 100%. A setting of 100 causes the spawned particle to travel in a random direction.

Specify a new value for the **Lifespan Value** parameter for the spawned particles.

❏ Link the particle source (the emitter) to the fire-plug.

❏ Create the gravity and place it anywhere within the scene (the gravity vector should be directed downwards):

Tab panel → Particles → Gravity Space Warp

❏ Bind the gravity field with the particle system:

Main Toolbar → **Bind to Space Warp** button 🔲

❏ Select the gravity settings to direct the liquid jet to the desired point (fig. 4.31, a).

❏ Create the deflector corresponding to the surface:

Tab panel → Particles → Deflector Space Warp

❏ Bind the deflector to the particle system and specify the settings to imitate the floor struck by the jet of water (fig. 4.31, b).

Create a lustrous material for the particles using the Blinn shader. In the **Falloff** group of the **Advanced Transparency** rollout, set the **In** radio button and enter a value of 60 into the **Amt:** field. It's also helpful to use a map. For example, I used the reflect.tif file, which can be found on the companion CD.

*NOTE*  To make the patches of light more interesting, I also applied a map to the **Specular Level** parameter. It wasn't necessary to mention that I made this material two-sided.

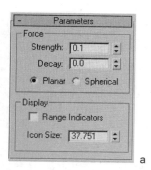

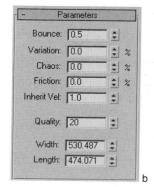

**Fig. 4.31.** Settings for gravity (a) and deflection (b)

# Animating the Fireman

Animation of the fireman includes animation of the fire-plug and fireman's arms. You can also animate any other part of the fireman's body as necessary.

**TIP** Don't use any additional controllers. In this example, confine yourself to creating keys.

❏ Tune the animation settings, if you haven't already done so. Set the frame rate to 15 frames per second, and the duration to 200 frames.

❏ Enable the animation mode by pressing the <N> key and go to frame 15.

❏ Change the fire-plug position (make sure that the fireman's hands move with the fire-plug).

❏ Go to frame 30 and change the fire-plug position again.

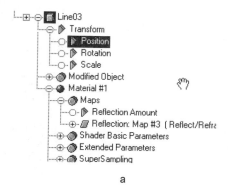

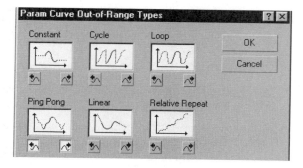

a                                                                        b

**Fig. 4.32.** Setting animation parameters in the **Param Curve Out-of-Range Types** window

❑ Open Track View for the fire-plug:

Right-click menu → Track View Selected

❑ Expand the animation tracks tree and select the **Position** track (fig. 4.32, a).

❑ To specify how an object is to behave outside the range of the keys you've defined, open the **Param Curve Out-of-Range Types** window and select the **PingPong** type (fig. 4.32, b).

Now try to playback the animation in the viewport window.

Proceed the same way to animate the head and the other bones.

# Animating Supplementary Objects

The Christmas tree is the only object in this scene that requires additional animation. Make it melt while it burns (after all, it's a toy).

❑ Apply the Melt modifier to the Christmas tree:

Right-click menu → Modifiers → Melt

I think you're capable of tuning and animating the settings of the modifier all by yourself. The settings that I've specified for the starting and ending points of the animation are shown in fig. 4.33.

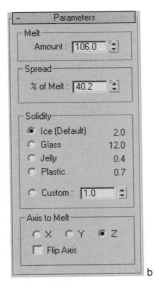

**Fig. 4.33.** Parameters of the Melt modifier for the melting Christmas tree: (a) at the starting point and (b) at the ending point of animation

# The Fire

Now let's add the most important element of the scene — the fire.

❏ Create a spherical gizmo for the atmospheric effects and place it at the center of the Christmas tree (fig. 4.34, a):

Tab panel → Helpers → SphereGizmo

❏ In the **Sphere Gismo Parameters** rollout, set the **Hemisphere** checkbox.

❏ Stretch the gizmo along the vertical axis to make it "envelope" the Christmas tree (fig. 4.34, b).

❏ Add the Fire Effect to the scene by opening the environment window and binding it to the gizmo:

Main menu → Rendering → Environment → **Atmosphere** rollout→ **Add** button

Select the **Fire Effect** item from the list of effects

Click the **Pick Object** button and select the Gizmo

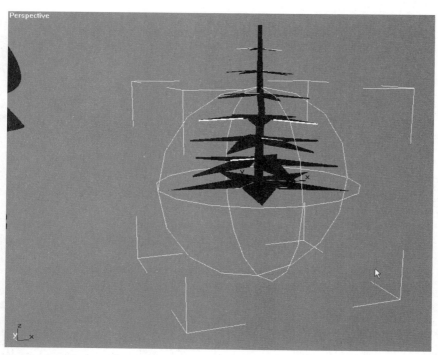

**Fig. 4.34, a.** Creating the fire gizmo

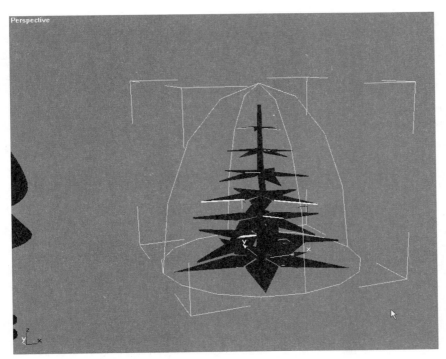

**Fig. 4.34, b.** Creating the fire gizmo

When performing test rendering operation in the Perspective viewport, adjust the fire parameters. First of all, change its type from FireBall to Tendrill and increase the density. Other settings can be adjusted as you wish.

***Self-study*** Create several copies of the gizmo and add them to the list of Fire Effect control objects. To get rid of the "similarity" of the flames, change the **Seed** value for each gizmo (the starting value of the randomizer). You can also animate the size of each gizmo to create the effect of "dancing flames".

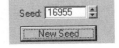

One final point. There can't be a smoke without a fire. One can also say, that there can't be fire without smoke. Now try to create the smoke. For this purpose, you can use the particle system or Combust (or even the same Fire Effect) plug-in module. Now it's all up to you.

# Setting the Lights

The fire is the only source of light in this scene. However, you'll need to create two additional lights (fig. 4.35). One of them is directional (Spot), and you'll need to place it under the Christmas tree. This light shouldn't produce any shadows since it's only intended to emphasize the Christmas tree. The second light is the point source of illumination that shoots out in all directions (Omni). This light must produce shadows. You'll need to fine-tune the color and intensity, along with shadow parameters. Furthermore, the Christmas tree must be excluded from the list of objects illuminated by the second light.

Control panel → ... → **Exclude** button

You can select the particle system and clear the **Cast Shadows** and **Receive Shadows** checkboxes in the parameters of this object.

Right-click menu → Properties → ... → **Rendering Control** group → clear the **Cast Shadows** and **Receive Shadows** checkboxes

The final stroke will be to animate the **Multiplier** parameters so as to make the light change intensity.

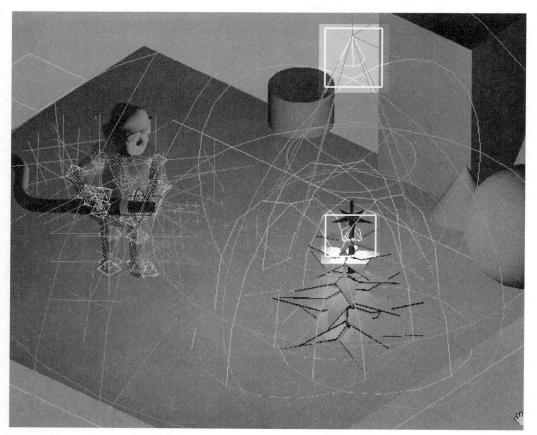

**Fig. 4.35.** Lighting the scene

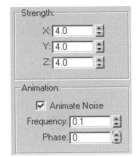

***Self-study*** You can produce an interesting effect by applying the animated Noise modifier to the lights. An example of the animated Noise modifier settings is shown in fig. 4.36.

**Fig. 4.36.** Settings for animated Noise modifier

# Setting the Camera and Rendering

❑ Set the camera to view both the Christmas tree and the fireman (fig. 4.37).

**Fig. 4.37.** Camera view

☐ Start the rendering process after setting all the desired parameters. Don't forget to save the rendering results (fig. 4.38) under any name, having saved the project first. Pay special attention to selection of the anti-aliasing algorithm. Recently I came to like the results produced by this algorithm more and more.

**_NOTE_**    The completed version of this project (lesson04.max) can be found in the \Lessons\Lesson04\Scenes directory on the companion CD. It has the only difference from the project which, as I hope that you have completed is, that the hose is modeled using Loft.

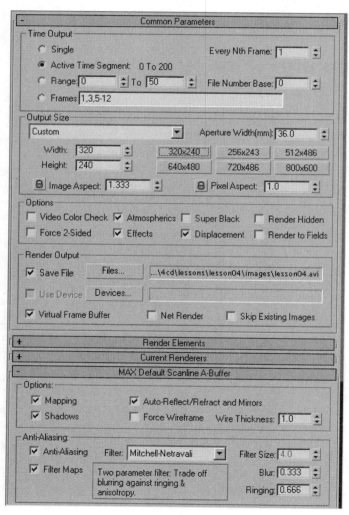

**Fig. 4.38.** Rendering settings

# Summary

If this project is nothing more than a draft, then everything looks all right! It would hardly be possible to produce something better in just one night. However, if you want to show this project to anybody else besides your boss or your customer, refining the project will take you a great deal of time.

First of all, the lighting is horrible. It doesn't emphasize either the burning fire, or other events that take place in reality (it doesn't matter that this reality is virtual). The lighting isn't sufficient, and we need additional lights for lighting the Christmas tree, the fireman, and the fire-hose. All these sources are needed to emphasize the main characters of the scene and highlight them in comparison to the background. Concerning the material of the Christmas tree, it would be good to add self-illumination and create a small glow around it.

For the light source imitating the illumination from fire, it's necessary to use an animated map assigned as a projector.

All of the other details aren't bad. Of course, it would be better to create several cameras, render several fragments from different viewpoints, and them mount them into the movie.

Animation of the fireman is done at a primitive level. It should be noted that character animation is the most difficult task in any 3D software package. No wonder that at many companies concentrate exclusively on developing supplementary animation tools. If you wish to investigate various aspects of this problem in more detail, I recommend you to complete the character animation lessons that you can find in the on-line tutorials supplied with 3ds max 4.

Furthermore, I recommend that you assign unique and meaningful names to all your objects and materials. If you call them something like Circle01 or Line07, you'll have trouble even in a small project containing about 10 objects, to say nothing of complex projects containing hundreds of objects!

# Lesson 5

# Martian Rally

I n this lesson, we're going to create an episode from a science fiction film. You can view this episode by opening the Lesson05.avi file stored on the companion CD in the \Lessons\Lesson05\Images directory.

## Aims of this Lesson

After completing this lesson, you'll know how to:

- ❏ Create and texturize landscapes
- ❏ Model simple objects using NURBS
- ❏ Use particle systems and create effects based on them
- ❏ Create animation using surface animation, motion capture, constraints, and equations

## Preliminary Notes

This lesson is the most difficult of all the others presented in this book. However, after viewing the movie, I'm sure you'll agree that the result was worth trying. When performing this lesson, you may disagree with some of the methods used and come up with your own ideas for solving certain problems. If this is the case, then I'm happy for you. This means that you've found your own way and your own style. This is the best reward for me!

If you can't complete the whole lesson, try to do as much as you can and perform the tasks that are interesting to you.

I intentionally miscalculated when performing a preliminary evaluation of the project. Of course, at first I thought about redoing it completely. However, after some consideration, I decided that you'd be interested in finding solutions for difficult situations and managing to accomplish a project that may, at first, seem hopeless. After all, this is just another aspect of the skill.

## Scenario and Details

### Scenario

The scenario is quite simple — the jet vehicle rushes along the surface of a planet (we'll pretend it's Mars), skirting obstacles and trying to avoid clefts.

# Details

**Landscape**. The surface of the planet is pitted and craggy. The lower areas are covered with sand, dust, and some vegetation; the hills consist of gravel and the mountain peaks are solid rock, possibly covered with ice.

**Jet vehicle**. A three-wheeled streamlined vehicle, with small nose wheels on a helical spring suspension. In the rear part of the vehicle, there are two jet engines, one to the left and one to the right of the large rear wheel. The hull of the jet vehicle is metallic; the back-up light is made from panels of multi-layered plastic attached to racks, which are made of the same material as the hull.

**Camera**. The camera follows the jet vehicle, flying around it from front to back, and then to the right.

**Environment**. Yellowish sky, with some suspended dust. The light source is high above the horizon.

**Special effects**. Dust from the wheels, and tracks left by the wheels on the planet's surface.

We'll try to implement all of this in the lesson.

# Initial Settings

Our episode will take approximately 10 seconds, at a frame rate set to 15 frames per second. Based on these settings, we need to set the animation parameters.

Open the **Time Configuration** settings and specify the appropriate values (fig. 5.1).

    Time Control → Time Configuration

> ***NOTE***   In the third lesson, we used the SMPTE time format. For a change, in this lesson we'll use an ordinary frame numbering notation.

> ***NOTE***   The SMPTE abbreviation stands for Society of Motion Picture and Television Engineers, the organization that proposed this format as a standard for time recording in TV and cinematography. The JPEG format (Joint Photography Experts Group) is another example of an abbreviation of this type.

Let's set a standard right now concerning measurement units. In general, this isn't required. However, to avoid problems when pasting objects from one scene to another, it would be easier to work on the scenes using a

common scale. For example, one measurement unit for the landscape can be set to 1 meter, and to 1 centimeter for the jet vehicle.

Set the measurement unit for the scene to 1 meter:

    Main menu → Customize → Preferences → General

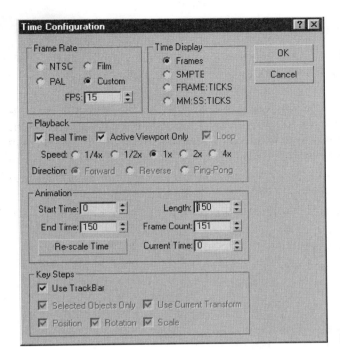

**Fig. 5.1.** Time settings

# Creating the Landscape

## Modeling

As a starting point for creating the landscape, we can use the following three object types: *patch grid*, *NURBS surface* or *plane*. Generally speaking, this isn't very important, because we'll have to convert the landscape to editable mesh anyway. It's necessary, though, for correctly calculating the path of the jet vehicle. Don't forget that the jet vehicle follows the relief precisely as it moves along the planet's surface.

Landscape modeling also can be performed using various techniques. First of all, we can create the plane and the relief we want by moving the vertices. We can also use the Displace modifier. Or, we can use the material with the Displace map. If you decide to use the first or second technique, you will need to specify a large number of steps to produce a smooth relief. The third method undoubtedly has a significant advantage over the first two, because it provides the capability of controlling the settings interactively. This allows you to set the parameters to produce an optimum result (considering it from both a complexity and quality point of view).

*NOTE*    Normally, the process used for creating the landscape isn't traditional (from the point of view of the instrument usage). However, this method is quite efficient.

Now let's create the landscape using the Plane primitive and the Displace modifier.

Before going any further, we need to evaluate the landscape size.

The jet vehicle will move at a velocity of approximately 150—160 kilometers per hour, which is equal to about 45 meters per second. So, in 10 seconds, the vehicle will cover a distance of 450 meters. Because we don't want the horizon to appear in the field of vision while the camera rotates over the jet vehicle, let's assume that the landscape will be approximately 1500×1500 meters.

Now, if you've already specified the scale, let us proceed with the modeling.

Go to the **Top** viewport and expand it to a full-screen by pressing the <W> key.

Create a plane (1500×1500 meters in size) and place its center at the origin of the coordinate system:

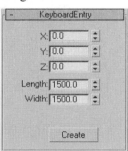

Tab panel → Objects → Plane Object

*TIP*    Create the object using manual keyboard entry.

❑ Don't forget to set the **Generate Mapping Coords** checkbox.

❑ Switch to the editing mode and rename the object "Land":

Right-click menu → Modify Mode

❑ Open the material editor (by pressing the <M> key) and select any sample slot.

❑ Go to the **Maps** rollout and specify the bitmap type for the Displacement map.

Select the landscape.tif file, which can be found on the companion CD in the \Lessons\Lesson05\Maps directory.

*TIP*    The map for Displace can have any color depth, but the best method to use is the Grayscale image (256 shades of grey). Besides which, this image requires fewer resources when being processed in 3ds max 4. Lighter areas represent bulges (higher areas). Dark areas represent lowlands. Also notice that gray  is used to represent zero level (rather than black). This allows you to create both highlands and lowlands.

❑ Rename this material  "Landscape" and assign it to the newly created landscape.

You can't view your landscape in the viewport right now. To view the landscape, apply the Displace Mesh modifier.

*NOTE*    The main idea of the Displacement map is to create more complicated objects during rendering. Tuning of the rendering parameters is done using another modifier — Disp

Approx, or the appropriate settings in the Editable Mesh parameters. For example, if we were going to create an aircraft flying through a canyon, we could use any of these methods. In our case, however, we need to create an object that will be used as a surface along which our jet vehicle moves.

❑ Apply the Displace Mesh modifier:

Control panel → Modifier List → Displace Mesh

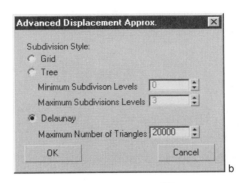

Specify the settings in order to make the object actually correspond to the height map. Don't forget that the camera will be placed very close to the surface. Because of this, you need to produce the highest quality setting possible (fig. 5.2, a, b).

**Fig. 5.2.** Basic and advanced settings for the Displace Mesh modifier

❑ Go to the Displacement map parameters in the material editor and set the **Blur** value to 30, and the **Amount** value to 80.

*NOTE*   To trace all the changes in the viewport window, click the **Update Mesh** button in the Displace Mesh modifier parameters.

Now you've created the landscape (fig. 5.3). I enabled Displacement mapping in the viewport. You can do the same by clicking the **Show Map** button in Viewport while editing the parameters of the map.

Now you should convert the object to Editable Mesh, thus retaining the landscape and avoiding a height map. Straightforward converting won't work since the Displace Mesh modifier is a specific one. It is a so-called "world-space modifier" and is always in the stack. This task can be done by either creating an object of the Mesh type or using a snapshot:

Main menu →TOOLS → SnapShot

You'll get a new object — Land01.

❑ Select the initial Land object and delete it by pressing the <Del> key.

❑ Rename the Land01 object "Land".

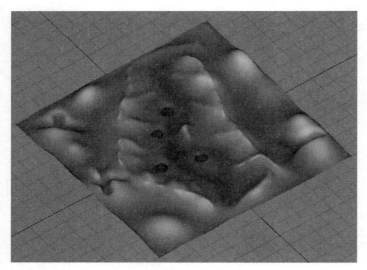

**Fig. 5.3.** The draft landscape

❑ In the Land material parameters, disable the Displacement map by clicking the map type button and selecting the **None** option or by dragging "None" from any other map button.

# Creating and Editing the Landscape Material

There are several methods of creating a complex landscape map. However, all these methods are based on one common principle — creating a mixed map based on masks.

**The first method** — creating the mask based on the existing height map.

❑ Open the material editor by pressing the <M> key.

❑ Select any sample slot and load the Landscape.tif file into it:

Material editor → **GetMaterial** button

Material/Map Browser → Browse From: New

❏ Select the Bitmap map type and then select the Landscape.tif file.

You'll see the map in the sample slot.

> **TIP** To have better control over the map parameters, you can expand the map for viewing in a larger, separate window.

❏ Open the **Output** rollout in the map parameters.

❏ Set the **Enable Color Map** checkbox.

❏ Add two extra points to the line by clicking the **Add Point** button.

When moving these points, notice the changes in the map.

❏ Make the curve and the map look like what's shown in figs 5.4, a and 5.4, b.

> **TIP** Everything's clear — at a later time, the black area will be filled with the first map, the white area will be filled with the second map, and the gray area will be filled with the mixed map.

❏ Rename the map to Mask1 — we'll need it later on.

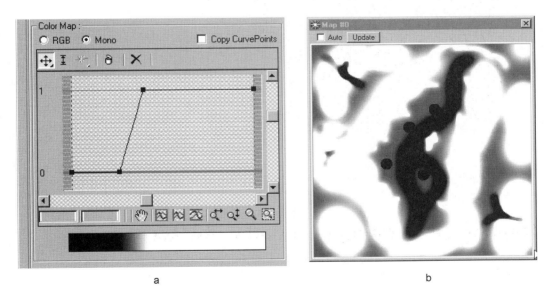

a                                          b

**Fig. 5.4.** Shape of the curve and corresponding gradient map

By copying the map and changing its settings in the **Output** rollout, you can create any number of levels. Based on these levels, you can create a natural texture for any type of landscape. By animating the parameters, you can create interesting effects, such as the melting of snow, and vegetation growth. However, we don't need these effects in our current project.

**The second method**. The main idea of this method is to use the gradient map applied to the landscape.

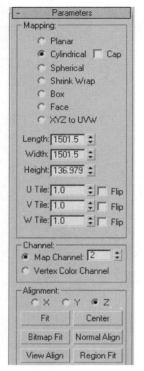

❑ Select any sample slot and load the gradient map into it:

Material editor → **GetMaterial** button

Material/Map Browser → Browse From: New

❑ Select the Gradient type for the map.

In the sample slot, you'll see the map.

❑ Go to the **Front** viewport (by pressing the <F> key).

❑ Select the Land01 object and apply the UVW Map modifier:

Modifier List → UVW Map

❑ Set the modifier parameters as shown in fig. 5.5.

*TIP* Change the type to Cylindrical.

The **Map Channel** setting should be set to 2. I'll explain the reason for this later, just in case you don't understand.

Specify the alignment along the Z-axis.

To make the modifier gizmo match the object proportions, click the **Fit** button.

**Fig. 5.5.** The settings for the UVW Mapping modifier

❑ Return to editing the gradient settings in the material editor and set the Map channel to 2.

❑ Rename the map "Mask2".

Now edit the gradient so that it corresponds to the landscape height map. Perform this operation in the viewport window while viewing the map display.

What a nuisance! You can't assign this map to the object! Now you'll have to work with the Land material.

❑ Select the sample slot containing the Land material.

❑ Move the Mask2 map to the Diffuse channel of the Land material using the instance method.

❑ Start editing the map and enable map display in the viewport. 🖼

❑ Enable the Smooth+Highlights rendering mode by pressing the <F3> key.

❑ Rotate the viewport to make editing the map settings easier (fig. 5.6).

Now edit the gradient settings as shown in fig. 5.7.

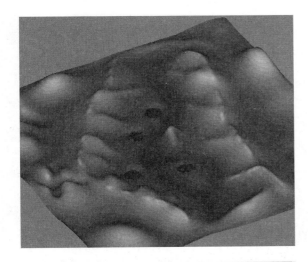

**Fig. 5.6.** Landscape displayed in the viewport with the applied gradient map

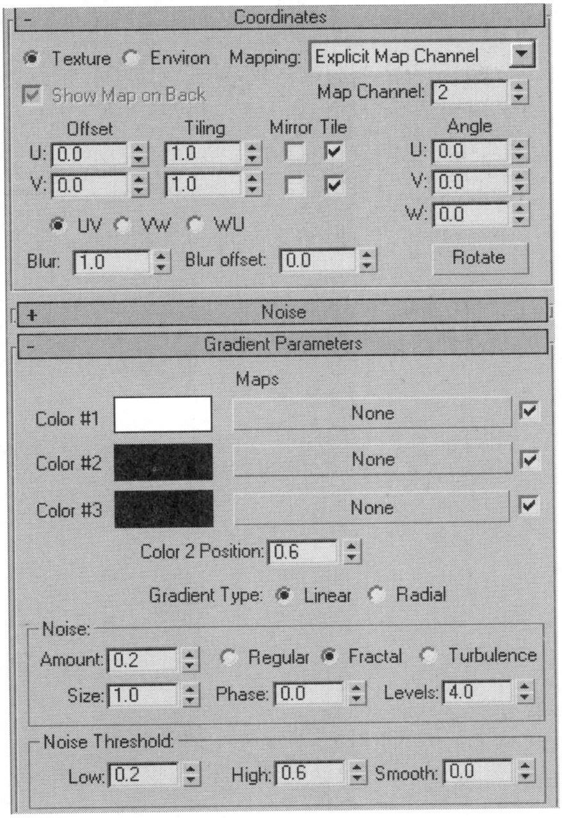

**Fig. 5.7.** Gradient settings for the mask

**TIP** Reverse colors #1 and #3 (black and white). Make color #2 the same as color #3 (black).

Change the **Color 2** setting to 0.6. This will raise the upper boundary.

If you apply the Noise effect, you'll get the effect of wind erosion.

Both of these methods have one common drawback — they don't provide full control over the final look of the landscape. For example, you can't create the glaciers or rockslides that slope down from the rocks to the vegetation-covered surface and the mountain riverbed. You can play with the Top/Bottom material, but this won't solve all your problems. Furthermore, the first method isn't applicable for the landscapes you created using the method of stretching the vertices and edges.

So, to achieve a high level of precision when displaying the landscape structure, you'll have to use the method described below.

The main idea of this method is to assign an absolutely white material to the landscape and to create a supplementary object, namely, an absolutely black plane. By moving the black plane along the vertical axis and performing intermediate rendering operations in the **Top** viewport, and then saving the results in files, you'll get a set of masks, which subsequently can be edited in any bitmap editor. You can use the contents of the individual files as masks for your maps.

In our lesson, we'll use the first two methods, since the masks are already provided.

However, before you start applying maps, edit the basic settings of the Land material.

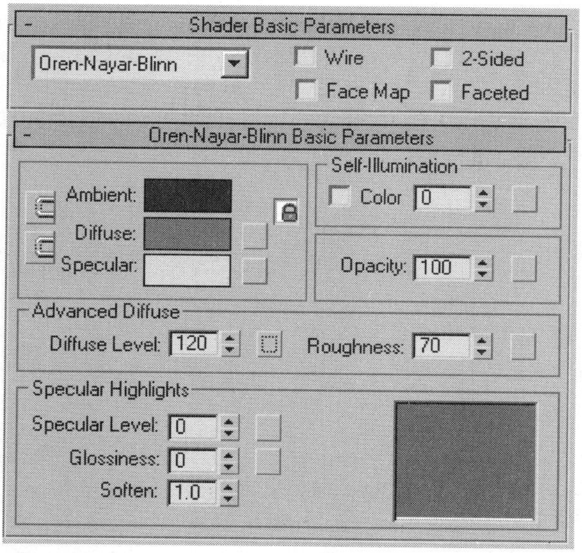

**Fig. 5.8.** Basic settings for the Land material

For a desert landscape (as in our case), the most appropriate shader type will be Oren-Nayar-Blinn. This shader type allows you to create materials that imitate various fleecy tissues or surfaces covered with dust.

- ❏ Start editing the Land material and change the shader type to Oren-Nayar-Blinn.
- ❏ Delete the previous map applied to the Diffuse channel. To do this, drag "None" from another button.
- ❏ Specify the material settings as shown in fig. 5.8.

    ***TIP***   Make the color for the Diffuse channel yellowish-brown (**Hue:** — 33, **Sat:** — 166, **Value:** — 144), the Ambient color — dark-brown (**Hue:** — 11, **Sat:** — 121, **Value:** — 55).

    The Specular color doesn't have an important role in our case. A yellowish color will work fine.

    Set the **Specular Level** and **Glossiness** parameters to 0, and **Soften** to 1 since the material we need isn't lustrous.

    Also, set **Roughness** to 70, and **Diffuse Level** to 200.

    ***Self-study***   Try to experiment with settings such as **Roughness** and **Diffuse Level**. Also try to "come down to the earth" – go to the **Perspective** viewport (by pressing the <P> key). Perform several test-rendering operations using different viewpoints, or run Active Shade in a separate window with the help of the **Active Shade Floater** button in the Main Toolbar.

Now let's create the maps and apply them to the planet's surface.

In the second and third lessons, we worked with the Blend material. In this lesson, we'll use the Mix map. This is very similar to the Blend material, except that now you'll mix maps rather than materials.

- ❏ Apply the Mix texture to the Diffuse color of the Land material.

For the moment, don't change colors. As for the **Mask** button, assign the Mask1 map to it by dragging it from the sample slot, using the instance method.

- ❏ Rename the map "Mix1".
- ❏ Click the **None** button in the **Color #2** string and change the map type to Mix.
- ❏ Assign the Mask2 map as a mask by dragging it from the sample slot.
- ❏ Rename the map "Mix2".
- ❏ Select red for Color #1.
- ❏ Perform test rendering (fig. 5.9).

Well, everything seems to look all right. Now we can edit the **Color 2 Position** setting of the Mask2 map (reduce it to 0.55 to make the "snow line" somewhat lower).

It would also be a good idea to make the separation line for the sand and the other maps more precise. You can do this by setting the **Use Curve** checkbox in the settings for the Mix1 map. To get the appropriate effect, set the **Upper** and **Lower** settings for the transition zone to 0.65 and 0.35, respectively.

**Fig. 5.9.** The landscape with masks applied

Now let's consider implementation of the snow, vegetation, and sand.

Obviously, for the snow we'll use a white material with clefts. Those can be simulated by using Noise as a Bump map. The size of the map should be big enough, and it should also be shifted to one of its components. There is no need to simulate the sand specially. However, a Noise map of little size can be used as Diffuse to simulate the uneven color of the sand. A larger and slighty stretched Noise will be suitable as a Bump map for simulating folds on the sandy surface. For stones and vegetation you'll have to use a Noise map whose components are "natural" Bitmap textures.

> **NOTE** Of course, you are free to use any other appropriate procedure map except for Noise.

Let's start with the sand.

❑ Open the Material/Map Navigator and start editing the Mix1 map (fig. 5.10).

❑ Select the Noise map for the **Color #1** string.

☐ Set the parameters to make the colors soft and not very different from each other (fig. 5.11).

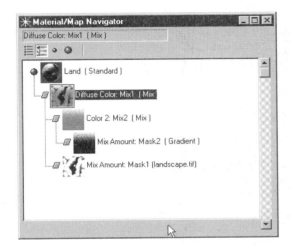

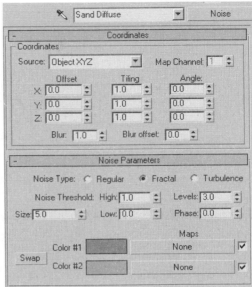

**Fig. 5.10.** The **Material/Map Navigator** dialog

**Fig. 5.11.** Settings for the Sand Diffuse map

☐ Rename the map "Sand Diffuse".

☐ Start editing the Mix2 map.

☐ Select the Noise map for the **Color #1** string.

☐ Specify the map size (the **Size** parameter) to 10, and set the **Noise Threshold: High** and **Low** parameters to 0.55 and 0.45, respectively. This is necessary to provide a sharp boundary line between the components.

**NOTE** Don't forget that you selected 1 meter as a measurement unit, so the Noise map size will be equal to 10 meters.

☐ Rename the map "Mud & Stones".

☐ Select the Bitmap type for the first component and load the Mud001.tga file, which can be found in the \Lessons\Lesson05\Maps directory on the companion CD.

☐ Enable map display in the viewport. By changing the values of the **U:Tiling** and **V:Tiling** parameters, select the appropriate values to make the map size comparable to the size of the landscape.

**TIP** For better control over the scale, create a primitive (Box, for example), almost equal in size to the jet vehicle (about 4×2×1.5 meters). Place this primitive on the surface of the landscape.

❏ For the second component of the Mud & Stones map, select the Stones.tif file and tune its parameters as described above.

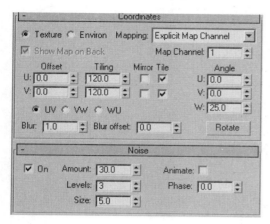

After performing test rendering, you'll notice one undesirable effect — the map is tiled as wall-paper. You can partially get rid of this effect by including and tuning the Noise property in the settings of the Stones map. You can also rotate the map around the W axis (fig. 5.12). Unfortunately, these modifications won't be displayed in the viewport. Because of this, you'll need to perform several test-rendering operations to achieve the desired result.

**Fig. 5.12.** The settings for the Stones map

Now the Diffuse maps are ready. Let's proceed with the Bump maps.

❏ Return to editing the basic parameters of the Land material and drag the Mix1 map from the Diffuse channel to the Bump channel, using the copy method.

**NOTE** Notice, that in this case, it's very important to drag the map using the copy method! The Bump map will match the Diffuse map only with the Mix mask structure. All the other properties of the maps will be different. To avoid corrupting the initial map, it's necessary to make both components independent from each other.

Before we start editing the Bump map, let's decide which areas of the landscape we're going to apply Bump maps to. If you've performed several test renderings, you've probably noticed that they're time-consuming, even at this stage of the project. Also notice that by now there aren't any lights, environment, or atmospheric effects for any of the supplementary objects. After applying the Bump map, rendering time will become even longer. This isn't a problem when we're rendering a static picture, because we can afford to spend several hours of calculation for the sake of quality. However, for animation, the time required for rendering is critically important.

The map for the sand relief is vitally important, because the sand will be one of the main "features" of our movie. As for the rocky surface, it doesn't require a Bump map, because these surfaces will be located at a significant distance from the camera. It'll be barely noticeable whether or not these surfaces have a relief. This is even truer, since the maps themselves are embossed. It's also possible to emboss the areas of transition from rocks and stones to snow caps — this will look striking.

❏ Start editing the Bump map and rename it "Mix1 Bump".

❏ Start editing the map assigned to the Color #1 channel.

❏ Change the map settings as follows: Color #1 and Color #2 should be changed to black and white, respectively. To make the map look stretched, go to the **Coordinates** parameters and change the **X Tiling** to 2.

❏ Rename the map "Sand Bump".

❏ Return to editing the Mix1 Bump map.

Now you need to disable all the other maps, and, at the same time, assign the transition map from the stones to the snowcaps. You can do this by assigning the Mask2 map to the Color #2 channel of the Mix1 Bump map.

If one of the sample slots in Material editor contains the Mask2 map, drag it to the Color #2 channel of the Mix1 Bump map, using the instance method.

If the Mask2 map isn't present in any of the sample slots, proceed as follows:

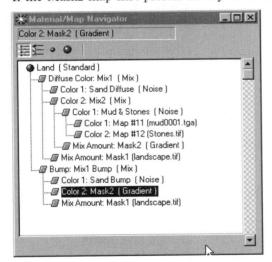

❏ Start editing the map of the Color #2 channel of the Mix1 map by clicking the **Color #2** button.

❏ Click the **Type:Mix** button.

❏ In the **Material/Map Browser** window, set the **Scene** option of the **Browse From** group.

❏ Select the Mask2 map from the list by double-clicking it.

❏ To make the Mask2 map parameters automatically change for the Bump map as well, use the inheritance method (the Instance option).

The **Material/Map Navigator** window will now look like what's shown in fig. 5.13.

**Fig. 5.13.** The **Material/Map Navigator** window for the Land material

If you perform test rendering now, you'll see that the Mask2 map produces a very sharp relief. This can be easily corrected by decreasing the influence factor of the map.

❏ Start editing the Mask2 map and open the **Output** rollout.

❏ Enter a value of 0.2 into the **Bump Amount** field.

Now let's do one last thing. Let's make the snowcaps and glaciers glitter in the sun.

❏ Start editing the basic parameters of the Land material.

❏ Set the **Glossiness** and **Specular Level** checkboxes, apply the Mask2 map to like channels, and enter the values of 60 and 100 into the appropriate fields.

*NOTE* In 3ds max 4, you can apply a map to any parameter of the material. Depending on the parameter, this map can influence the color or, in our case, the value of the parameter. The black on the map corresponds to a value of 0%, while white corresponds to 100%. By changing the map amount, you can significantly change the values of the parameters to produce the desired effect.

*Self-study* Temporarily disable the maps on the Glossiness and Specular Level channels by clearing the appropriate checkboxes. Then change the values of these settings in the basic parameters to select the required factor of influence (amount).

# Creating Environment and Atmosphere

The sky will have a yellowish tint near the horizon, and turquoise near its zenith.

For creating the sky, let's use the Gradient Ramp type of the map.

❏ Open the environment window:

Main menu → Rendering → Environment

❏ Assign the Gradient Ramp map to the environment:

Environment → **Environment Map** button

Material/Map Browser → Browse From: New

Material/Map Browser → Gradient Ramp

❏ Drag the map to any sample slot using inheritance (the Instance option).

❏ Rename the new map "Sky".

*TIP* You'll need to perform a lot of test renderings when editing this map. To speed-up the process, select the Land01 object and exclude it from the rendering process:

Right-click menu → Properties... → **General** tab → **Rendering Control** rollout → clear the **Renderable** checkbox

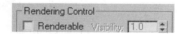

❏ Set the camera horizontally.

❏ Edit the mapping coordinates of the Sky map:

• Select the Environ coordinate type and set the Spherical Environment option.

• Rotate the map by 90° around the W coordinate.

• Set the **U:Mirror** and **V:Mirror** checkboxes. This is necessary to avoid the appearance of a seam after applying the Noise map, and to make one of the gradient boundaries correspond to the horizon.

❏ Set the gradient colors, as shown below:

- The first and the second colors (from left to right) — **Hue:** — 120, **Sat:** — 255, **Val:** — 255 (turquoise).
- The third color — **Hue:** — 40, **Sat:** — 100, **Val:** — 200 (dark yellow).
- Move the second color to the right to a position of 80%.

❏ The settings from the **Noise** group should be set like what's shown in fig. 5.14.

**Fig. 5.14.** The Noise map settings

***Self-study***     Animate the **Phase** parameter. This will make the "clouds" change smoothly during rendering. However, don't make the phase change too rapidly. For example, set the parameter to 0 for the first frame, and to 3-4 for the last frame.

Now we're going to add fog to our scene.

❏ Open the environment settings window:

Main menu → Rendering → Environment...

❏ Add some fog:

Environment → **Atmosphere** rollout → **Add** button

From the atmospheric effects list, select the **Fog** item.

❏ Specify the settings as shown in fig. 5.15, a.

***NOTE***   Select the Standard type.

Make the fog light yellow by setting the following values: **Hue:** — 40, **Sat:** — 40, **Val:** — 255.

The **Fog Background** checkbox controls the fog influence in the background picture (in our case, this will be the Sky map).

Set the fog density for the far boundary (Far %) to 30%, lest the fog should cloud the sky.

***NOTE***   Standard fog is based on the **Range** parameter of the camera. Later, you'll need to set it for the camera that will be used for final rendering.

However, the standard fog isn't right for our scene. We need to add layered fog.

❏ Add another Fog effect and rename it "Layered Fog".

❏ Specify the parameters for this fog as shown in fig. 5.15, b.

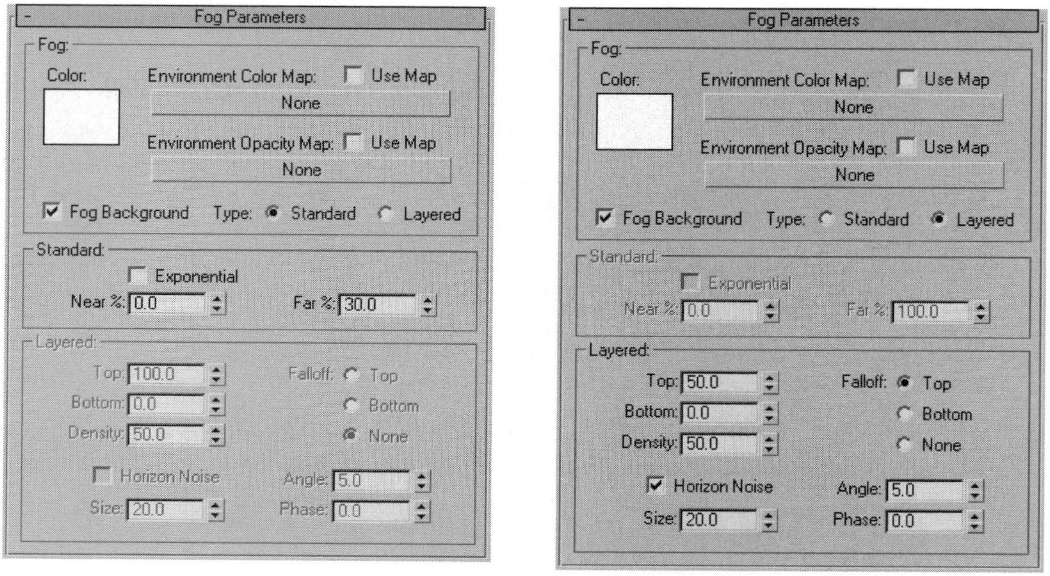

**Fig. 5.15.** Settings for standard and layered fog

*TIP* Select the Layered type.

Specify the same color as was used for the standard fog: **Hue:** — 40, **Sat:** — 40, **Val:** — 255.

The **Top** and **Bottom** parameters specify the boundaries for the fog (from above and from below, respectively). In our case, these parameters are set to 0 and 50 meters .

The **Falloff** parameter allows you to make the fog density decrease smoothly along the vertical axis.

The **Horizon Noise** checkbox isn't required in our case. However, I recommend that you set this checkbox. For example, imagine a case when the camera accidentally captures the horizon during animation. In this situation, the even line of the fog on the horizon will spoil the whole impression produced by your movie.

*Self-study* You have probably noticed two buttons in the fog parameters: **Environment Color Map** and **Environment Opacity Map**. By using these buttons, you can assign maps to the color and opacity parameters, thus making the fog look like clouds of smoke or dust. You can assign this to any map. There's just one limitation: you can only use the Environment mapping coordinates.

❑ Rename the landscape "Land" and save your project in the file named Land.max.

# Jet Vehicle

A sketch of our jet vehicle is shown in fig. 5.16. Now we need to model the hull, wheels, spring suspension, and the jet engines.

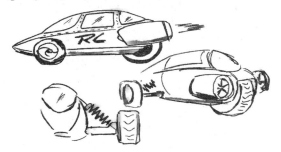

All of these details need to be linked to each other in such a way as to provide the capability of animating them when modeling the vehicle motion along the planet's surface.

**Fig. 5.16.** A sketch of a jet vehicle

# Specifying the Initial Settings and Creating the Auxiliary Objects

Before we start modeling the jet vehicle, we have to specify a scale.

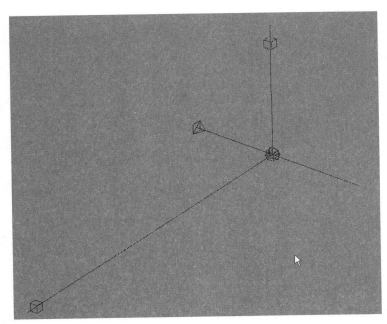

**Fig. 5.17.** Specifying Tape Measure Helper objects

❑ Select one centimeter as the measurement unit to be used in 3ds max 4:

Main menu → Customize → Preferences → **General** tab

You can also set several tapes, and specify their size to 400, 200, and 150 centimeters, respectively (fig. 5.17):

Tab panel → Helpers → Tape Measure Object

After settings the tapes, select and freeze them by pressing the <6> key.

# Modeling the Hull

To create the hull, let's use the NURBS technology.

*TIP*   3ds max 4 has a very powerful mechanism that lets you snap to specific scene elements. For example, you can snap not only to the main grid, but to any part of existing geometry as well.

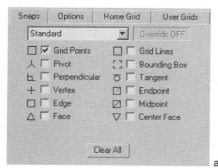

a

Right-click the **3D Snap Toggle** button in the status controls to open the snaps settings dialog.

Specify the snaps settings as shown in fig. 5.18. This will simplify the procedure of creating curves for the surface frameworks.

3ds max 4 also provides the capability of temporarily disabling global snaps settings. To use this capability, right-click anywhere in the viewport while pressing and holding down the <Shift> key. I hope that you'll be able to easily understand how to do this.

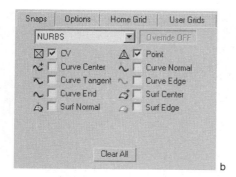

b

*NOTE*   Obviously, it's not necessary to model the hull using NURBS. In all of the previous lessons, we created various models using every technique available in 3ds max 4. You probably have your own favorite methods by now. If so, go ahead and create the hull of the jet vehicle using one of them.

It should be noted that the NURBS module has more stringent requirements to the hardware than any other module in 3ds max 4. If your computer isn't powerful enough, NURBS modeling may turn into a nightmare!

**Fig. 5.18.** Snaps settings основного интерфейса (a) и NURBS (b)

❑ In the left viewport, create the NURBS point curve, sequentially adding the points from right to left (fig. 5.19, a):

Tab panel → Shapes → NURBS Point Curve

Finish creating the curve by clicking the right mouse button

❑ Switch to the editing mode. To do so, convert the curve to the NURBS type:

Right-click menu → Convert To: → Convert to NURBS

❑ Rotate the viewport to make the modeling process easier (click the central mouse button while holding the <Alt> key) and create another curve (to be precise, a straight line segment), connecting the starting and ending points of the initial curve (fig. 5.19, b).

NURBS Toolbox → Create Point Curve

❑ Add two points to the new curve and move them to produce a smooth curve (fig. 5.19, c):

**NOTE** The developers of 3ds max 4 did not include the necessary commands into the Right-click Menu. You may do it yourself if you wish. As for me, I am going to use the standard features.

Right-click menu → Sub-objects → Point

Control panel → Refine

Move the cursor to the curve you need to add the point to and click the mouse button

Right-click menu → Move

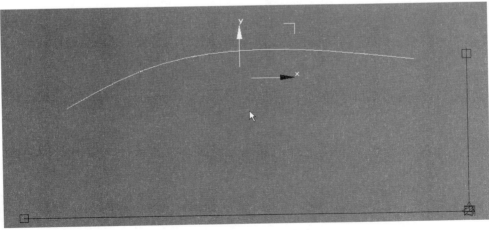

**Fig. 5.19, a.** Modeling sequence used for creating the cockpit

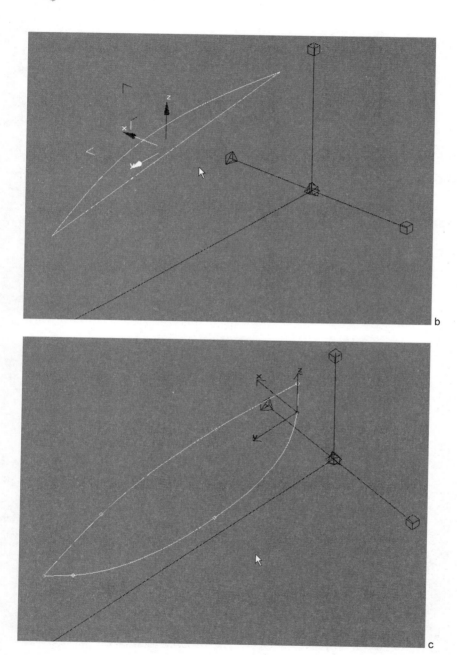

**Fig. 5.19, b, c.** Modeling sequence used for creating the cockpit

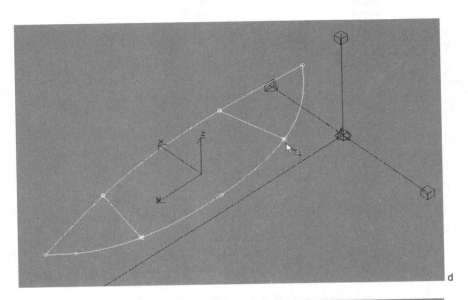

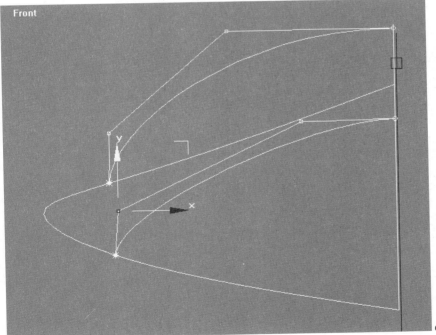

**Fig. 5.19, d, e.** Modeling sequence used for creating the cockpit

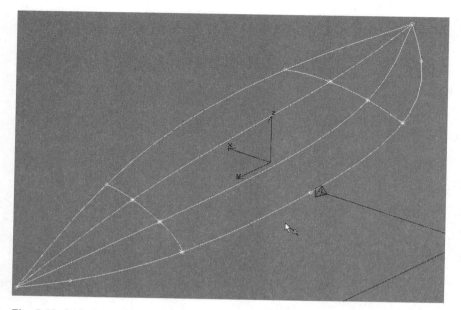

**Fig. 5.19, f.** Modeling sequence used for creating the cockpit

> *TIP*   To control the shape of the curve, resize the viewport as needed.

❑ Now add the points to the second curve. These points will be used for creating the cross-section:

NURBS Toolbox → Create → Curve Point

> *NOTE*   These points won't be control vertices. Rather, they're separate sub-objects connected to the curve.

❑ Create two new curves using the vertices of the initial curve and newly created points (Fit Curve) (fig. 5.19, d):

NURBS Toolbox → Create Fit Curves

❑ Select the newly created curves and make them independent. Notice that they are CV curves (that is, curves built using control vertices).

Right-click menu → Sub-objects → Curve

Control panel → ... → **Make Independent** button

❑ Edit the control vertices (CV) to level the upper parts of the curves horizontally (fig. 5.19, e):

Right-click menu → Sub-objects → Curve CV

**NOTE** This operation is necessary to provide seamless welding of the surface halves.

**TIP** Edit the control vertices in the **Front** viewport.

❑ Add two additional points to each curve and draw two curves through these points (fig. 5.19, f):

NURBS Toolbox → Create Curve Point

NURBS Toolbox → Fit Curve

❑ Construct a U Loft Surface using four longitudinal curves:

NURBS Toolbox → **Create U Loft Surface**

Create the surface by selecting the longitudinal curves sequentially

**NOTE** This operation will be easier if you enable the Smooth+Highlights mode in the viewport (by pressing the <F3> key). If you can't view this surface in the viewport, it means that the surface orientation is incorrect. To correct the orientation of the surface, set the **Flip Normals** checkbox.

☐ Flip Normals

Half of the cockpit is now ready.

❑ Select it and make it independent:

Right-click menu → Sub-objects → Surface

Control panel → ... → **Make Independent** button

❑ Now select and delete all the curves and points:

Now it's time to construct the longitudinal curves for the hull. Try to create a similar number of points and vertices in each curve.

❑ Create two CV curves, as shown in fig. 5.20, a:

Right-click menu → Create CV Curve

**NOTE** Why did I propose point curves for modeling the cockpit and CV curves for the hull? This is due to a serious drawback of point curves — that it's very difficult to produce a curve of the required shape. So, I recommend point curves for simple surfaces, and CV curves if you need to create a complex surface.

❑ Modify the shape of the upper curve by editing the control vertices (fig. 5.20, b):

Right-click menu → Sub-objects → Curve CV

❑ Go to the **Front** viewport by pressing the <F> key.

❏ Select the lower curve and move it along the X-axis, while pressing and holding down the <Shift> key.

❏ Set the **Independent Copy** radio button in the **Sub-Object Clone Options** dialog.

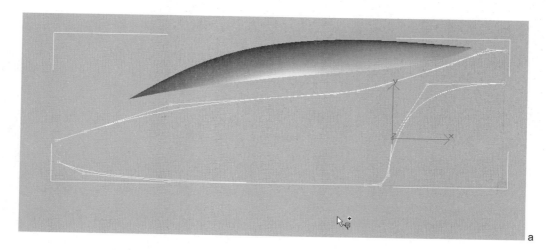

a

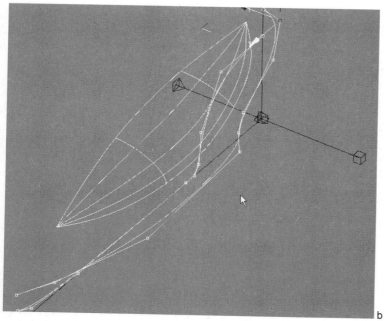

b

**Fig. 5.20, a, b.** Modeling sequence for the lower part of the hull

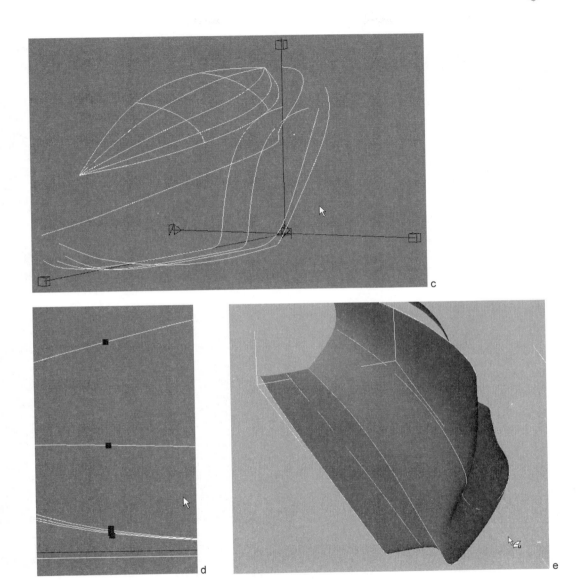

**Fig. 5.20, c, d, e.** Modeling sequence for the lower part of the hull

**TIP**   If the **Independent Copy** radio button is selected, you'll get an independent copy of the cloned object.

If you select the **Copy as TRANSFORM Object(s)** option, you'll get a dependent copy that will reflect the changes done to the source object.

Create the hull framework by copying and editing the curves (fig. 5.20, c).

*TIP* Hide any unnecessary control vertices. Select all the control vertices in the curves that you're not going to edit, and click the **Hide** button in the control panel.

You can also disable the display of the lattice and surfaces:

Right-click menu → the radio buttons in the **TOOLS 1** menu

❏ Break the longitudinal curves in the nose part (fig. 5.20, d):

Right-click menu → Sub-objects → Curve
Control panel → **Break** button on the **Curve Common** rollout

Select the curve and break it by clicking the left mouse button

Now you can delete the curves in the nose part, since they're no longer needed.

❏ Create two surfaces using the longitudinal sections. One surface will be formed by the curves of the lower part of the hull, while the other will be based on the curves of the lateral parts (fig. 5.20, e):

NURBS Toolbox → **Create U Loft Surface**

*NOTE* Don't forget that the direction of the normals needs to point outwards.

The surface we just created is far from perfect. To make it look better, I recommend that you experiment with control vertices to generate a smooth, flawless surface.

This can be done using two methods.

The first, with the exception of a small number of generating curves, is the easiest to use. Simply switch to the editing mode of the curve CV:

Right-click menu → Curve CV Level

The second method includes using an additional level of surface editing.

Let's go ahead and create some exercises.

❏ Switch to the surface-editing mode and select a surface which is built using curves and is not independent.

Right-click menu → Surface Level

The surface parameters will be displayed in the control panel.

Click the **Edit Curves** button at the bottom of the control panel.

The curve editing rollout will open.

Select the curves in the list. You'll notice that the appropriate curves are highlighted in blue in the viewport.

Open the appropriate rollouts; now you'll be able to edit the curves and their elements.

*TIP* It is worth it to use a new feature of 3ds max 4 interface. In order to avoid unnecessary scrolling, arrange the parameters in the control panel into several columns.

*NOTE* If you have a newer, more powerful computer, you will be able to track the changes introduced to the surface while editing vertices by clearing the **TRANSFORM Degradate** checkbox:

You can also simplify the surface in the viewport, thus improving the performance by changing the rendering settings for the NURBS surfaces in the viewport:

Right-click menu → Sub-objects → Top Level

Control panel → ... → **Surface Approximation** rollout

❑ Hide the curves:

Right-click menu → Display Curves

❑ Now it's time to create mirror copies for all of the surfaces (fig. 5.21, a):

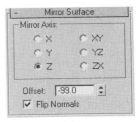

NURBS Toolbox → Create → Mirror Surface

Select each surface and click the left mouse button. If necessary, change the axis, in relation to how you created the mirror copy

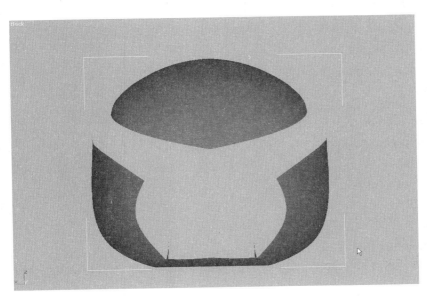

**Fig. 5.21, a.** Two surfaces of the hull of the jet vehicle

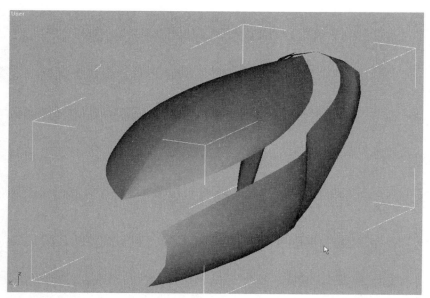

**Fig. 5.21, b.** Two surfaces of the hull of the jet vehicle

❑ Join the surfaces forming the light:

Right-click menu → Sub-objects → Surface
Control Panel → **Join** button on the **Curve Common** rollout

Select the right part of the light (the seam will be blue)

Move the cursor by selecting the appropriate edge of the left part and click the left mouse button

Proceed, using the same method to connect all of the surfaces of the lower part of the hull.

Finally, you'll get two surfaces (fig. 5.21, b).

View these surfaces carefully by rotating them in the viewport. You'll notice two flaws.

First of all, there's a seam between the two parts of the light. This can be easily corrected. To do so, select the control vertices on the surface of the seam and delete them. Select the whole group of vertices at once.

The second defect is represented by wrinkles in the stern and beak parts of the cockpit.

**NOTE**  If you've created surfaces without any defects, then you've done your job well and much better than I did. Congratulations!

I'll try to explain why my surfaces had these defects. When I prepared the lessons, I always did more operations than necessary to make sure I was doing things the right way. For example, the hull of the jet vehicle was redone at least three times.

To get rid of these problems, proceed as follows:

❑ Magnify the viewport to make it as large as possible in order to view any wrinkles that may appear if the control vertices don't match (fig. 5.22).

❑ Fuse the control vertices to one of the surface vertices:

Right-click menu → Sub-objects → Surface CV
Control Panel → Fuse

Select the control vertices (CVs) sequentially and fuse them to the vertices belonging to the second surface (while clicking down and holding the left mouse button)

You'll notice that the wrinkles disappear.

Proceed the same way to eliminate the wrinkles in the beak of the hull.

**Fig. 5.22.** Uncoordinated control vertices

***NOTE***   There's an alternative method of achieving the same purpose, used by my friends and me. Select all the control vertices that you want to join (or, to be more precise, to make their coordinates match) and right-click the mouse, pointing the cursor to the **Select and Uniform Scale** button in the **Main Toolbar** rollout. The **Scale TRANSFORM Type-In** dialog will open. Enter "0" into the **Offset: Screen** field and press <Enter>. You'll need to set the transform center to the center of your selection.

In 3ds max 4 this procedure is simplified; you need only to enter the corresponding values into the coordinate panel.

Now finish all the surfaces to create the hull of the jet vehicle.

❑ Create the blend surfaces between the appropriate faces of the hull and the light surfaces (fig. 5.23, a):

NURBS Toolbox → Create → Blend Surface

Select the appropriate hull surface edge (it will be blue)

Click the left mouse button and move the cursor to the appropriate light surface face

❑ Change the parameters to achieve a smooth transition between the two surfaces.

Proceed the same way to create the surface for the opposite side.

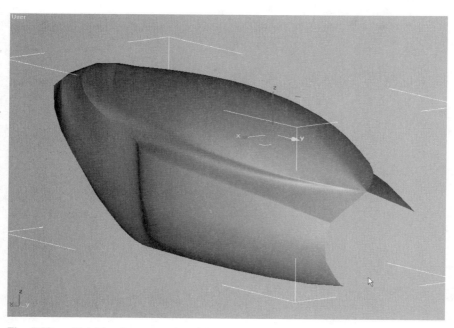

**Fig. 5.23, a.** Finishing the geometry of the jet vehicle

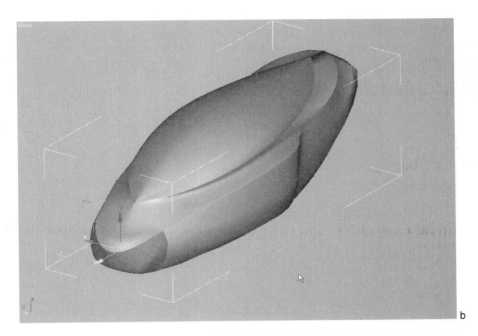

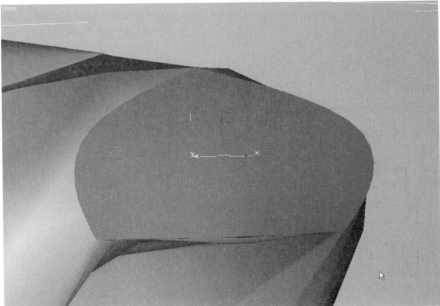

**Fig. 5.23, b, c.** Finishing the geometry of the jet vehicle

Now let's proceed with the beak.

❑ Create a transitional surface between the two surfaces you just created.

❑ Make this surface independent and edit the beak by editing its control vertices:

Right-click menu → Sub-objects → Surface CV

*TIP*  To speed up this process, use Soft Selection.

❑ Finally, create the beak part of the hull by joining the newly created surface with the bottom part of the hull (fig. 5.23, b).

❑ Create a surface to cover the stern of the hull (fig. 5.23, c):

NURBS Toolbox → Create Cap Surfaces

Select the hull surface and the edge that defines the surface of the stern (they'll be blue)

Click the left mouse button

You can finish the hull to make it look better. The only thing that you need to remember is that the rendered object will differ from the object shown in the viewport. Thus, some of the unmatched surfaces in the viewport are of no importance.

Now let's determine which materials will correspond to each surface of the hull. Unfortunately, the NURBS module does not fully support the drag-and-drop technique for submaterials as it does for, say, polygons. That is why you should explicitly set the Material ID parameters of every surface. By default, all the surfaces have the **Material ID** value set to 1. This is satisfactory for all of the surfaces except the cockpit surface.

❑ Select the cockpit surface:

Right-click menu → Surface Level

❑ Change the **Material ID** value to 2:

Control panel → ... → **Material Properties** rollout

❑ Set the **Generate Mapping Coordinates** checkbox.

❑ Rename the object to "Mobil_Body".

# Modeling Other Parts of the Jet Vehicle

I won't discuss the entire process of creating the wheels and the elements of suspension in detail. Rather, I'll provide some general notes.

The wheels will include two main parts — the tire and the disk.

❑ The tire can be created using the Torus primitive in the Top viewport:

Tab panel → Objects → Torus Object

❑ Apply the Edit Mesh modifier to the newly created object. Select one of the side vertices and move it aside in the **Front** viewport.

❑ Perform the same operation in relation to the vertices on the opposite side.

❑ Apply the UVW Map modifier and specify the cylindrical coordinates.

*NOTE*  Remember that the modifier should be applied to the whole object.

❑ Create the wheel disk and convert it to lathe:

Tab panel → Shapes → Line

Modifier List → Lathe

Don't forget to set the **Generate Mapping Coordinate** checkbox

❑ Attach the disk to the tire by selecting the tire, then applying the Edit Mesh modifier and clicking the Attach button in the control panel.

❑ Switch to editing elements:

Right-click menu → Sub-objects → Elements

❑ Select the tire and set the **Material ID** parameter to 2.

❑ Select the disk and set the **Material ID** parameter to 1.

Rename the wheel to "Mobil_Fwheel".

Proceed the same way to create the rear wheel. The only difference will be that the curve for the disk needs to be doubled. Rename it to "Mobil_Bwheel".

*NOTE*  You can create the rear wheel by copying the front wheel and changing its size. The best way to perform this operation is to apply the XForm modifier and edit its gizmo.

To create the double-sided disk, select the disk and detach it from the object. Then edit the disk, mirror it using the copy method, and reattach it to the object.

*TIP*  When renaming the object, you can use the Windows clipboard. Select the Mobil_ prefix and copy it (using <Ctrl>+<C> or <Ctrl>+<Ins> keyboard shortcut). To rename the object, select its name and use the <Ctrl>+<V> or <Shift>+<Insert> keyboard shortcut. Then add the suffix.

Now create the chassis.

Go to the **Top** viewport and create the curve. Next, mirror the curve using the copy method, attach the source curve and connect the appropriate vertices. Then create the chassis object using the Bevel modifier.

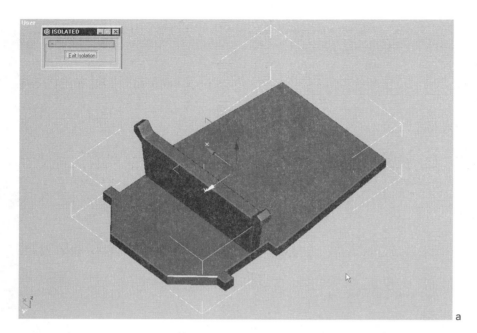

a

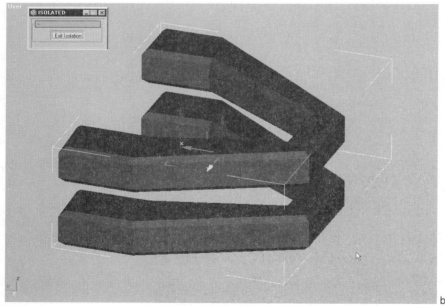

b

**Fig. 5.24.** Chassis and levers of the jet vehicle's suspension

Create vertical posts for fastening the springs and attach them to the chassis (which needs to be converted to Editable Mesh).

The chassis (fig. 5.24, a) is ready. Rename it to Mobil_Rama.

Proceed the same way to create the levers for the front suspension (fig. 5.24, b). Rename them to Mobil_Tag.

*TIP*   Use the Copy/Paste function of the Modifier Stack.

*Self-study*   You can create the same elements using other capabilities of 3ds max 4. Try to make all the elements of the construction look as realistic as possible. However, always remember that you're preparing this model for animation, and any extra faces could result in extra minutes, or even hours, of rendering process.

Now let's create the suspension springs. I'll discuss the process of creating the springs in greater detail.

☐ First of all, create two dummy objects and place them at the supposed points of attachments for the spring endpoints (fig. 5.25, a):

Tab panel → Helpers → Dummy Object

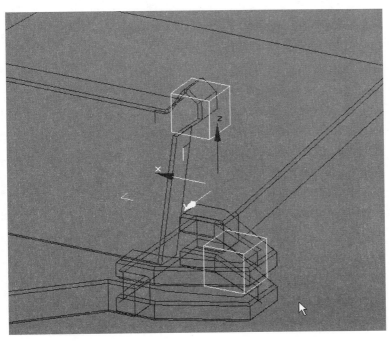

**Fig. 5.25, a.** The front suspension spring

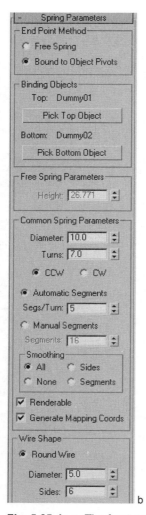

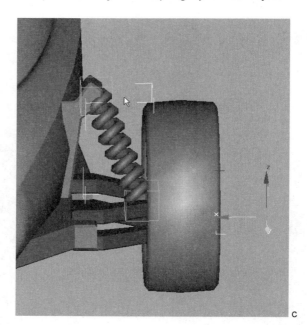

**NOTE**   Dummy objects are fictitious objects that aren't subject to rendering. For example, they're needed as helpers in the hierarchical chains. You can also use any other objects of this class (for example, the point object which, in 3ds max 4, has changed so drastically that one can hardly call it "a point" any more).

❏ Rename these objects to Mobil_Dummy1 and Mobil_Dummy2.

❏ Now create the spring in any point of the viewport:

Tab panel → Objects → Spring Dynamics Object

**Fig. 5.25, b, c.** The front suspension spring

Set the spring type option (End Point Method) to the **Bound to Object Pivot** option. Select Mobil_Dummy1 as the first object and Mobil_Dummy2 as the second object.

Now set the spring parameters as shown in fig. 5.25, b.

**NOTE**   There's no need for detailed explanations. However, I would like to mention that the spring and the damper have very interesting properties for imitating dynamics. Unfortunately, because of the limited size of the book, we won't be able to cover this topic. If you're interested, though, I recommend that you find out more about it in the user's manual.

We've finally completed the process of creating the spring (fig. 5.25, c).

Now we need to create the jet engine. It's up to you, now, to select the method used to accomplish this task. The engine shouldn't present any serious problems to those of you who have already created the hull of the jet vehicle. I decided to use the Torus primitive (in the Top viewport) and applied the Edit Mesh modifier to it (fig. 5.26). Then I renamed the newly created object "Mobil_Engine".

The basic geometry of the jet vehicle is ready now. However, we only have the left part of the jet vehicle. All you need to do, though, is to create copies for the right part of the vehicle.

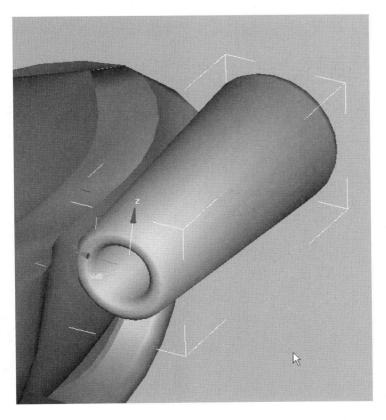

**Fig. 5.26.** The jet engine

❑ Go to the **Top** viewport, select all the objects that need to be copied, and mirror them using the copy method.

Notice that the copy of the spring isn't bound to any object. Thus, you need to select it and bind it to the appropriate objects.

The result of this operation is shown in fig. 5.27.

As you can see in the illustration, the vehicle's wing is in the stern. Even though I didn't describe it, you should, by now, already know the procedures you'll need to follow in order to create the wing. I'll briefly explain what I've done.

First, I converted one of the engines to Editable Mesh and attached another engine to it. Then, I edited the polygons using the Bevel and Extrude modifiers. Next, I collapsed the appropriate vertices and finally applied the MeshSmooth modifier to that part of the object.

The results of all these transformations is shown in the Mobil_02.max file, which can be found in the \Lessons\Lesson05\Scenes directory on the companion CD.

**Fig. 5.27.** The jet vehicle

**NOTE** Why is the wing necessary? The main idea is that the stern part of the jet vehicle is far from perfect. The wing (or any other object) will help distract the viewer's attention. This may seem strange but, in most cases, it works. Of course, you may not agree. My reasons, however, are fairly easy to understand. Suppose, for example, that you're watching a movie full of computer graphics. Do you notice little details like how minor objects are textured? Most people don't. All your attention is drawn to the central character or object. Of course, if you're watching the movie carefully or have seen it several times, then you'll start to notice that something's wrong. Most of the time, however, it takes an experienced person to detect these things. Until someone qualified explains to them, people usually aren't aware of just when and how they were fooled.

Let's return to our stern wing, and I'll explain the important task it performs. In our example, its shadow shades the hull in such a way that it hides the stern part of the hull, eliminating the details.

Sometimes, there may be even comical aspects. For example, in one blockbuster film, there's a colonel, dressed in an appropriate uniform (in fact, it's so appropriate that when you're viewing the film for the first time, you only have a vague feeling that something's wrong). What actually is wrong is that the character's badges of rank are attached upside down! So, remember this when you try to produce something realistic.

Fortunately, our Martian Rally is supposed to take place in the remote future (and in abstract space), so we don't have to bother with minor details.

# Creating the Materials for the Jet Vehicle

You'll need the following basic materials: red metal for the hull, a surface covered with dust for the lower part of the hull, dark plastic for the cockpit, chrome for the wheel disks, rubber for the tires, and dark metal for the chassis and suspension details. Using these basic materials, you'll also create the other materials needed for this scene at a later time.

## Red Metal

❏ Press the <M> key to open the material editor. Select any sample slot.

❏ Rename the selected material to M_RedMetal.

> *TIP*   Use meaningful names to simplify material navigation in the subsequent stages of modeling where you need to assemble all the objects in a single project.

❏ Select the Multi-Layer shading type. This type of shading will allow you to create surfaces with additional coating such as painted metal. In our movie, we'll use this type of material to imitate red metal covered with a layer of dust.

❏ Specify the basic settings as shown in fig. 5.28, a.

> *TIP*   For the diffuse color, select dark red.

Set the color of the first specular layer to light rose, and the color of the second specular layer to light yellow.

The anisotropic parameters for the glossy layer should be set in such a way to produce a patch of light, stretched along the horizontal axis.

To make the material look more stunning, apply the Noise map (fig. 5.28, b) to the patch of light on the second layer. Decrease the intensity by setting the **Specular Color 2** value in the **Maps** rollout to 70.

Normally, polished metals reflect their surrounding objects. Our material also needs this property. 3ds max 4 provides several methods for creating realistic reflections. However, all these methods have one common drawback: they're resource-consuming and require additional time for final rendering. Let's do a trick, that is apply the Environment map stored in the Land.max file to the M_RedMetal material.

❏ Select a sample slot and load the Environment map from the Land.max file into it:

    Material editor → **Get Material** button

    Material/Map Browser → **Browse From: Mtl Library** rollout

    Click the **Open** button in the **File** rollout , select the *.max file type, and load the materials

    Select the Sky map from the list

    Drag this map to the reflection map channel and rename it to M_Sky

❏ Set the **Amount** value for this map to 25.

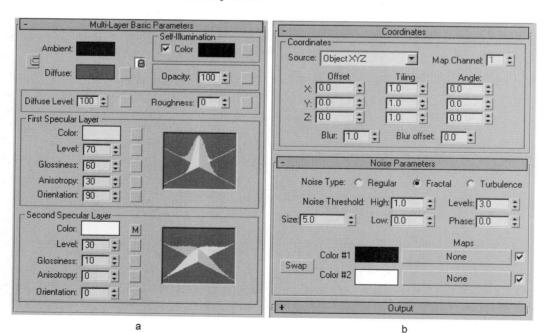

a                                     b

**Fig. 5.28.** Basic parameters of the M_RedMetal material and the map applied to the patch of light at the second layer

To make the map reflection more realistic, go to the **Reflection Dimming** group in the **Extended Parameters** rollout and set the **Apply** checkbox. Experiment with other parameters to produce a better result.

> *TIP* The **Dim Level** and **Refl Level** parameters specify reflection factors for the dark and illuminated parts of the object. This method is not optimal, however. Using a map of type Falloff would be more proper. You may do it if you wish.

## Dark Plastic

❑ For this material, select the Anisotropic shading type. Specify other parameters as shown in fig. 5.29.

❑ Rename this material to M_Plastic.

> *TIP* Make the diffuse color very dark, almost black and a bit blue. Use M_Sky as a reflection map. Set the parameters at will.

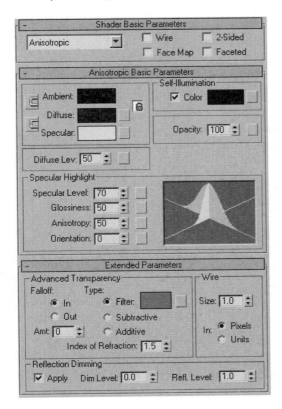

**Fig. 5.29.** Basic parameters of the M_Plastic material

# Creating Combined Materials for the Hull

You'll remember that when we started editing the hull, we specified the **Material ID** parameters for each surface of the jet vehicle. And you've probably guessed that we'll use the Multi/Sub-Object material. However, this isn't all. For the cockpit, we'll need the Blend material, produced by blending the materials with the mask for creating the racks. For the lower part of the hull, we'll need to produce a smooth transition from the dust-covered to the glossy material in the upper part. This effect can be achieved using the Blend type of material. However, for a change we'll use the Top/Bottom material for this purpose.

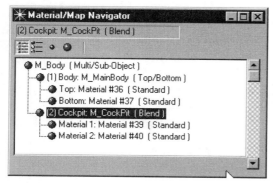

❏ Select any unoccupied sample slot in material editor and create a structure similar to that shown in fig. 5.30. Notice the naming convention used for naming materials and submaterials.

❏ Assign the M_Body material to the hull of our jet vehicle.

**Fig. 5.30.** Structure of the material used for the hull

❏ Go to the M_MainBody (Top/Bottom) material. Make the M_RedMetal material the upper submaterial by dragging it from the sample slot with the help of the Instance method.

❏ Go to the material parameters and set the **Local** option in the **Coordinates** group. Thus, you'll specify material orientation in relation to the object's coordinate system.

❏ Perform test rendering.

The result you get probably won't be what you expected. Instead of a Top/Bottom transition, you may get a Left/Right or even a Front/Back transition. This is because the local coordinates normally don't match the World coordinate system. In other words, the upper part of your object may be anywhere.

Let's match the local coordinate system to the World coordinate system.

❏ Apply the **Reset Xform** procedure to the Mobil_Body object:

Control panel → Utilities → Reset XForm

❏ Switch to the editing mode. You'll see the Xform modifier in the object's modifier stack.

❏ Convert your object to NURBS:

Right-click menu → Convert To: → Convert to NURBS

Perform test rendering. Now everything's all right. We'll proceed with editing the materials.

❏ Set the **Blend** and **Position** parameters to 5 and 35, respectively. This will produce a smooth transition in the lower part of the hull.

❏ For the lower part, create a new standard material with any type of shading. For example, you can use normal Blinn or Strauss type. Make this material suffused, specify a yellowish color, and apply the Noise map as a Bump texture. The relief level should be low. Finally, don't forget to rename this material in the same manner as the others in this project were.

*Self-study*   Don't be afraid to experiment! You'll probably consider the Top/Bottom material interesting. If so, try using the Blend material and experiment with various map types and parameters. After all, the material selection is up to you. The only thing you always need to remember is that the more complex the materials and maps are, the more time will be required for final rendering.

Now let's proceed with the most interesting part of our task.

❏ Start editing the M_CockPit material.

❏ For the first submaterial, select the M_Plastic material. Drag it from the sample slot, using the Instance method.

❏ For the second submaterial, select the M_RedMetal material. Drag it from the sample, slot using the Copy method.

*NOTE*   Notice that, in this case, you need to use the Copy method! You're going to modify the parameters of this material, and because of this there shouldn't be a relation to the source material!

❏ For the mask, select the mobil__pit_mask.tif file, which you can find on the companion CD in the \Lessons\Lesson05\Maps directory.

❏ Enable map display in the viewport.

Notice that you can't view the map in the viewport because you haven't specified the mapping coordinates.

❏ Select the Mobil_Body object and start the editing surfaces:

Right-click menu → Surface Level

❏ Select the cockpit surface and set the **Generate Mapping Coordinates** checkbox in the Material properties:

Control panel → ... → **Materials Properties** rollout

Now the map will be displayed in the viewport.

Most probably, the texture mapping will be wrong. The square of the front side should be greater than that of the rear. You can correct this by changing the **Tiling** parameter in the control panel or in the map parameters in the material editor. Set this value to "–1" along the V coordinate. By doing this, you're modifying the coordinates for all of the maps that will be applied to this channel.

If you're satisfied with the look of the map, leave it as it is. Otherwise, change it to meet your needs. Go to the control panel and set the **User Defined** option in the **Texture Surface** group. Two gray buttons will become available, allowing you to correct the mapping coordinates.

*Self-study* In my opinion, it isn't necessary to describe this process in detail since it is quite similar to editing the coordinates of UVW unwrap. By now, you should be able to accomplish the task yourself.

Now edit the second submaterial of the M_CockPit material.

❐ Add the mobil_pit_bmp.tif file to the Bump channel. You can find this file on the companion CD in the \Lessons\Lesson05\Maps directory.

Because this map is applied to the same channel as the mobil_pit_mask.tif map, you need to be sure that the rivets created by applying this texture are placed appropriately.

❐ Set the **Amount** parameter to 30.

## Other Materials

I think, by now, you're experienced enough to create the other materials for this scene. I'll just provide some brief comments and notes for you.

Create the wheels using the Multi/Sub-Object material. For the tires, select a matted material. For the tread, you can use the Bump map from the mobil_protector.tif file. Apply this map as shown in fig. 5.31.

*NOTE* Assign mapping coordinates when you create the tires and disks. You can do this by selecting the tire element and applying the UVW Map modifier.

For the Diffuse map, use the Noise texture with a large element size. This allows you to imitate dirty tires. Also, you can add the Noise map with small elements to the Bump channel, and combine the noise with the tread using the Mix texture. If necessary, increase the influence of the mobil_protector.tif texture by increasing the **Bump Amount** value in the **Output** rollout.

For the disks, use an Anisotropic type lustrous light material. Use the mobil_wheel.tif file as a texture for the Bump channel by mapping it to the disk and disabling the tiling along all of the coordinates.

To complete this task, select the disk element and apply the UVW Map modifier. Next, edit the coordinates:

Right-click menu → Sub-objects → Elements

As a texture for reflection, select any file (for example, the Mud0001.tga file from the companion CD). Select the mapping parameters. Don't forget to edit the other parameters, such as **Reflection Dimming** and **Amount**, as well.

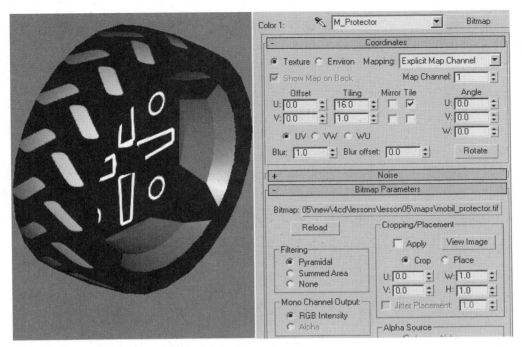

**Fig. 5.31.** Tread map applied to the wheel

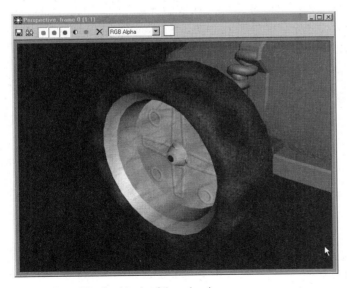

**Fig. 5.32, a.** The final look of the wheel

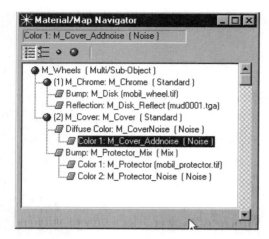

The final look of the wheel is shown in fig. 5.32, a. To view the example on-screen, open the \Lessons\Lesson05\images\Wheel01.tif file on the companion CD. Fig. 5.32, b illustrates the structure of the wheel material.

Assign the M_Wheels material to the front right and driven wheels. You'll probably need to edit the mapping coordinates of the wheel disks. You can copy the UVW map modifier applied to the left wheel and drag it to the modifier stacks of the other wheels. Also, you'll need to apply the Mesh Select modifier and select the disks. Don't forget that the rear wheel has two visible disks.

**Fig. 5.32, b.** Structure of the wheel material (b)

For the chassis and suspension levers, create a compound Blend material with the gradient transition mask.

For the upper material, you can select M_RedMetal. For the lower material, use the material of the lower part of the hull.

To apply the gradient transition map, select all the objects comprising the chassis and suspension, and apply the UVW Map modifier of cylindrical type.

*TIP*    Hide the objects that you aren't working with:

Right-click Menu → Hide Unselected

Apply the M_RedMetal material to the jet engines. For the springs, create a new material like the material used for the wheel disks. Make this material darker and decrease the **Amount** parameter of the reflection map.

The final structure of materials and maps is shown in fig. 5.33.

Now, your jet vehicle looks quite impressive (fig. 5.34 and files mobil01.tif and mobil02.tif on the companion CD)!

Save the project file (for example, name it Mobil.max).

*Self-study*    Try to improve the model you just created, especially the front part of the hull. My results are shown in the Mobil_03.max file, which you can find on the companion CD (\Lessons\Lesson05\Scenes).

Finally, we need to complete one of the most important transformations of the Mobil_Body object.

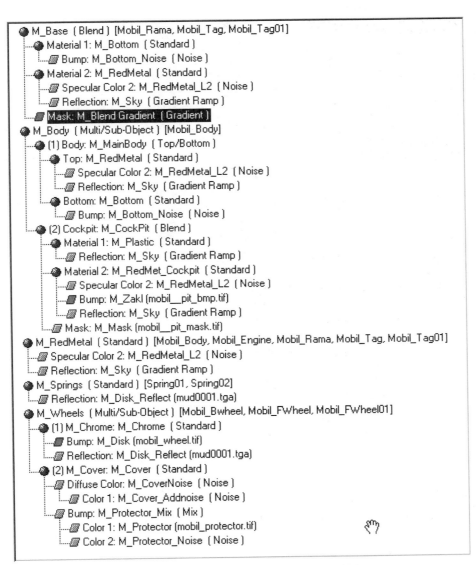

**Fig. 5.33.** Final structure of all materials and textures of the jet vehicle

This object contains several elements that may create some problems for you later on. When I mention this, I'm talking about the dependent surfaces. To avoid these problems, select all the surfaces and make them independent:

    Control panel → ... → **Make Independent** button

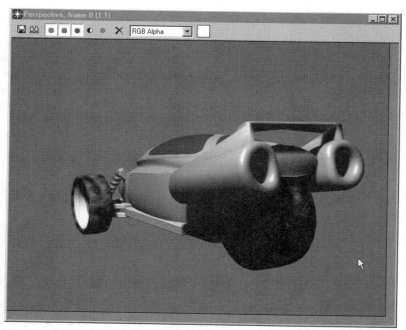

**Fig. 5.34.** Jet vehicle with applied materials

# Creating Hierarchical Links

The details of your jet vehicle will be animated. During animation, they should behave as follows.

First of all, the wheels should rotate around the axles. Furthermore, the driving wheels must turn in the direction of movement. Finally, both the wheels and the suspension elements must move in response to the landscape relief.

Because of this, you can't assemble all the parts into the whole object. Rather, you'll need to create and tune hierarchical links between these objects.

Before starting to link the objects, transform them to the basic type (NURBS, Editable Mesh) and reset the transformation matrices for all of the objects.

❑ Select one object at a time and convert it to NURBS, Editable Mesh. Notice that this doesn't relate to the dummy objects and springs:

Right-click menu → Convert To:

*TIP* You can speed up this process by selecting several objects of the same basic type and converting them.

❑ Select objects sequentially and reset the transformation matrices:

> Control panel → Utilities → Reset XForm

This operation will probably produce some undesirable effects. For example, when I was preparing this lesson, I noticed flipped normals of the objects created by mirroring with the Copy method. In this lesson, I won't provide a detailed description of the reasons that this effect was produced. However, I will note that you should use the XForm modifier and perform all transformations over its gizmo.

❑ Once again, reconvert the objects to the basic type and edit the flipped object by selecting all the polygons and flipping the normals:

> Control panel → **Surface Properties** rollout → Normals → Flip

Now link the objects. Object linking is applied from child to parent. To link tow objects, click the **Select and Link** button in the **Main Toolbar**.

The linking sequence is as follows:

> Mobil_Fwheel → Mobil_Tag, Mobil_Tag → Mobil_Rama
>
> Mobil_Fwheel01 → Mobil_Tag01, Mobil_Tag01 → Mobil_Rama
>
> Mobil Dummy2 → Mobil_Tag, Mobil Dummy1 → Mobil_Rama
>
> Mobil Dummy04 → Mobil_Tag, Mobil Dummy03 → Mobil_Rama
>
> Mobil Engine → Mobil_Body, Mobil_Body → Mobil_Rama
>
> Mobil_Bwheel → Mobil_Body

The links created using this sequence are shown in fig. 5.35.

> **NOTE**  You'll probably prefer to perform this operation in the Schematic View.

Now the chassis is the main "parent" object.

Try to select the chassis and move it. You'll notice that all the objects follow the chassis. Now select and move the hull. As you can see, all the objects, except for the engines, remained where they were.

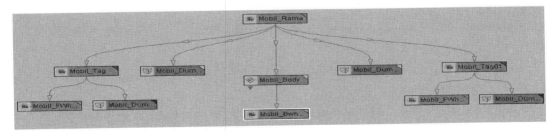

**Fig. 5.35.** Structure of links in the **Schematic View** window

Now it's time to adjust the pivot points for all of the objects.

❑ Select all of the objects.

❑ Go to the **Pivot** rollout:

Control panel → Hierarchy → Pivot

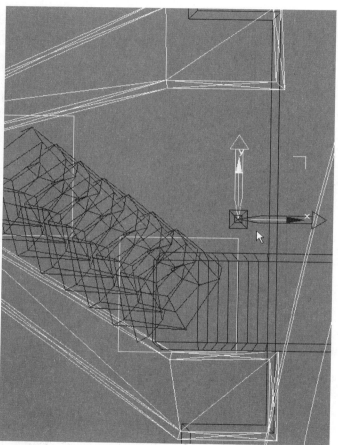

**Fig. 5.36.** Adjusting the pivot point of the suspension levers

❑ Move the pivot points to the centers of the objects and adjust them in relation to the World coordinates:

Control panel → Hierarchy → Pivot → click the **Affect Pivot Only** button

Click the **Center to Object** and **Align to World** buttons

Now it's necessary to adjust the suspension lever pivot points.

❑ Select the Mobil_Tag object and move its pivot point, as shown in fig. 5.36. This is necessary to make the suspension work correctly during subsequent animation.

❑ Perform the same operation over the Mobil_Tag01 object.

Thus, everything's prepared for the animation. Save the project under the Mobil.max name.

# Creating the Basic Animation
# of the Jet Vehicle

First, we need to imitate the suspension work. This can be done in the Mobil.max project.

❑ Make sure that the animation settings specified are the same as in the Land.max project (fig. 5.1). If they aren't, correct them now:

Time Control → Time Configurations

❑ Select the Mobil_Bwheel object.

❑ Open the animation track of the object:

Right-click menu → TrackView Selected

Now you'll start the most important function of 3ds max 4 — the Track View.

❑ Open the controller tree for the Mobil_Bwheel object by clicking the <+> key (fig. 5.37, a).

❑ Replace the current Position controller by the Position XYZ controller:

TrackView → **Assign Controller** button

❑ Select the Position XYZ controller and click **OK**.

Now you just have another controller subtree. Expand it and select the Noise Float controller for the movements along the Z-axis.

> *TIP* By coordinates, I mean the local coordinates of each object. To avoid confusion, adjust the viewport options to display the local coordinates.
>
> Main ToolBar → **Reference Coordinate System** drop-down list → select the **Local** option

❑ Right-click the controller name (fig. 5.37, b), select the **Properties** command, and specify the parameters as shown in fig. 5.37, c.

> *TIP* The **>0** checkbox specifies that only the positive part of the curve is used. Set this checkbox so the wheels won't sink into the ground.

Now it's necessary to assign a controller of this type to the rotation of the Mobil_Tag and Mobil_Tag01 objects (suspension levers of the left and right wheels) around the axis.

***NOTE*** This is correct, since the front wheels are fastened to the front suspension.

❑ Select the Mobil_Tag object, expand the controller tree and replace the Rotation controller to the Euler XYZ (fig. 5.37, d).

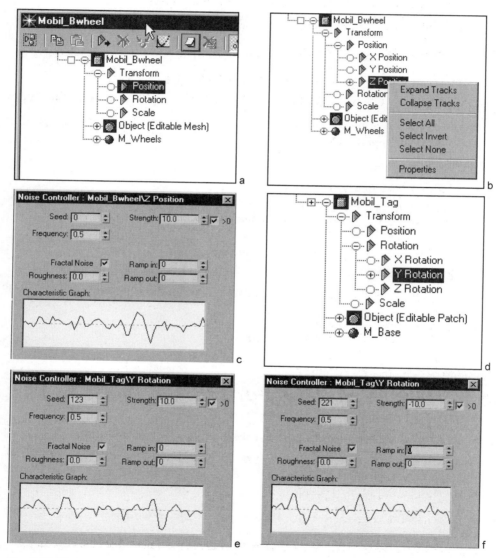

**Fig. 5.37.** The sequence of assigning Noise controllers to the back wheel and suspension levers

❑ Select the Noise Float controller as a controller for rotation about the Y-axis.

❑ Specify the settings as shown in fig. 5.37, e.

> **NOTE**  Specify the **Seed** parameter (initial value for the randomizer) to a nonzero value, since the vibration phase must be different from that of the back wheel.

❑ Copy the parameters of this controller for future use:

   TrackView → **Copy Controller** button ▣

❑ Proceed in a similar way to adjust controllers for the Mobil_Tag01 object.

❑ For rotation about the Y axis, assign the copied Noise Float controller using the Copy method:

   TrackView → **Paste Controller** button ▣

   Select the Copy method

❑ Specify the parameters as shown in fig. 5.37, f.

> **TIP**  Set the **Strength** setting to a negative value. This will mirror the coordinates of the object in the **Top** viewport.

Now play back the animation in the viewport. Notice that the springs follow the movements of the suspension levers. It looks great!

Thus, the basic animation for the jet vehicle is complete. Now it's time to start more complicated tasks.

Save this project under the name "Mobil_animated.max".

# Animating the Movement
# of the Jet Vehicle over the Surface

To animate the movement of the jet vehicle over the surface we don't actually need the vehicle itself. We're going to animate a fictional object that will represent our jet vehicle.

❑ Open the Land.max file. If you have not set the time parameters, do this right away (see fig. 5.1).

❑ Go to the **Top** viewport by pressing the <T> button.

❑ Create a box of the following size: 4×2×1.5 meters.

> **TIP** It would be convenient to create the objects by entering the values from the keyboard.

❏ Move the box to the intended starting point of the path and place it above the landscape surface making it visible in the viewport on the landscape background. Select the Smooth +Highlights rendering type:

❏ Go to the last frame.

❏ Switch to the animation mode (by pressing the <N> key).

❏ Move the Box01 object along the Y-axis to its final position.

A brief explanation is needed here. The object has to move skirting the obstacles. You can achieve this by simply drawing the path along which the object moves. However, using Motion Capture is a more interesting method.

❏ Resize the viewport display to view both the starting and final points of the object's path.

❏ Select the Box01 object and start editing the animation:

Control panel → Motion

❏ Open the **Assign Controller** rollout and select the **Position: Bezier Position** option.

❏ Change the controller type to Position XYZ:

Control panel → Motion → **Assign Controller** rollout → **Assign Controller** button

Select the Position XYZ controller and click **OK**.

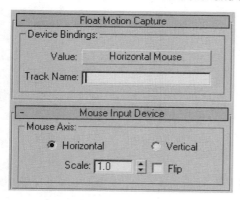

Now you can assign the Motion Capture controller to the motion along the X-axis.

❏ Select the X Position controller from the **Position** list and change its type to Float Motion Capture.

❏ In the parameters window, bind the motion along the X-axis to the mouse motion along the horizontal axis (fig. 5.38).

**Fig. 5.38.** Parameters of the Motion Capture controller

Now we need to record the animation.

❏ Go to the **Utilities** rollout and click the **Motion Capture** button.

❏ Set the capture parameters as shown in fig. 5.39.

    ***TIP***    Activate the **Box01\X Position** track.

Specify the **Out** parameter in the **Record Range** rollout to a value equal to the ordinal number of the last frame.

◄ **Fig. 5.39.** Parameters of the motion capture

You will be able to get a little training if you click the **Test** button.

> **TIP**  It's necessary to record the animation evenly, without omitting any frames. Your computer performance probably isn't sufficient for recording real-time animation. You can decrease the speed (the **Speed** parameter), for example, as shown in fig. 5.40.

❑ Record the motion by pressing the **Start** button. You'll probably need to repeat this operation several times.

◄ **Fig. 5.40.** Decreasing the playback speed

Now let's convert the object's path to the curve. Why do we need this? The point is that making an object move over a polygonal surface is not a simple task. In 3ds max 4, there is a controller which lets an object move over the surface of another one, yet the object has to be a NURBS. So we are going to build a NURBS track for the jet vehicle to move along.

❑ Start editing the animation and switch to the path editing mode:

Control panel → Motion → **Trajectories** button

In the viewport, you'll see the path the object moves along.

❑ Specify the parameters for converting the trajectory to spline (fig. 5.41). To convert the trajectory into a curve, click the **Convert To** button in the **Spline Conversion** rollout.

> **TIP**  The larger the **Samples** value is, the more precise the shape of the trajectory will be.

❑ Make an outline for your spline so that the path is slightly wider than the front wheels' gage.

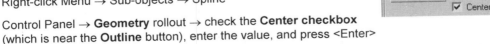

Right-click Menu → Sub-objects → Spline

Control Panel → **Geometry** rollout → check the **Center checkbox** (which is near the **Outline** button), enter the value, and press <Enter>

Now we need to image the curve on the surface of the Land object.

❏ Select the Land object.

❏ Create the curve projection object (ShapeMerge) based on the Land object:

Control panel → Compounds→ ShapeMerge  Compound Object

❏ Click the **Pick Shape** button and select the curve obtained as a result of trajectory conversion (in my example, this curve is called Shape01).

❏ Specify the settings as shown in fig. 5.42. Be sure to use Copy or Instance!

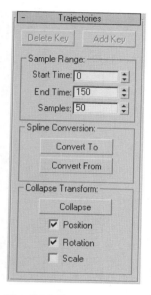

**Fig. 5.41.** Conversion parameters used to convert the motion trajectory to curve

**Fig. 5.42.** Parameters of projection of the curve to the landscape's surface

*TIP* The **Cookie Cutter** radio button and the set checkbox **Invert** in the **Operations** rollout indicate that a tape having the shape of the curve will be cut out.The **Edge** radio button in the **Output Sub-Mesh Selection** rollout specifies that the edges will be selected for subsequent conversion.

❏ Switch to the editing mode and apply the Edit Mesh modifier to the object:

<Ctrl>+Right-click menu → Modifiers

❏ Start editing the edges:

Right-click menu → Sub-objects → Edge

You'll notice that the edges resulting from projecting the spline to the surface were selected.

❑ Convert the selected edges to curve:

Control panel → ... → **Edit Geometry** rollout → **Create Shape from Edges** button

❑ Set the parameters as shown in fig 5.43. Enter the "Path" name and click **OK**.

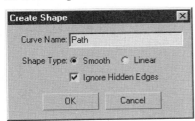

Now you may delete the Land object, because it's no longer needed. However, change the name of the initial curve Shape01 to Steps and then hide it, — you are going to use it later.

**Fig 5.43.** The parameters for converting edges into a curve

❑ In the Path object, delete the butt-end segments to get two parallel splines.

Right-click menu → Sub-objects → Segment

❑ Convert your curve to NURBS.

Right-click menu → Convert To: → Convert to NURBS

**_NOTE_** This might take a long time.

Before creating a surface you should simplify the curves.

❑ Select either curve.

Right-click menu → Sub-objects → Curve

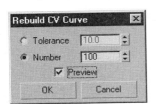

❑ Set the number of controlling curves to 100 (fig. 5.44).

Control Panel → ... → **CV Curve** rollout → **Rebuild** button

**Fig. 5.44.** The **Rebuild CV Curve** window

❑ Repeat the same procedure with the other curve.

❑ Create a U-Loft type surface.

NURBS Toolbox → Create U-Loft Surface

Now adjust Box01's motion along the Path surface.

❑ Select the Box01 object and start editing the animation:

Control panel → Motion

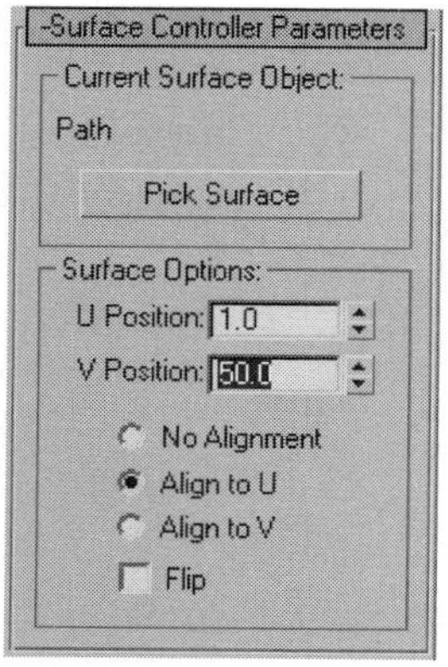

❏ Open the **Assign Controller** rollout and select the **Position** string.

❏ Change the controller type to Path (motion along the path):

Control panel → Motion → **Assign Controller** rollout → **Assign Controller** button

❏ Select the Surface controller and click **OK**.

❏ Specify the settings as shown in fig. 5.45.

**Fig. 5.45.** Parameters of the controller for motion along the surface

*TIP*   Click the **Pick Surface** button and select the Path surface as a path.

Set **Align to U** and then set the value of **V Position** to 50, so that the object moves along the central line of the track, responding to folds of the surface.

Animate the movement of the box along the U-coordinate.

❏ Go to the first frame and set **U Position** to 1.

❏ Go to the last frame, click the **Animate** button, and set **U Position** to 99.

❏ Run animation and watch the box moving along the path.

❏ Save the project in the Land Path.max file.

It is time now to animate the jet vehicle.

❏ Now load the jet vehicle from the Mobil_animated.max file:

Main menu → File → Merge

❏ Select all the objects and click **OK**.

Before animating the movement of the jet vehicle along the surface, model the rotation of the wheels. Use the Expression controller to do this.

❏ Select the back wheel and go to the **Track View** window:

Right-click menu → TrackView Selected

❏ Replace the Rotation controller to Euler XYZ.

❏ Select the Float Expression controller as a controller for rotation about the X-axis. The **Create Variables** window will open (fig. 5.46). From this point on, you will be able to edit its parameters by right-clicking the controller and selecting the **Properties** command.

**Fig. 5.46.** The **Create Variables** window

❑ Create the scalar variable and name it SurfacePos, for example:

Enter the name into the **Name**: field and click the **Create** button

❑ Link the variable value to the position of the Box01 object at the path:

Select the **SurfacePos** variable and click the **Assign to Controller** button

Select the controller from the Objects\Box01\TRANSFORM\Position:Surface\U:Besier  Float branch in the list.

**NOTE**   Notice that most controllers are grayed. They're unavailable because of the variable type mismatch.

❑ Enter the variable name into the **Expression** field, click the **Evaluate** button and try to play back the animation in the viewport.

You'll see that the wheel rotates very slowly and in the wrong direction. You probably already know what caused this problem. The value of the variable changes from 0 to 100, and because of this the wheel rotates at a 100° angle maximum.

You can correct this situation by adding a factor to the expression (77, for example) and changing the sign.

**NOTE**   Of course, you can specify the correct expression based on the wheel diameter.I In our case, however, we don't need to be so precise.

❑ Select all three wheels and open the **Track View** window.

Right-click menu → Track View Selected

❑ Copy the Rotation controllers of the Mobil_Bwheel by clicking the **Copy Controller** button.

Replace the rotation controllers for all the wheels by selecting the corresponding tracks and clicking the **Paste** button.

As I mentioned earlier, there's no need to specify a precise expression. The wheels rotate fast. To emphasize this fact, apply Motion Blur to them:

Right-click menu → Properties → General tab

❑ Set the **Enabled** checkbox and select the **Image** radio button in the **Motion Blur**.

If you perform test rendering in any frame, you'll see that each wheel is blurred and looks like a solid circle. It's impossible to identify the rate of their rotation. The only important thing is that they rotate very fast!

Now let's make our jet vehicle move.

❑ Go to the **Top** viewport and then go to frame 0.

❑ Select zoom to make the Box01 object visible.

❑ Select the Mobil_Rama object using the select by name method (the \<H\> key).

❑ Align the position and orientation of the Mobil_Rama object in relation to the Box01 object:

Main Toolbar → **Align** button

❑ Select the Box01 object and specify the parameters as shown in fig. 5.47.

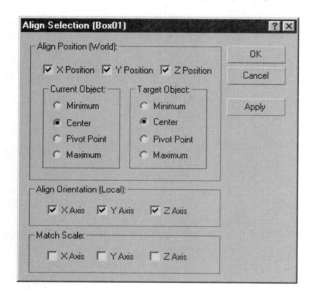

**Fig. 5.47.** Alignment parameters

❑ Link the Mobil_Rama object to the Box01 object:

Main Toolbar → **Select and Link** button

❑ By modifying the viewport view and moving the Mobil_Rama object along the local vertical axis and rotating it about the same axis make the wheels touch the lower face of the box (fig. 5.48).

❑ Select and hide the Box01 object:

Right-click menu → Hide Selected

Now the jet vehicle is moving along the path.

We're a little off. The speed of the jet vehicle is too high. To correct this situation, it's necessary to edit the time scale by stretching it to make it approximately three times longer. Go to the time controls and click the **Rescale Time** button.

Enter the values of 0 and 450 for the starting and final frames of the animation. Click **OK**.

Don't worry if all your controllers lose their settings. 3ds max 4 will automatically recalculate the parameters with one exception — it won't recalculate factors in expressions. If you wish, you can correct these factors. However, there's no need to do it.

**Fig. 5.48.** Initial position of the jet vehicle when moving over the surface

**NOTE**    Obviously, before assembling the whole scene, you'll need to perform a similar action in the Land.max project.

Now the length of our movie is tripled. What can we do about it? That's easy — you can calculate only part of the animation when performing the final rendering.

❑ Create a camera (fig. 5.49, a) that will fly around the jet vehicle in the course of its movement:

Tab panel → Light & Cameras → Targeted Camera

❑ Rename this camera "Mobil_Cam".

❑ Align the camera's target in relation to the center of the Mobil_Body object by all coordinates. Then link the camera to this center.

❑ Go to the **Top** viewport and create a circle, as shown in fig. 5.49, b.

❑ Rename the circle "M_Cam_Path". As you know, this circle will serve as a path for the camera.

❑ Center this circle by all coordinates with the Mobil_Body object and then link it to the object.

❑ Go to the **Left** viewport and move the circle along the vertical axis. Position the circle slightly above the jet vehicle (fig. 5.49, c).

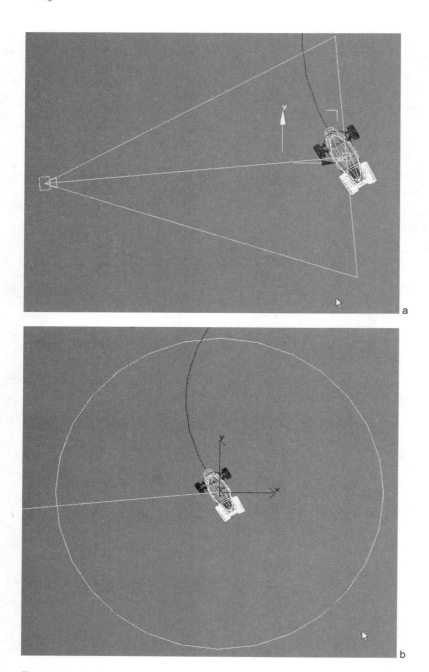

**Fig. 5.49, a, b.** Creating and animating the camera

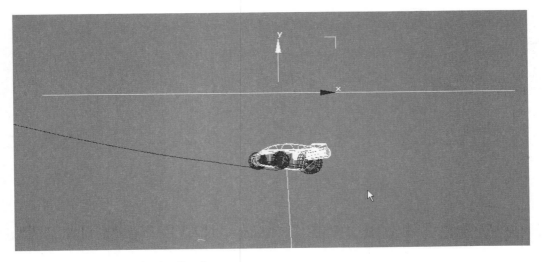

**Fig. 5.49, c.** Creating and animating the camera

Now it's necessary to adjust the link between the path and the object to create the illusion of the camera following the jet vehicle " from a helicopter".

❏ Select the M_Cam_Path object and start editing the linking parameters.

Control panel → Hierarchy → **LinkInfo** rollout

❏ Clear the **X**, **Y**, and **Z** checkboxes in the **Rotate** group of the **Inherit** rollout to disable inheritance of rotation about all the axes.

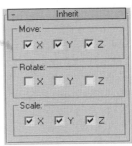

*Warning* All modifications for the links should be done in one predefined frame (frame 0 is the preferable place for this operation). Otherwise, the results may be unpredictable.

❏ Select the camera and assign the path controller to it:

Control panel → Motion → **Assign Controller** rollout

Select the Path controller

Specify the M_Cam_Path circle as a path

❏ Toggle to the animation recording mode by pressing the <N> key. Go to frame 0 and set the **% Along Path** value to 80, then go to the last frame and set this value to 30.

# Animating Steering of the Front Wheels

Our jet vehicle looks wonderful! However, it is missing steering for the front wheels. Let's correct the situation. I spent a great deal of time thinking over the problem of how to animate the wheels without using MAXScript language. Finally, I found a solution.

At first, this solution seems very simple. We have to create a dummy object, which will move along the surface, leaving the jet vehicle slightly behind. Now let's assign the Look At Constraint controller to the wheels and select the dummy object as a control object. That's all there is to it! However, this task isn't that simple. First of all, we'll lose the capability of rotating the wheels. Secondly, the toe-in will be too large.

As it turned out, though, these problems weren't very hard to solve. To avoid them, you'll need to use two controlling dummy objects instead of one. They will move over the surface along the gage of the front wheels. Besides which, it's necessary to create two additional dummy objects placed in the center of the wheels. Assign the Look At controller to these objects. For the control objects, select the appropriate objects moving along the way. Link the wheels to each of them and link the objects to the suspension levers.

❏ Create two dummy objects (M_ Surf _Dummy_Left and M_ Surf _Dummy_Right)

> Tab panel → Helpers → Dummy

In the animation tracks editing mode, copy the path of the controllers of the Box01 object and assign it to the corresponding paths of the objects M_Surf_Dummy_Left and M_Surf_Dummy_Right by using copying.

❏ Adjust the **U Position** and **V Position** parameters in such a way that the objects run ahead of the corresponding wheels.

❏ Create two more dummy objects and name them M_LW_Dummy and M_RW_Dummy.

❏ Align these objects with the center of the left and right wheels by all coordinates (fig. 5.50):

> Tab panel → Main ToolBar → **Align** button

Now it's necessary to position these objects between the wheels and chassis levers.

❏ Link the objects as shown below:

> Mobil_FWheel → M_LW_Dummy, M_LW_Dummy → Mobil_Tag

> Mobil_Fwheel01 → M_RW_Dummy, M_RW_Dummy → Mobil_Tag01

❏ Select the Look At controller as a controller for the M_LW_Dummy and M_RW_Dummy objects, and then select the M_Path_Dummy_Left control object:

> Control panel → Motion → ... → **Assign Controller** rollout

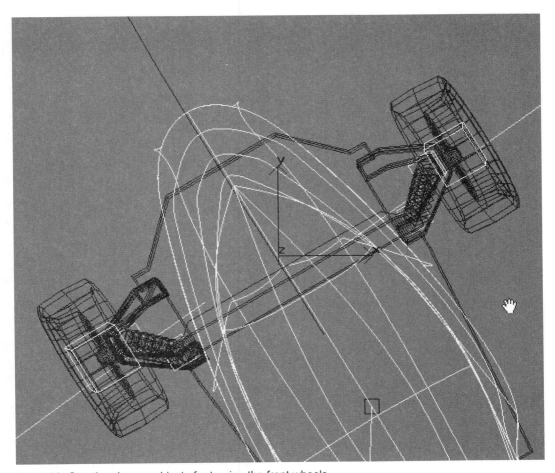

**Fig. 5.50.** Creating dummy objects for turning the front wheels

❏ Select the **Rotation: Look At Constraint** item and reassign the controller:

   Click the **Add LookAt Target** button and select the M_Path_Dummy_Left object

❏ Perform the same operation for the M_RW_Dummy object.

That's all. Now the wheels are steering, while each is following its own object.

❏ Hide the Box01 and Path objects.

Save the project as Land Path01.max. Beginning with its first version, 3ds max provides numbering of files automatically. Just select **Save As...** in the Main menu and click the "+" button.

# Creating the Tracks of the Jet Vehicle and Dust from the Wheels

It is time now to assemble all the elements.

❑ Open file Land.max.

❑ Change the parameters of the time scale by setting the animation length to 450 frames.

❑ Load all the objects from the Land Path01.max file.

   Main menu → Merge...

❑ Now unhide the previously hidden object Steps.

   Control Panel → Display → **Hide** rollout → Unhide By Name

❑ Delete the butt-end segments to get two parallel splines.

❑ Convert the object to NURBS and create a U-Loft surface. Be sure to set the **Generate Mapping Coordinates** checkbox.

Now you should project this object onto the landscape surface without any type conversions. You can do this with the Conform space warp.

❑ Create the space warp at any spot within the scene.

   Tab Panel → Space Warps → Conform Space Warp

❑ Select Land as a warped object.

❑ For **Standoff Distance** set a small but nonzero value.

❑ Bind the Steps object to the Conform warp.

   Main Toolbar → Bind to Space Warp

❑ Select the Steps object and bind it to the Conform Object01 object.

   *NOTE*  This might take a long time.

As you can see, the tracks are shown on the surface now. Adjust the approximation parameters of the Steps object so that it corresponds to the surface as exactly as possible. However, don't go too far!

   Right-click menu → Sub-objects → Surface

   Control Panel → **Surface Approximation** rollout → **Tessellation** rollout

   *TIP* You may easily control the degree of tessellation by pressing the <Q> key, thus enabling an indicator in the left corner of the viewport.

Create a material for the tracks. It will be based on that in the sand.

❑ Open the Material Editor by pressing the <M> key.

❑ Start editing the Land material. In the event of its absence in the Material Editor, load it using the **Pick Material from Object** option.

❑ Copy the material to any material slot and rename it "Steps".

First, simplify the material.

❑ Start editing the map applied to the Diffuse channel.

❑ Copy the Sand Diffuse map to any material slot.

❑ Move this map to the Diffuse channel of the Steps material.

❑ Disable all other maps by dragging "None" from the buttons of the map channels.

❑ Apply the gradient map with the parameters shown in fig. 5.51.

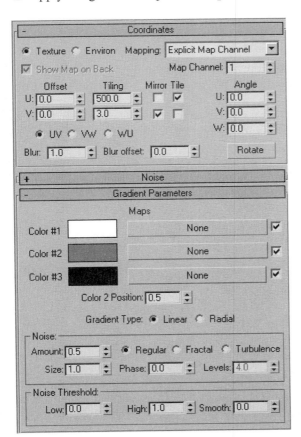

**Fig. 5.51.** The parameters of opacity and smoothness for the Steps material

*TIP* Swap the colors Color #1 and Color #3. To obtain three parallel tracks, set **V Tiling** to Mirror and **Tiling** to 3. Set the **Noise** parameters however you would like to. For **Noise** to look proper, set **U Tiling** to a large enough value. All changes are conveniently controlled in the viewport of the Mobil_Cam camera if you have applied the Steps material to the Steps object.

❏ Copy this map to the Bump channel using the Instance method.

❏ To inverse the map action, set the value of Amount to −20.

| ☑ Bump . . . . . . . . | -20 ⬍ | Map #26 ( Gradient ) |

❏ Animate the process of the tracks emerging. To do this, the map applied to the opacity channel should be converted to the Gradient Ramp type, the Noise map being one of its components.

**Replace Map**

○ Discard old map?

◉ Keep old map as sub-map?

[ OK ]   [ Cancel ]

❏ Set **Solid** interpolation among the parameters of the map.

❏ Set the second color to black and its position to 1 in the starting frame.

All you need now is to animate the position of this parameter.

You might encounter a problem. More precisely, the position of the jet vehicle might not correspond exactly to its track. This is because it moves with variable speed due to the unevenness of the Path surface. You will have to correct the situation by adjusting the position of the front of the Gradient Ramp map. You should use the "interval bisecting" method. Go to intermediate frames, gradually making the intervals smaller.

*NOTE* A map of the Gradient Ramp type has an unpleasant feature. The value of the color position can only be an integer from 1 to 100. To overcome this disadvantage, you can adjust the **Offset** parameter of mapping coordinates instead.

I hope you obtained satisfactory results. Now fulfil the final conversion of the Steps object. Since it is slightly above the surface, make it not cast shadows.

Right-click menu → Properties → **Rendering Controls** rollout → clear the **Cast Shadows** checkbox

Now we'll create the dust rising behind the jet vehicle. You'll accomplish this using the particle system.

*TIP* It would be logical to create the dust using a large number of small particles. Unfortunately, this method isn't the best one in our case. The path of the jet vehicle is very long, and thus will require a large number of particles (tens of thousands). The total number of additional faces won't be very large when using particles of the Face type. However, I wouldn't recommend this method for our example, either.

The main idea of the second method is to use  spherical particles that gradually increase in volume and "dissolve" in the air. To make the spheres look like clouds of dust, use the **Opacity Falloff** parameter in material settings. Polygons directed precisely to the reviewer will be totally opaque in this case, while all the other polygons will vary their opacity depending on the angle of vision. Most 3D software packages (LightWave 3D, for example) provide excellent results when using this method. 3ds max also implements this capability, but, unfortunately, it doesn't produce  the desired results. Borders of the spheres will still remain visible.

The best result can be obtained by using the Falloff map applied to the Opacity channel. This type of map is more flexible than the **Opacity Falloff** parameter. I recommend that you use this method.

Create the SuperSpray system as a source of particles.

❏ Go to the **Top** viewport and create the particle system:

Tab panel → Particles → SuperSpray Particle System

❏ Turn and move the particle source to position it under the left front wheel of the jet vehicle. Place it so that the particles fly out and upwards.

❏ Rename this object "M_Dust".

❏ Set the M_Dust particle parameters as shown in fig. 5.52.

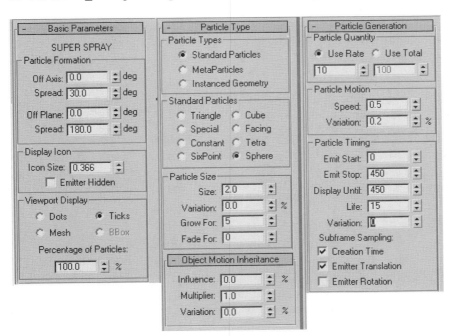

**Fig. 5.52.** Parameters for creation of the dust plume

*TIP*  Set the particle spread in relation to the direction vector to produce a cone.

Set the **Rate** parameter to a small value. This parameter specifies the number of particles emitted in each frame.

Particle velocity should also be set to a small value. Specify a spread in velocity values.

Particles should be emitted and be visible the entire time the jet vehicle is moving along its path. Specify a small value for the lifetime.

The **Subframe Sampling** checkboxes are very important. By setting these checkboxes, you'll achieve time uniformity for the emission of the particles. This is important in our case, because the distance between the particle source in the previous and next frames will be significant.

I've selected a large value (2 meters) for the particle size. Don't be worried, though, because the **Grow** parameters specify that the particles won't achieve this size immediately, but rather three frames later.

Select the **Sphere** option for the particle type.

The **Object Motion Inheritance** parameter is set to zero in order to create a plume of dust.

## *Self-study* Try to apply gravitation and wind to the particles.

❏  Link the M_Dust object to the hull of the jet vehicle.

❏  Copy the particle emitters and place them under each wheel.

Go to any frame and perform test rendering.

The dust is top notch!

Create a material for it.

We'll create material for the dust based on three main principles. First, the opacity must change as a function of the lifetime of the particles. 3ds max 4 implements the Particle Age texture for this purpose. Second, it's necessary to use the Falloff map applied to the opacity channel. Third, it's necessary to create the illusion of dust. We'll need to apply an additional map for this purpose.

❏  Open the material editor and select any unused sample slot.

❏  Specify the basic parameters for this material as shown in fig. 5.53, a.

*TIP*  Make the Ambient, Diffuse, and Specular colors the same, and specify a light yellowish color setting for each of them.

❏  Start editing the Opacity parameters.

❏  Select the procedural map of the Particle Age type.

By default, all parameters are specified in such a way as to make the particles transparent at the beginning of their lifetime (black), and opaque at the end of their life (white). This isn't correct in our case, though, because of the color change.

❏ Rename the map "M_Dust_Age".

Now make the particles transparent near the edges. Use the Falloff map for this purpose.

❏ Select any unused sample slot, and edit the map as shown in fig. 5.53, b:

Material editor → **Get Material** button

Material /Map Browser → Browsing from: New

*TIP* Select white for color 1 and black for color 2.

Set the falloff type to Perpendicular/Parallel, and select the falloff direction relative to the camera (along the Z-axis). Thus, the map will always be correctly oriented towards the viewing direction.

Edit the curve to make the falloff more intense.

❏ Rename the map "M_Dust_Falloff".

❏ Select another unused sample slot and create the fractal Noise structure. Replace the white color of the map to a finer noise (fig. 5.53, c, d).

*TIP* A higher noise level is necessary to hide the spheres and create rippling patterns in the dust clouds. Lower noise levels imitate the dust itself.

❏ Rename the maps "M_Dust_Frac" and "M_Dust_Frac_Low", respectively.

Now let's assemble all the maps.

❏ Switch to the editing mode and start editing the M_Dust_Falloff map. Move the M_Dust_Frac map to the channel of the white map. The copying method isn't important here, because we'll edit these maps later.

❏ Start editing the M_Dust_Age map of the M_Dust material and move the M_Dust_Falloff map to all color channels using the copy method.

❏ Don't modify the maps on the white channel.

❏ For all other channels, go to the lowest map level (fine fractal noise) and change the white color to light gray and dark gray , respectively.

❏ Rename the maps accordingly.

The structure of the M_Dust material will look like what's shown in fig. 5.53, e. As you can see, I moved the whole map structure to the Bump channel.

❏ Go to the parameters of the M_Dust material and set the **Self Illumination** parameter to 80%. This allows you to eliminate the influence of the light sources, which can easily turn your magnificent dust to plain, dull, gray dirt.

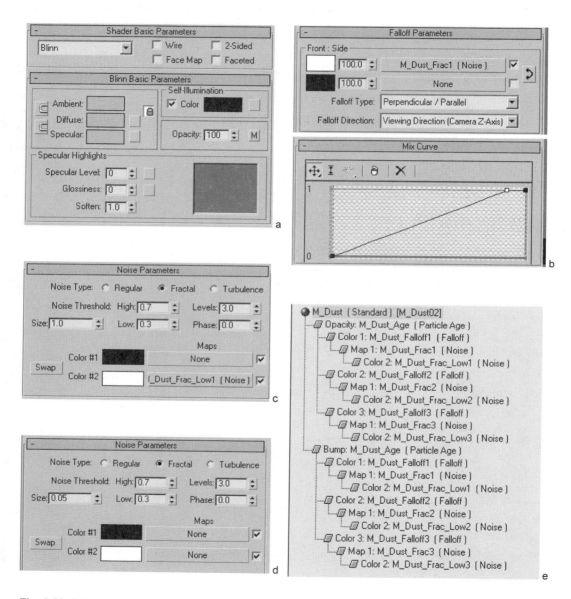

**Fig. 5.53.** Parameters of material and maps for the dust

***TIP***    Why did I set the value of self-illumination to 80%, rather than 100? If you have ever looked at the dust clouds carefully, you'll have noticed that the light influences the dust in the same way that it influences all the other objects. So, to make the dust look realistic, you should allow the light source to influence the look of the dust.

Now everything's ready.

Perform the test rendering to make sure that everything's correct.

☐ Save the project in the file named Mobil_Complete.max.

# Rendering the Whole Scene

## Setting the Light

You'll need at least two light sources. The first source will simply illuminate the jet vehicle and cast shadows from it. This source will be placed high above the horizon. Since the landscape is gently sloping, there's no need to create shadows from the landscape itself. Because of this, the first directional light will have a size slightly larger than that of the jet vehicle, and will be linked to it.

The second light will imitate the reflection of light from the jet vehicle to the landscape. It will also be linked to the jet vehicle, but it will illuminate the landscape.

***Self-study***    Recently, an illumination method called "Sky Dome" has became fairly popular. If you have completed Lesson Two, you'll understand what I mean. Recall that its essence is that it uses a lot of light sources of different colors which are positioned over a hemisphere. You might want to create such a system by yourself.

☐ Go to frame 0.

☐ Create the source of parallel light that will illuminate the jet vehicle at a small angle, and place it high above the horizon (fig. 5.54, a):

Tab panel → Lights & Cameras → Targeted Directional Light

☐ The target of this light should match the center of the hull.

☐ Go to the **Light** viewport by pressing <Shift>+<4>. Set the **Falloff** and **Highlight** parameters to illuminate only the jet vehicle (fig. 5.54, b).

☐ Specify the settings for the light source as shown in fig. 5.54, c.

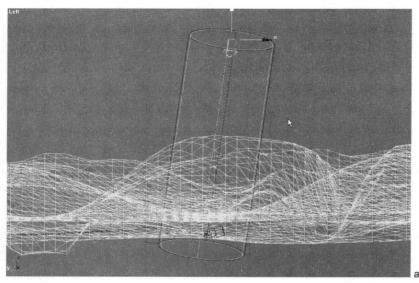

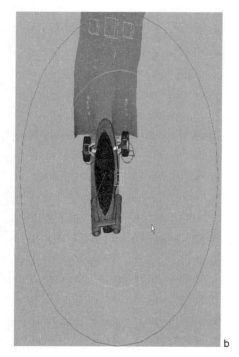

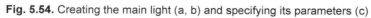

**Fig. 5.54.** Creating the main light (a, b) and specifying its parameters (c)

*TIP*  Make the light color slightly yellowish.

Set the **Cast Shadows** checkbox.

Increase the brightness by setting the **Multiplier** value to 1.2.

Set the **Overshoot** checkbox to make the light illuminate the whole landscape. Now the light will cast shadows only in the area limited by the **Falloff** parameter.

Link the light and its target to the hull of the jet vehicle.

❐ Disable rotation inheritance in the light parameters:

Control panel → Hierarchy → Link Info → **Inherit** rollout

❐ Select all the sources of dust and clear the **Cast Shadows** and **Receive Shadows** checkboxes in the object parameters:

Right-click menu → Properties → **Rendering Control** rollout

Now perform test rendering from the **Mobil_Cam** camera.

❐ You'll notice that the shadow is too intense. Decrease its intensity (fig. 5.55):

Control panel → ... → **Shadow Parameters** rollout

**Fig. 5.55.** Decreasing the shadow density

You can also make the shadow look washed out by increasing the **Sample Range** parameter:

Control panel → ... → **Shadow Map Params** rollout

❐ Create the second source of light that will imitate patches of light from the jet vehicle at the surface of the landscape. Any spotlight will be sufficient for this purpose:

Tab panel → Lights & Cameras → Free Spot

❐ Place the light at an angle from the shadow side, somewhere above the cockpit (fig. 5.56, a).

❐ Link this light to the hull of the jet vehicle without changing the linking parameters.

❐ The settings for this additional light are shown in fig. 5.56, b.

*NOTE*  Only the Land object should be included into the illuminated area (fig. 5.80). Make the light rectangular by selecting the **Rectangle** option.

Also don't forget to make the source map for the texture. Click the **Map** button and select the **Bitmap** option. For the texture, select the light_map.tif file, which you can find on the companion CD.

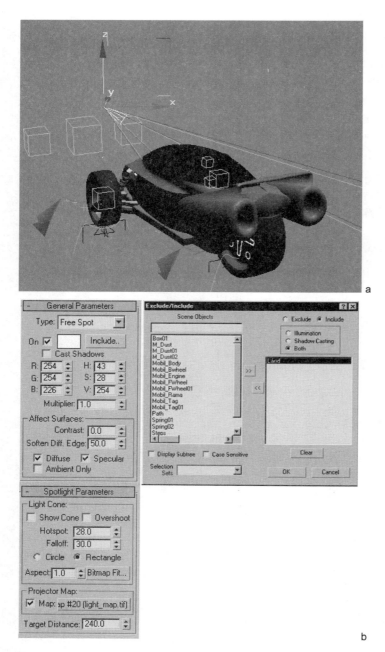

**Fig. 5.56.** Setting additional source of light (a), setting parameters for additional light (b)

*TIP*  Add the falloff for this light.

*Self-study*  Highlight the jet vehicle from both sides and from below. Create several omni lights with falloff, and exclude all objects except for the jet vehicle from the lighted area.

Now, everything is ready for final rendering.

# Final Rendering

Before we start discussing rendering settings, I'd like to draw your attention to one important aspect. Most novice animators try to render the animation directly to AVI or MOV files. This is certainly the fastest and easiest way of obtaining the results. More experienced animators, however, save the animation to the sequence of TGA or TIFF files, where they subsequently create animation using the software like Adobe Premier or Ulead Media Studio. As a matter of fact, if you save your animation to video files (AVI or MOV), the quality is usually degraded, and can't be restored later. If you process this animation, you'll only achieve further quality degradation. Furthermore, the programs of video rendering have much more powerful capabilities, including special effects and adding titles. Selection of the rendering format is up to you. The general rule, in this case, is simple. If you're not planning any further processing of your movie, or simply create a preview, then save the results in video files. If you're planning further processing of your movie, including special effects and titles, the best way is to save it as a sequence of files that support compression without quality degradation. Some file formats (TGA, TIFF) support alpha channel. As for the RLA format and a new format from Discreet, RPF — they support and preserve many other parameters, such as Z-Buffer. Notice, however, that you'll need professional video processing software like Discreet effect* in order to use this capability. Finally, some formats are cross-platform, which means that you can render the scene in the Windows environment, and assemble the movie on SGI, Amiga, or Mac.

And, finally, let's consider one more favorable feature of the file sequence. Rendering of some large projects may take hours (sometimes days). During this time, some unexpected failures may happen (for example, there may be a power failure or system hang-up). After rebooting the system, your results will be lost, and you'll need to start the rendering process from the beginning. On the other hand, if you render the animation into the sequence of files, you can restart rendering at the point the failure occurred.

However, let's return to our project.

The parameters of the final rendering are shown in fig. 5.57. Let's discuss these parameters. The length of the whole movie is now 450 frames, which corresponds to 30 seconds. To limit the animation length by 10 seconds, specify the appropriate number of the starting and final frames.

You can select the frame size according to your requirements.

Don't forget to set the checkboxes that enable special effects and shadows. The same is also true for Motion Blur.

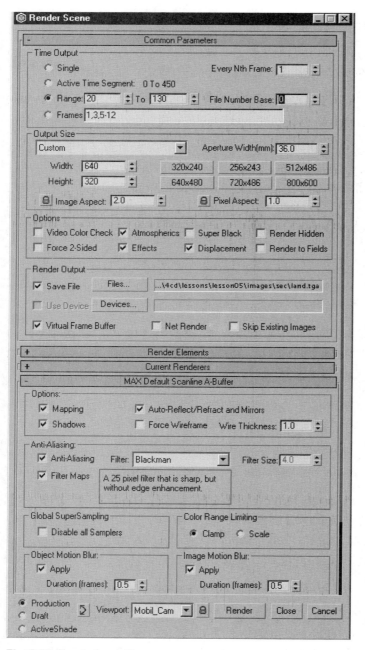

**Fig. 5.57.** Rendering settings

Save the rendering results in a sequence of files named Land0100.tga, Land0101.tga, and so on. Of course, if you wish, you can save the rendering results in AVI or MOV file. A description of the settings of these parameters goes beyond the limits of this book.

The Anti-Aliasing, however, is worth a separate discussion.

All 3ds max 4 releases of earlier than R 3.0 supported only one anti-aliasing algorithm, which was far from perfect. Moreover, this algorithm was absolutely identical to the algorithm implemented in 3ds max for DOS. One of the main drawbacks of early releases of 3ds max was the rendering quality. Images created in 3 ds max 4 were easily recognizable by their washed-out textures and object contours.

| Area |
| Blackman |
| Blend |
| Catmull-Rom |
| Cook Variable |
| Cubic |
| Mitchell-Netravali |
| Plate Match/MAX R2 |
| Quadratic |
| Sharp Quadratic |
| Soften |
| Video |

Developers have taken user comments into account and provided a set of at least 12 anti-aliasing and 5 SuperSampling algorithms. Selection of any specific algorithm depends on the circumstances. For example, the Video algorithm is ideal for cases when animation is prepared for subsequent rendering using video cards supporting Motion JPEG and MPEG formats. The Catmull-Rom algorithm is the best selection if you intend to create sprites for video games. More detailed information on the anti-aliasing and SuperSampling algorithms is provided in the User's Manual or in the Help system.

Now you can click the **Render** button.

Don't be hasty, however. First, save the project file. Then close all resource-consuming applications, and disable the screen saver and other applications that may switch your system to the waiting state. Make sure that there's sufficient space on your hard disk (it must be sufficient to store your animation). After this is done, click the **Render** button, switch off the monitor and, depending on the time of day, either get some other work done or go to sleep!

# Summary

First of all, let's consider the scenario and preliminary settings. We made a serious mistake when evaluating the velocity of our jet vehicle and the size of the surrounding landscape. We didn't need to create such a large landscape. It would have been sufficient to create the canyon, smoothly curving in the **Top** viewport. To create the peaks at the horizon, we could have created them in a separate project, rendered them, processed the results in any 2D graphics editor and assigned the image to a cylindrical surface.

I have to confess that the methods used so far are much too complex. I beg your pardon, yet I tried to cover as many 3ds max 4 features as possible.

Finally, let's take a critical look at the composition itself. We've spent a long time creating the environment, but it is actually almost invisible. Because of this, the movie can only be considered as a part of another and longer one. I tried to create such a movie. You can view the result, which is stored on the companion CD in the \Lessons\Lesson05\Images\ MarsRacers.avi file. Though made for my previous book, the movie will be of use here.

To produce this movie, I created some additional cameras set in various places of the scene. Further, I rendered each fragment separately and assembled the final movie using Adobe Premiere. If you don't have a program like this available, you can use the VideoPost module supplied with 3ds max 4.

Now let's discuss the biggest mistake we made when developing this project.

You're probably aware of some of the secrets of creating movies. As you know, the filming is done in small fragments. Each scene requires its own lighting, camera positions, and such. However, in the movies, everything is much simpler, because you're working with real objects. The sand will always look like sand, no matter what angle you're shooting from. On the other hand, you can also limit yourself to just a part of the object (for example, most aviation movies show just the cockpit model).

In 3D graphics, everything's much more complicated. You always have to sacrifice quality for the sake of time or vice versa. Because of this, if you ever need to create a scene like the one presented in this lesson, never try to create it as a whole. The best method for creating movies like this is to create several scenes and achieve the best possible quality for each of them, while minimizing the required rendering time.

Now let's discuss our particular scene in detail.

From a bird's eye view, the textures look far from perfect. In future projects, I recommend that you use large (I would even say gigantic) texture no less than 2000×2000 pixels, carefully prepared and applied to the landscape. If you can't afford this, use correctly mixed procedural textures. There are  a large number of procedural textures, including freeware ones that are an excellent choice for creating the landscape elements.

There's no need to use a detailed object instance. It will be sufficient to have a dummy that's simply very much like the object. Of course, there's no need to animate the wheels or create any other special features — from a distance, they're just not visible. The tracks from this view can also be simplified. The dust cloud can be represented by a simple textured object linked to the main object.

However, when viewing from a camera placed near the object, all the shortcomings of the landscape's surface become visible. When creating a view like this, you can't do without stones, shrubs, and other objects. As for the maps, they should be more detailed.

The view from the camera placed at the hull implies ideal and very detailed work on all the objects of the jet vehicle, including the joints of the springs and the chassis, tires, and other elements of the suspension and undercarriage. You'll still need to create realistic reflections and light patches. The dirt and dust, in this case, must be created using a large number of particles. This, by the way, is not as frightening as it seems, because the lifetime of these particles is limited to three or five frames. Besides this, you can use the Particle Motion Blur maps. The landscape details are of minor importance here, because they'll look blurred from this distance from a camera. Furthermore, you can simply delete most parts of the jet vehicle which aren't visible from this viewpoint.

One of the most interesting capabilities provided by 3ds max 4 is worth a special mention. This is  the module named Level Of Detail. This module allows you to dynamically replace complicated objects with simpler ones, depending on the area taken by the object on-screen during final rendering. This module will prove to be very useful when you model the asteroid belt or moving through the jungle.

There are many other interesting ways of improving 3ds max 4 productivity. I think that while performing the lessons, you've often seen the capabilities of selecting parameters that work differently in the viewports and during rendering. The NURBS module can be considered an example.

And, finally, I would like to quote the interactive Help system provided with one of the beta versions of 3ds max 4 (for some unknown reason, it wasn't included with the commercial release). "If a certain object will not be visible in your rendering under any conditions, do not create it. If during the final rendering some elements are less than one pixel in size — do not bother to create the details of such objects". Isn't this great?

# Appendix 1

# 3D Graphics Brief Glossary

This brief glossary includes the main terms and concepts of 3D graphics related to 3ds max 4 in general and to this book in particular.

If you're interested in more detailed information on this topic, you can find it in the User Manual supplied with the 3ds max 4 software or in the interactive Help system. It's also recommended that you have 3ds max 4 reference literature at hand.

## General Concepts

**Scene**. A scene in 3ds max 4 is a set of objects, materials, animation and program settings. Actually, the scene contains everything that has to be written to the project file.

**Viewport**. Viewports are program windows where you edit objects. Viewports can display shading modes or objects such as a wireframe.

**Object**. A 3ds max 4 object is any scene element. Objects can be renderable (for example, graphics primitives) or non-renderable (lights, space warps, and helpers).

**Sub-Object**. This is one of the main concepts in 3ds max 4. A sub-object is a subset of an object's geometry, including vertices and faces. Many objects and modifiers in 3ds max have various types of sub-objects that you can work with independently. However, all sub-objects must be a part of an object. Each object type has its own set of sub-objects.

**Transformation Matrix**. When you create any object, 3ds max records its position, rotation, and scale information in an internal table called a transformation matrix. Subsequent position, rotation, and scale adjustments are called transforms.

**Normal**. A face normal is a vector that defines which way a face is pointing. The direction of the normal indicates the front, or outer surface of the face. You can manually flip or unify face normals to fix surface errors caused by modeling operations or by importing meshes from other programs.

**Modifier**. Modifiers are special procedures, applied to an object, set of objects, or sub-objects to modify an object's geometrical structure.

**Modifier Stack**. A list of modifiers applied to an object. The effect of modifiers is directly related to their sequence, or order, in the stack. Where you put a modifier in the stack is critical, because the program applies modifiers in their stack order, beginning at the bottom, and carries the cumulative change upward. You can always return to any position within the modifier stack and change the settings of the current modifier. Any modifier within a stack can be moved, copied, or deleted at any level. You can also move modifiers from stack to stack.

**Gizmo**. A wireframe that initially surrounds the selected object. A gizmo acts like a kind of mechanical apparatus that transfers the modification to the object it's attached to.

**Material**. Material is the data that you assign to the surface or faces of an object so that it appears a certain way when rendered. Materials affect the color of objects, their shininess, their opacity, and so on.

**Rendering**. The process of turning the scene into an image based on object geometry, material settings, lights and camera parameters.

# Modeling
## Polygon Modeling

When working with 3ds max 4 it is necessary to distinguish mesh objects from "true" polygons (Poly Mesh). Although all these objects will be converted to mesh in the course of rendering, the editing procedure for these objects may sometimes be different.

**Editable Mesh**. The basic state of a polygonal object.

**Vertex**. A point positioned in 3D space. Object geometry is created based on vertices. Generally speaking, a vertex is an "atom" of any object in 3ds max 4.

**Face**. Minimal surface created based on three vertices. To continue with our analogy, this is a "molecule" of any 3ds max 4 object.

**Edge**. A line connecting two vertices.

**Border**. A group of open edges, i. e. edges that have adjoining polygons only on one side. For polygonal objects only.

**Polygon**. Several coplanar faces joined by "invisible" edges. In 3ds max 4, a polygon is a conditional concept introduced with version 3. It was mainly introduced for convenience purposes during low-level modeling.

**Element**. A combination of several polygons. Elements in an object can be separated by space, like letters in a title, or they can be contiguous faces that are touching or attached.

**Smooth/Smoothing Group**. Each model has a limited set of faces. 3ds max 4 provides the smoothing operation to produce the impression of a smooth model (a ball, for example) after the final rendering, while in reality this model is composed of flat faces. The renderer attempts to create smooth transitions between faces. Sometimes this is not necessary (for example, when modeling a multidiameter shaft). Just for such cases, 3ds max 4 provides the ability to group faces or polygons according to the smoothing characteristic.

## Bezier Curves

**Editable Spline**. One of the basic states of an object. The curve editing process in 3ds max 4 is very similar to the one used in vector graphics software packages. The only difference is that in 3ds max 4 you edit curves in 3D space.

**Vertex**. A point in 3D space, used as the basis for creating and editing curves. In contrast to the vertex within a polygonal object, spline vertex can be of several types: Smooth, Bezier, and Corner. The vertex type influences the curve shape.

**Handle**. Each Bezier vertex has two handles that control the curve shape.

**Segment**. The portion of a curve between two of its controlling points or CVs. Also, the portion of a spline between two vertices.

**Spline**. A set of segments sequentially connected by common vertices.

# Patch Modeling

**Editable Patch**. One of the basic object states. Generally speaking, patches are surfaces created basing on the same principles as Bezier curves.

**Vertex**. In contrast to the curve vertex, a patch vertex has three or four handles that control the surface shape. The surface can contain outer vertices (ones that belong to edges) and inner vertices. Both types of surface vertices control the patch shape.

**Edge**. Very similar to the edge in a polygonal model. The only difference, in this case, is that the edge is a segment of a curve.

**Patch**. Minimal editable surface.

# Materials

**Shader**. An algorithm used to calculate how the faces, materials, and lighting all combine to create a surface. Different shaders are used to create specific effects such as chrome, glass, gold, or wood. Shaders and materials have unique sets of controls and parameters.

**Ambient Color**. Ambient color is the color of the object when it's in a shadow. This color is what the object reflects when illuminated by ambient light rather than direct light.

**Diffuse Color**. The color that the object reflects when illuminated by "good lighting"; that is, by direct daylight or artificial light that makes the object easy to see.

**Specular Color**. The color that the object reflects when illuminated by the light incident at an angle close to a right angle.

**Highlight graph**. This curve defines a ratio of color mixing in relation to the angle of incidence of the rays of light.

**Map**. Any image you assign to the materials. There are several different types of maps you can use in 3ds max 4. By assigning the maps to different attributes of the materials, you can affect the color, opacity, or the smoothness of the surface, and much more. The different types of maps you can use range from the common bitmap to the flexible procedural map, created basing on a math algorithm and calculated in the course of rendering.

# Animation

**Keyframe**. Keyframes record the beginning and the end of each transformation of an object or element in the scene. The values at these keyframes are called keys. You should have at least two keyframes for animation — the starting and the ending ones.

**Controller**. An algorithm controlling animation of a specific parameter. There are many other types of animation controllers, each with its own controls and abilities. There are controllers based on the keyframes that define the intermediate values of controlled parameters within the ranges between keyframes. There are also controllers based on mathematical algorithms (Noise, for example) or external effects (Sound).

**Pivot Point**. The point belonging to the object about which the object is transformed during animation. Pivot point can be located anywhere, even outside the object. Furthermore, its position can also be animated.

# Rendering

**Antialiasing**. Removing the effect of granularity (Aliasing) from the final image during rendering.

**Motion Blur**. The effect of blurring the moving object in relation to the static camera. In real life, this effect can be a result of non-zero exposition of the camera. In graphics, this effect is applied to make images more realistic.

# Appendix 2

# Keyboard Shortcuts

Table A2.1 lists default keyboard shortcuts in 3ds max 4. A complete list of all commands for main interface and plug-in modules is provided in 3ds max 4 online help (see the section named Default Keyboard Shortcuts).

**Table A2.1. Default Keyboard Shortcuts in 3ds max 4**

| Keyboard shortcut | Command | Description |
|---|---|---|
| | **Viewport and file commands** | |
| \<O\> | Adaptive Degradation Toggle | Toggle the viewport optimization mode |
| \<Shift\>+\<Ctrl\>+\<A\> | Adaptive Perspective Grid Toggle | Toggle the grid correction in the Perspective viewport |
| \<Alt\>+\<Ctrl\>+\<B\> | Background Lock Toggle | Toggle the background lock in the viewport |
| \<K\> | Back View | Change the viewport display to the back view |
| \<B\> | Bottom View | Change the viewport display to the Bottom view |
| \<C\> | Camera View | Change the viewport display to the camera view |
| \<F\> | Front View | Change the viewport display to the front view |
| \<U\> | Isometric User View | Change the viewport display to the isometric user view |
| \<L\> | Left View | Change the viewport display to the left view |
| \<P\> | Perspective User View | Change the viewport display to the perspective user view |
| \<R\> | Right View | Change the viewport display to the right view |
| \<Shift\>+\<4\> | Spot/Directional Light View | Change the viewport display to Spot/Directional Light view |

*continues*

**Table A2.1 Continued**

| Keyboard shortcut | Command | Description |
| --- | --- | --- |
| | **Viewport and file commands** | |
| <T> | Top View | Change the viewport display to the Top View |
| <E> | Track View Viewport | Change the viewport display to the Track View |
| <D> | Disable Viewport | Disable the changes display in the viewport (if the viewport isn't active) |
| <Shift>+<C> | Hide Cameras Toggle | Toggle the camera display in the viewport |
| <Ctrl>+<E> | Display Edges Only Toggle | Toggle the Display Edges Only mode |
| <Alt>+<1> | Display First Tab | Go to the first tab in the tab menu |
| <Shift>+<O> | Hide Geometry Toggle | Toggle the Display Geometry mode in the viewport |
| <G> | Hide Grids Toggle | Toggle the Grid display mode in the viewport |
| <Shift>+<H> | Hide Helpers Toggle | Toggle the Display Helpers mode in the viewport |
| <Shift>+<L> | Hide Lights Toggle | Toggle the Display Lights mode in the viewport |
| <Shift>+<P> | Hide Particle Systems Toggle | Toggle the Display Particle Systems mode in the viewport |
| <Shift>+<F> | Show Safeframes Toggle | Toggle the Display Safeframes mode in the viewport |
| <Shift>+<W> | Hide Space Warps Toggle | Toggle the space warps display in the viewport |
| <F4> | View Edged Faces Toggle | Toggle the Edged Faces mode in the viewport shading mode |
| <Ctrl>+<X> | Expert Mode Toggle | Toggle the Expert mode |
| <Alt>+<Ctrl>+<F> | Fetch | Restore the state saved using the Hold command |
| <Shift>+<G> | Show All Grids Toggle | Toggle the Grid Display All mode |
| <3>, <Q> | Show Command Panel Toggle | Toggle the display of control panel |
| <4> | Show Floating Toolbars Toggle | Toggle the display of floating toolbars |

*continues*

**Table A2.1 Continued**

| Keyboard shortcut | Command | Description |
|---|---|---|
| | | **Viewport and file commands** |
| <Alt>+<6> | Show Main Toolbar Toggle | Toggle the main toolbar display |
| <2>, <Y> | Show Tab Panel Toggle | Toggle the Tab Panel display |
| <Alt>+<Ctrl>+<H> | Hold | Save the current state |
| <I> | Pan Viewport | Interactive move in the viewport |
| <[> | Zoom Viewport In | Interactive zooming in the viewport |
| <]> | Zoom Viewport Out | Interactive zooming out in the viewport |
| <Ctrl>+<C> | Match Camera To View | Aligning the camera to the view |
| <M> | Material Editor | Starting the material editor |
| <W> | Maximize View Toggle | Maximizing the viewport |
| <Ctrl>+<N> | New Scene | Creating a new scene |
| <Alt>+<L>, <Ctrl>+<4> | NURBS Shaded Lattice Toggle | Toggle the NURBS grid display in the Shaded mode |
| <Ctrl>+<1> | NURBS Tessellation Preset 1 | Selecting the first set of presets for displaying NURBS in the viewport |
| <Ctrl>+<2> | NURBS Tessellation Preset 2 | Selecting the second set of presets for displaying NURBS in the viewport |
| <Ctrl>+<3> | NURBS Tessellation Preset 3 | Selecting the third set of presets for displaying NURBS in the viewport |
| <Ctrl>+<O> | Open File | Opening a file |
| <Ctrl>+<P> | Pan View | Toggle to the Pan View mode |
| <Shift>+<Ctrl>+<P> | Snap Percent Toggle | Toggle the snap mode when re-scaling objects |
| <Shift>+<Q> | Quick Render | Quick rendering using the latest settings |
| <Ctrl>+<A> | Redo Scene Operation | Redo the undone scene operation |
| <Shift>+<A> | Redo Viewport Operation | Redo the undone viewport operation |
| <1> | Redraw All Views | Redraw display in all viewports |
| <Shift>+<E>, <F9> | Render Last | Render the viewport using the latest settings |
| <Shift>+<R>, <F10> | Render Scene | Render the whole scene |
| <Ctrl>+<R>, <V> | Rotate View Mode | Rotate viewport |

*continues*

**Table A2.1 Continued**

| Keyboard shortcut | Command | Description |
|---|---|---|
| **Viewport and file commands** | | |
| <Ctrl>+<S> | Save File | Save a file |
| <Alt>+<X> | See-Through Display Toggle | Toggle the semi-transparent display mode for displaying selected objects |
| <F2> | Shade Selected Faces Toggle | Toggle the shaded display mode for selected faces |
| <Ctrl>+<I> | Show Last Rendering | Show the result of the previous rendering |
| <\> | Sound Toggle | Toggle the sound |
| <Ctrl>+<T> | Texture Correction | Toggle the texture correction mode in the viewport |
| <X> | Transform Gizmo Toggle | Toggle the transform gizmo display mode |
| <=> | Transform Gizmo Size Down | Decrease the size of the transform gizmo |
| <-> | Transform Gizmo Size Up | Increase the size of the transform gizmo |
| <Ctrl>+<Z> | Undo Scene Operation | Undo the last scene operation |
| <Shift>+<Z> | Undo Viewport Operation | Undo the last viewport operation |
| <Alt>+<Shift>+ +<Ctrl>+<B> | Update Background Image | Redraw the background image in the viewport |
| <Alt>+<B> | Viewport Background | Toggle background display in the viewport |
| <Shift>+<B> | Viewport Box Mode Toggle | Toggle the viewport Box Mode |
| <1> (numeric keypad) | Virtual Viewport Toggle | Toggle virtual viewport display |
| <2> (numeric keypad) | Virtual Viewport Pan Down | Move downwards in the virtual viewport |
| <4> (numeric keypad) | Virtual Viewport Pan Left | Move leftwards in the virtual viewport |
| <6> (numeric keypad) | Virtual Viewport Pan Right | Move rightwards in the virtual viewport |
| <8> (numeric keypad) | Virtual Viewport Pan Up | Move upwards in the virtual viewport |
| <7> (numeric keypad) | Virtual Viewport Zoom In | Increase the scale in the virtual viewport |

*continues*

**Table A2.1 Continued**

| Keyboard shortcut | Command | Description |
|---|---|---|
| | **Viewport and file commands** | |
| <9> (numeric keypad) | Virtual Viewport Zoom Out | Decrease the scale in the virtual viewport |
| <F3> | Wireframe / Smooth+ +Highlights Toggle | Toggle the shading mode in the viewport |
| <Alt>+<Ctrl>+<Z> | Zoom Extents | Set the viewport scale to display all objects |
| <Shift>+<Ctrl>+<Z> | Zoom Extents All | Set the scale in all viewports to display all objects |
| <Shift>+<Grey +> | Zoom In 2X | Double the viewport display |
| <Z> | Zoom Mode | Enable the Zoom mode in the viewport |
| <Shift>+<Grey –> | Zoom Out 2X | Decrease the viewport display twice |
| <Ctrl>+<W> | Zoom Region Mode | Enable rectangular region zoom mode |
| | **Object commands** | |
| <Alt>+<A> | Align | Start aligning objects |
| <A> | Angle Snap Toggle | Toggle the angle snap mode |
| <F5> | Restrict to X | Constrain transforms to the X-axis |
| <F6> | Restrict to Y | Constrain transforms to the Y-axis |
| <F7> | Restrict to Z | Constrain transforms to the Z-axis |
| <F8> | Restrict Plane Cycle | Cycle the plane of transform coordinates |
| <Ctrl>+<F> | Cycle Selection Method | Cycle the selection method (rectangle, circle, freeform) |
| <Ins> | Sub-object Level Cycle | Cycle the sub-object levels |
| <Alt>+<Space> | Snaps Cycle | Cycle the types of snaps (2, 2.5, 3) |
| <Ctrl>+<L> | Default Lighting Toggle | Toggle the default lighting |
| <Del> | Delete Objects | Delete the object or sub-object |
| <H> | Select-By-Name Dialog | Open the Select By Name dialog |
| <6> | Freeze Selection | Freeze selected objects |
| <Alt>+<N> | Normal Align | Align the object in relation to the other object's normals |
| <Ctrl>+<H> | Place Highlight | Place the highlight from the light at the object |

*continues*

**Table A2.1 Continued**

| Keyboard shortcut | Command | Description |
|---|---|---|
| **Object commands** | | |
| <S> | Snap Toggle | Toggle snap when moving objects |
| <Page Up> | Select Ancestor | Select the parent object in the hierarchical chain |
| <Page Down> | Select Children | Select the child object in the hierarchical chain |
| <Space> | Selection Lock Toggle | Lock the selection |
| <Shift>+<I> | Spacing Tool | Start the spacing tool |
| <Ctrl>+<B> | Sub-Object Selection Toggle | Toggle the sub-object selection mode |
| <F12> | Transform Type-In Dialog | Open the dialog for manual input of the transform parameters |
| <7> | Unfreeze All | Unfreeze all objects |
| <5> | Unhide by Name | Open the Unhide by Name dialog |
| **Animation and time control commands** | | |
| <N> | Animation Mode Toggle | Toggle the animation recording mode |
| <,> (comma) | Backup Time One Unit | Move one frame or key back |
| <.> (period) | Forward Time One Unit | Go one frame or key forward |
| <End> | Go to End Frame | Go to the last frame |
| <Home> | Go to Start Frame | Go to the first frame |
| </> | Play Animation | Play animation in the viewport |

# Appendix 3

# Internet Resources

I f you're an experienced Internet user, you can easily browse the Net to visit the links provided on any of the sites listed below.

| | |
|---|---|
| http://www.discreet.com<br><br>http://www.autodesk.com<br><br>http://www.lightscape.com | The sites of developers and publishers of 3ds max. These sites provide the latest news and updates for both 3ds max and other products of the Autodesk group |
| http://www.digimation.com<br><br>http://www.cebas.com<br><br>http://www.maxplugins.com<br><br>http://www.afterworks.com<br><br>http://www.reyes-infografica.com<br><br>http://www.trinity3d.com | These are the sites of leading vendors and publishers of commercial plug-in modules for 3ds max. Here you can find the latest information on the new plug-ins and download updates for free, if you're a registered user |
| http://max3d.3dluvr.com<br><br>http://www.3dcafe.com<br><br>http://www.raph.com<br><br>http://www.3dartist.com | Interesting sites that provide lots of additional information on 3D software packages. Also provided are creations of independent 3D artists, both professional and amateur. Besides, you can download various shareware and freeware plug-ins for 3ds max |

# Appendix 4

# CD Description

T he companion CD contains all the files necessary to complete the exercises described in this book, along with images, maps, scenes, and movies for reference and use.

In the \Lessons\Lesson01 — Lesson05 directories, you can find all the files necessary to complete the lessons described in the book. The directory tree corresponds to the 3D Studio MAX directory structure. In the \Scenes subdirectories, you can also find intermediate and final versions of all the projects.

## System Requirements

❏ Intel or AMD-compatible processor at 300 MHz or better (dual Pentium III system recommended)

❏ Minimum 128 MB RAM and 300 MB swap space

❏ Video adapter supporting 1024×768 resolution at 16-bit color (OpenGL and Direct3D hardware acceleration support, 24-bit color, 3D graphics accelerator preferred)

❏ Windows-compliant pointing device (specific optimization for Microsoft IntelliMouse™)

❏ CD-ROM drive

❏ Operating system: Windows 98/ME or Windows NT 4.0 (Windows 2000 recommended)

# INDEX